Comparative Politics

Using MicroCase *ExplorIt*®

SECOND EDITION

Michael K. Le Roy

WHEATON COLLEGE

WADSWORTH

———✳———™

THOMSON LEARNING

Australia • Canada • Mexico • Singapore • Spain • United Kingdom • United States

Acquisitions Editor: *David Tatom*
Developmental Editor: *Sharon Adams Poore*
Developmental Editor: *Jodi Gleason*
Assistant Editor: *Kasia Zagorski*
Editorial Assistant: *Jonathan Katz*

Technology Project Manager: *Julie Aguilar*
Ancillary Coordinator: *Rita Jaramillo*
Printbuyer: *Doreen Suruki*
Printer: *Webcom Ltd.*
Duplicator: *Micro Bytes, Inc.*

For more information about our products, contact us at:
Thomson Learning Academic Resource Center
1-800-423-0563

For permission to use material from this text, contact us by:
Phone: 1-800-730-2214
Fax: 1-800-731-2215
Web: www.thomsonrights.com

Asia
Thomson Learning
60 Albert Complex, #15-01
Albert Complex
Singapore 189969

Australia
Nelson Thomson Learning
102 Dodds Street
South Street
South Melbourne, Victoria 3205
Australia

Canada
Nelson Thomson Learning
1120 Birchmount Road
Toronto, Ontario M1K 5G4
Canada

Europe/Middle East/South Africa
Thomson Learning
Berkshire House
168-173 High Holborn
London WC1 V7AA
United Kingdom

Latin America
Thomson Learning
Seneca, 53
Colonia Polanco
11560 Mexico D.F.
Mexico

Spain
Paraninfo Thomson Learning
Calle/Magallanes, 25
28015 Madrid, Spain

CONTENTS

Acknowledgments vii

Preface ix

Getting Started xi

PART I   Doing Comparative Politics with ExplorIt 5

Chapter 1   The Nation-State 7

Chapter 2   People, Populations, and State Capacity 29

Chapter 3   Organizing Political Systems: First, Second, and Third Worlds? 45

PART II   Politics and Government in Liberal Democracies 61

Chapter 4   Political Culture in Liberal Democracies 63

Chapter 5   Political Participation: Making Democracy Work 87

Chapter 6   Electoral Systems in Liberal Democracies 101

Chapter 7   Political Parties in the United Kingdom and Germany 115

PART III   Communist and Postcommunist Societies 137

Chapter 8   After Communism 139

Chapter 9   Russia, Poland, and Democratic Transition 155

PART IV   Newly Industrialized Countries 169

Chapter 10   Developing Nations: What Determines Wealth and Poverty? 171

Chapter 11   Newly Industrialized Countries in Asia 187

Chapter 12   Asian Values: Political Culture in South Korea and Japan 203

PART V   Less Developed Countries and the Islamic World 215

Chapter 13   Less Developed Countries and Marginal States in Africa 219

Chapter 14   Social Capital in Nigeria and South Africa 233

Chapter 15   Authority Patterns in Mexico and Brazil 253

Chapter 16   Islam and Politics in Pakistan and Turkey 279

Appendix: Variable Names and Sources A1

ABOUT THE AUTHOR

Michael Le Roy is an Associate Professor and Chair of the Department of Politics and International Relations at Wheaton College in Wheaton, Illinois, where he received the Faculty Achievement Award for excellence in teaching. He received his Ph.D. in Political Science at Vanderbilt University and his B.A. from Whitworth College in Washington state. Between 1992 and 1994, Michael was a Fulbright scholar at Gothenburg University in Sweden. His research on civil society, xenophobia, and the European Union has been published in *Comparative Politics*. Comments about this book from students and faculty are welcomed and may be sent directly to the author at the following e-mail address: Michael.LeRoy@wheaton.edu.

ACKNOWLEDGMENTS

I am delighted to acknowledge the efforts of many people who made this workbook possible. John Yoder, my first political science professor, introduced me to the study of comparative politics, and M. Donald Hancock, my advisor in graduate school, persuaded me of the value of empirical comparative research.

I am thankful for the support of Wheaton College and the encouragement of my colleagues in the Department of Politics and International Relations, Mark Amstutz, Amy Black, Sandra Joireman, Lyman A. Kellstedt, Helene Slessarev, and Ashley Woodiwiss. This workbook would not have been possible, or even desirable, if it were not for the many students at Wheaton College who have given feedback and input into the examples used in this text. I particularly wish to thank my student assistants who put in many hours testing the exercises and examples over the years: Sara De Master, David Fabrycky, Sara Gray, Kate Morley, Ivy Orr, Andrea Saul, Rob Vickery, and Marjory Winn. Working with these remarkable people makes my arrival at work each day a pleasure.

I am also very grateful for the careful reading and the many helpful contributions and insights of the reviewers of this text. In particular, I would like to thank Donald Baxter (College of William and Mary), Michael L. Bressler (Furman University), Michael Gold-Bliss (St. Cloud State University), Baogang Guo (Thomas County Community College), Charles Hauss (George Mason University), Richard Jankowski (SUNY Fredonia), Kay Knickrehm (James Madison University), Margaret E. Scranton (University of Arkansas at Little Rock), Andreas Sobisch (John Carroll University), and Jeff Walz (Concordia University – Wisconsin).

If this workbook achieves any distinction at all, it will be because I stood on the shoulders of giants who came before me. Rodney Stark pioneered the pedagogical use of statistical software in the social sciences and helped teachers better imagine how to engage students in social science research. David Smetters and his staff were instrumental in perfecting the software and the instructional resources that accompany it. In particular, I wish to thank David for sticking with me through the first edition of the project and giving me the necessary encouragement to bring it to completion.

For the second edition, I am indebted to Julie Aguilar and Sharon Adams-Poore for their editorial advice and assistance. I am also grateful to Jodi Gleason for her Herculean efforts to produce this manuscript so quickly and at a high level of quality. I have appreciated their professionalism, patience, and good humor.

I would also like to thank the sources of the data files accompanying this workbook. These data sets represent thousands of hours of work by many unsung heroes who have labored around the world to interview thousands of people, survey the state of human development, and document the state of the politics. In particular, I wish to thank Ronald Inglehart at the Institute for Social Research, University of Michigan, for his generosity in making the World Values Survey available to students and scholars. A comparative politics workbook like this would not have been possible if it were not for Professor Inglehart's diligent research over the past 30 years. I am pleased to thank the study staff at the CSES Secretariat, based in the Center for Political Studies, University of Michigan, for its very exciting work on the Comparative Study of Electoral Systems.

Finally, no academic project can ever go forward without the support of the people we love who give us the space to work and the time to think and travel. I thank my family: my wife Andrea, my son Dana, and daughters Hannah and Astrid. As always, I am indebted to them for their patience and support throughout the development of this book.

PREFACE

When I was a boy I could hardly think beyond the water's edge of Bainbridge Island, Washington, where I grew up. The border states of Idaho and Oregon meant little more to me than day-long trips in the back of our station wagon, and Washington D.C. seemed as far away as the moon. I still remember a teacher who made me and my classmates memorize the locations and capitals of countless countries throughout the world. But as a child I never thought about the people and politics of these distant lands.

The world became a bit smaller and the people in other countries became more real when I went on a short trip to Mexico while in high school. This led to a longer, six-month trip to Central America several years later. I have since spent a couple years in Sweden and have visited dozens of countries in Europe, Africa, Central America, and South America.

Even if you've never traveled abroad, you too have probably noticed how the world has grown smaller over the past ten years. Think about it. Someone in the United States can now pick up the phone and call Bangkok and pay just pennies a minute. A person in Great Britain can wake up someone in Hawaii with equal effort and cost. We have faxes, e-mail, the Internet, and a host of other telecommunications pulling us closer and closer every day.

Any illusion that we need not concern ourselves with the internal politics of other nations came crashing down as I sat writing the second edition of this text on September 11, 2001. This brutal attack on thousands of innocent people was instigated by political forces far from our shores, but hit the United States just as hard as it would have had it been hatched in our own backyard. The world is indeed a smaller place. And we must know more about it.

We are witnessing the uniting of economies and currencies in Europe. We are nervously watching democratic and economic transition in the former Soviet Union. The "Asian tigers" are roaring one day, silent the next, and then roaring once again with ever more determination and might. The Middle East keeps pumping and Africa keeps struggling. With so many different countries in the world, how does one make sense of it all? What political systems are most stable? Which countries have the best records for respecting human rights? Which political systems are the most corrupt? What factors lead to internal and external war? Which countries have the weakest infrastructures for dealing with education, health, and population growth?

The answers to these and many other questions can be found by comparing one nation to another. And that's exactly what these materials will teach you to do: compare nations. This workbook and its accompanying software allow you to explore the real world of comparative politics, using the same data and analytical tools used by professional researchers. The Student ExplorIt software is packaged inside the back cover of this workbook. In addition, you will find an incredibly rich assortment of data files, such as the GLOBAL data file which contains more than 100 variables for the 172 largest countries in the world. There are also regional files providing aggregate data for Asia, Europe, Africa, and Latin America. All data are from the best sources available, such as the World Values Survey, the World Bank, and the United Nations. The second edition is a significant revision thanks to the proliferation of new data sources. The most recent edition of the World Values Survey has new chapters that incorporate additional surveys from Russia, Poland, Brazil, Pakistan, and Turkey, and national election studies from Germany and the United Kingdom.

When I was in college, I had a political science professor who continually pushed us to "think beyond the water's edge." Sometimes it was difficult to meet this challenge because it required analytical tools that were not easily accessible to college students. It also called for the analysis of data sets that were not readily available. Times have changed. The software and workbook materials you are holding in your hands are unlike anything ever available for comparative politics courses. I wish I could say that I came up with this instructional concept myself, but I didn't. I undertook this project only after seeing how easily students in an introductory American government course were able to do real analysis using MicroCase's software-based workbook, *American Government: An Introduction Using ExplorIt*. The workbook and software considerably simplify what had previously been considered too complex for college freshmen, and they did so without compromising or dumbing down the content. If you've never encountered the Student ExplorIt or Student MicroCase software—even earlier versions of the software—you'll be amazed at how easily you can generate maps, analyze survey data, and do many other things.

When I started work on this project, a primary goal was to develop a set of materials that would allow undergraduate students to explore the real world of comparative politics research. The exercises in this workbook provide a great deal of guidance and structure, and I promise you will find nothing difficult about these materials if you simply read the text and follow the step-by-step instructions. However, I encourage you to do more than just try to get the "right answers" for the worksheet sections. With a little application and exploration, you'll discover that comparative politics is much more than learning facts and figures about distant lands.

I hope you enjoy this workbook. I took great pleasure in developing these materials. If I have been successful at my task, you too will experience the excitement of exploring politics beyond the water's edge.

Michael K. Le Roy
Wheaton, Illinois

GETTING STARTED

INTRODUCTION

Welcome to ExplorIt! With the easy-to-use software accompanying this workbook, you will have the opportunity to learn about comparative politics by exploring more than 170 countries and dozens of political issues with data from around the world.

Each exercise in this workbook deals with a theme in the study of comparative politics or the study of the countries in a specific region of the world. The preliminary section of each chapter uses data provided with the workbook to illustrate key issues related to the topic in question. You can easily create all the graphics in this part of the exercise by following the ExplorIt Guides you'll be seeing. Doing so will take just a few clicks of your computer mouse and will help you become familiar with ExplorIt. The ExplorIt Guides are described in more detail below.

Each exercise also has a worksheet section where you'll do your own data analysis. This section contains a series of questions that will either follow up on examples from the preliminary section or have you explore some new issues. You'll use the workbook's software to answer these questions.

SYSTEM REQUIREMENTS

- Windows 95 (or higher)
- 8 MB RAM
- CD-ROM drive
- 15 MB of hard drive space (if you want to install it)

To run the software on a Macintosh, you will need emulation software or hardware installed. For more information about emulation software or hardware, check with your local Macintosh retailer or try the website http://machardware.about.com/cs/pcemulation/.

NETWORK VERSIONS OF STUDENT EXPLORIT

A network version of Student ExplorIt is available at no charge to instructors who adopt this book for their course. It's worth noting that Student ExplorIt can be run directly from the CD on virtually any computer network—regardless of whether a network version of Student ExplorIt has been installed.

INSTALLING STUDENT EXPLORIT

If you will be running Student ExplorIt directly from the CD-ROM—or if you will be using a version of Student ExplorIt that is installed on a network—skip to the section "Starting Student ExplorIt."

To install Student ExplorIt to a hard drive, you will need the CD-ROM that is packaged inside the back cover of this book. Then follow these steps in order:

1. Start your computer and wait until the Windows desktop is showing on your screen.

2. Insert the CD-ROM into the CD-ROM drive of your computer.

3. On most computers the CD-ROM will automatically start and a welcome menu will appear. If the CD-ROM doesn't automatically start, do the following:

   Click [Start] from the Windows desktop, click [Run], type **D:\SETUP**, and click [OK]. (If your CD-ROM drive is not the D drive, replace the letter D with the proper drive letter.) To install Student ExplorIt to your hard drive, select the second option on the list: "Install Student ExplorIt to your hard drive."

4. During the installation, you will be presented with several screens, as described below. In most cases you will be required to make a selection or entry and then click [Next] to continue.

   The first screen that appears is the **License Name** screen. Here you are asked to type your name. It is important to type your name correctly, since it cannot be changed after this point. Your name will appear on all printouts, so make sure you spell it completely and correctly! Then click [Next] to continue.

   A **Welcome** screen now appears. This provides some introductory information and suggests that you shut down any other programs that may be running. Click [Next] to continue.

   You are next presented with a **Software License Agreement**. Read this screen and click [Yes] if you accept the terms of the software license.

   The next screen has you **Choose the Destination** for the program files. You are strongly advised to use the destination directory that is shown on the screen. Click [Next] to continue.

5. The Student ExplorIt program will now be installed. At the end of the installation, you will be asked if you would like a shortcut icon placed on the Windows desktop. We recommend that you select [Yes]. You are now informed that the installation of Student ExplorIt is finished. Click the [Finish] button and you will be returned to the opening Welcome screen. To exit completely, click the option "Exit Welcome Screen."

STARTING STUDENT EXPLORIT

There are three ways to run Student ExplorIt: (1) directly from the CD-ROM, (2) from a hard drive installation, or (3) from a network installation. Each method is described below.

Starting Student ExplorIt from the CD-ROM

Unlike most Windows programs, it is possible to run Student ExplorIt directly from the CD-ROM. To do so, follow these steps:

1. Insert the CD-ROM disc into the CD-ROM drive.

2. On most computers the CD-ROM will automatically start and a welcome menu will appear. (Note: If the CD-ROM does **not** automatically start after it is inserted, click [Start] from the

Windows desktop, click [Run], type D:\SETUP and click [OK]. If your CD-ROM drive is not the D drive, replace the letter D with the proper drive letter.)

3. Select the first option from the Welcome menu: **Run Student ExplorIt from the CD-ROM.** Within a few seconds, Student ExplorIt will appear on your screen. Type in your name where indicated to enter the program.

Starting Student ExplorIt from a Hard Drive Installation

If Student ExplorIt is installed to the hard drive of your computer (see earlier section "Installing Student ExplorIt"), it is **not** necessary to insert the CD-ROM. Instead, locate the Student ExplorIt "shortcut" icon on the Windows desktop, which looks something like this:

To start Student ExplorIt, position your mouse pointer over the shortcut icon and double-click (that is, click it twice in rapid succession). If you did not permit the shortcut icon to be placed on the desktop during the install process (or if the icon was accidentally deleted), you can alternatively follow these directions to start the software:

Click [Start] from the Windows desktop.

Click [Programs].

Click [MicroCase].

Click [Student ExplorIt—Cp].

After a few seconds, Student ExplorIt will appear on your screen.

Starting Student ExplorIt from a Network

If the network version of Student ExplorIt has been installed to a computer network, you need to double-click the Student ExplorIt icon that appears on the Windows desktop to start the program. Type in your name where indicated to enter the program. (Note: Your instructor may provide additional information that is unique to your computer network.)

MAIN MENU OF STUDENT EXPLORIT

Student ExplorIt is extremely easy to use. All you do is point and click your way through the program. That is, use your mouse arrow to point at the selection you want, then click the left button on the mouse.

The main menu is the starting point for everything you will do in Student ExplorIt. Look at how it works. Notice that not all options on the menu are always available. You will know which options are available at any given time by looking at the colors of the options. For example, when you first start the software, only the OPEN FILE option is immediately available. As you can see, the colors for this option are brighter than those for the other tasks shown on the screen. Also, when you move your mouse pointer over this option, it is highlighted.

EXPLORIT GUIDES

Throughout this workbook, "ExplorIt Guides" provide the basic information needed to carry out each task. Here is an example:

> ➤ *Data File:* **GLOBAL**
> ➤ *Task:* **Mapping**
> ➤ *Variable 1:* **12) POPULATION**
> ➤ *View:* **Map**

Each line of the ExplorIt Guide is actually an instruction. Let's follow the simple steps to carry out this task.

Step 1: Select a Data File

Before you can do anything in Student ExplorIt, you need to open a data file. To open a data file, click the OPEN FILE task. A list of data files will appear in a window (e.g., AFRICA, ASIA, EUROPE). If you click on a file name *once*, a description of the highlighted file is shown in the window next to this list. In the ExplorIt Guide shown above, the ➤ symbol to the left of the Data File step indicates that you should open the GLOBAL data file. To do so, click GLOBAL and then click the [Open] button (or just double-click GLOBAL). The next window that appears (labeled File Settings) provides additional information about the data file, including a file description, the number of cases in the file, and the number of variables, among other things. To continue, click the [OK] button. You are now returned to the main menu of Student ExplorIt. (You won't need to repeat this step until you want to open a different data file.) Notice that you can always see which data file is currently open by looking at the file name shown on the top line of the screen.

Step 2: Select a Task

Once you open a data file, the next step is to select a program task. Seven analysis tasks are offered in this version of Student ExplorIt. Not all tasks are available for each data file, because some tasks are appropriate only for certain kinds of data. Mapping, for example, is a task that applies only to ecological data and thus cannot be used with survey data files.

In the ExplorIt Guide we are following, the ➤ symbol on the second line indicates that the MAPPING task should be selected, so click the MAPPING option with your left mouse button.

Step 3: Select a Variable

After a task is selected, you will be shown a list of the variables in the open data file. Notice that the first variable is highlighted and a description of that variable is shown in the Variable Description window at the lower right. You can move this highlight through the list of variables by using the up and down cursor keys (as well as the <Page Up> and <Page Down> keys). You can also click once on a variable name to move the highlight and update the variable description. Go ahead—move the highlight to a few other variables and read their descriptions.

If the variable you want to select is not showing in the variable window, click on the scroll bars located on the right side of the variable list window to move through the list. See the following figure.

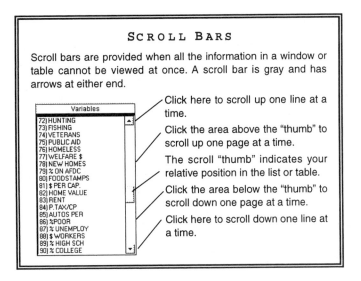

SCROLL BARS

Scroll bars are provided when all the information in a window or table cannot be viewed at once. A scroll bar is gray and has arrows at either end.

Click here to scroll up one line at a time.

Click the area above the "thumb" to scroll up one page at a time.

The scroll "thumb" indicates your relative position in the list or table.

Click the area below the "thumb" to scroll down one page at a time.

Click here to scroll down one line at a time.

By the way, you will find an appendix at the back of this workbook that contains a list of the variable names for key data files provided in this package.

Each task requires the selection of one or more variables, and the ExplorIt Guides indicate which variables you should select. The ExplorIt Guide example here indicates that you should select 12) POPULATION as Variable 1. On the screen, there is a box labeled Variable 1. Inside this box, there is a vertical cursor that indicates that this box is currently an active option. When you select a variable, it will be placed in this box. Before selecting a variable, be sure that the cursor is in the appropriate box. If it is not, place the cursor inside the appropriate box by clicking the box with your mouse. This is important because in some tasks the ExplorIt Guide will require more than one variable to be selected, and you want to be sure that you put each selected variable in the right place.

To select a variable, use any one of the methods shown below. (Note: If the name of a previously selected variable is in the box, use the <Delete> or <Backspace> key to remove it—or click the [Clear All] button.)

- Type the **number** of the variable and press <Enter>.

- Type the **name** of the variable and press <Enter>. Or you can type just enough of the name to distinguish it from other variables in the data—POPU would be sufficient for this example.

- Double-click the desired variable in the variable list window. This selection will then appear in the variable selection box. (If the name of a previously selected variable is in the box, the newly selected variable will replace it.)

- Highlight the desired variable in the variable list, then click the arrow that appears to the left of the variable selection box. The variable you selected will now appear in the box. (If the name of a previously selected variable is in the box, the newly selected variable will replace it.)

Once you have selected your variable (or variables), click the [OK] button to continue to the final results screen.

Step 4: Select a View

The next screen that appears shows the final results of your analysis. In most cases, the screen that first appears matches the "view" indicated in the ExplorIt Guide. In this example, you are instructed to look at the Map view—that's what is currently showing on the screen. In some instances, however, you may need to make an additional selection to produce the desired screen.

POPULATION -- POPULATION IN 1000S (IDB, 1998)

(OPTIONAL) Step 5: Select an Additional Display

Some ExplorIt Guides will indicate that an additional "display" should be selected. In that case, simply click on the option indicated for that additional display. For example, this ExplorIt Guide may have included an additional line that required you to select the Legend display.

Step 6: Continuing to the Next ExplorIt Guide

Some instructions in the ExplorIt Guide may be the same for at least two examples in a row. For instance, after you display the map for population in the example above, the following ExplorIt Guide may be given:

> Data File: **GLOBAL**
> Task: **Mapping**
> ➤ Variable 1: **78) CAP PUNISH**
> ➤ View: **Map**

Notice that the first two lines in the ExplorIt Guide do not have the ➤ symbol in front of the items. That's because you already have the data file GLOBAL open and you have already selected the MAPPING task. With the results of your first analysis showing on the screen, there is no need to return to the main menu to complete this next analysis. Instead, all you need to do is select CAP PUNISH as your new variable. Click the [🔄] button located in the top left corner of your screen and the variable selection screen for the MAPPING task appears again. Replace the variable with 78) CAP PUNISH and click [OK].

To repeat: You need to do only those items in the ExplorIt Guide that have the ➤ symbol in front of them. If you start from the top of the ExplorIt Guide, you're simply wasting your time.

If the ExplorIt Guide instructs you to select an entirely new task or data file, you will need to return to the main menu. To return to the main menu, simply click the [Menu] button at the top left corner of the screen. At this point, select the new data file and/or task that is indicated in the ExplorIt Guide.

That's all there is to the basic operation of Student ExplorIt. Just follow the instructions given in the ExplorIt Guide and point and click your way through the program.

ON-LINE HELP

Student ExplorIt offers extensive on-line help. You can obtain task-specific help by pressing <F1> at any point in the program. For example, if you are performing a scatterplot analysis, you can press <F1> to see the help for the SCATTERPLOT task.

If you prefer to browse through a list of the available help topics, select **Help** from the pull-down menu at the top of the screen and select the **Help Topics** option. At this point, you will be provided a list of topic areas. Each topic is represented by a closed-book icon. To see what information is available in a given topic area, double-click on a book to "open" it. (For this version of the software, use only the "Student ExplorIt" section of help; do not use the "Student MicroCase" section.) When you double-click on a book graphic, a list of help topics is shown. A help topic is represented by a graphic with a piece of paper with a question mark on it. Double-click on a help topic to view it.

If you have questions about Student ExplorIt, try the on-line help described above. If you are not very familiar with software or computers, you may want to ask a classmate or your instructor for assistance.

EXITING FROM STUDENT EXPLORIT

If you are continuing to the next section of this workbook, it is *not* necessary to exit from Student ExplorIt quite yet. But when you are finished using the program, it is very important that you properly exit the software—do not just walk away from the computer or remove your CD-ROM. To exit Student ExplorIt, return to the main menu and select the [Exit Program] button that appears on the screen.

Important: If you inserted your CD-ROM before starting Student ExplorIt, remember to remove it before leaving the computer.

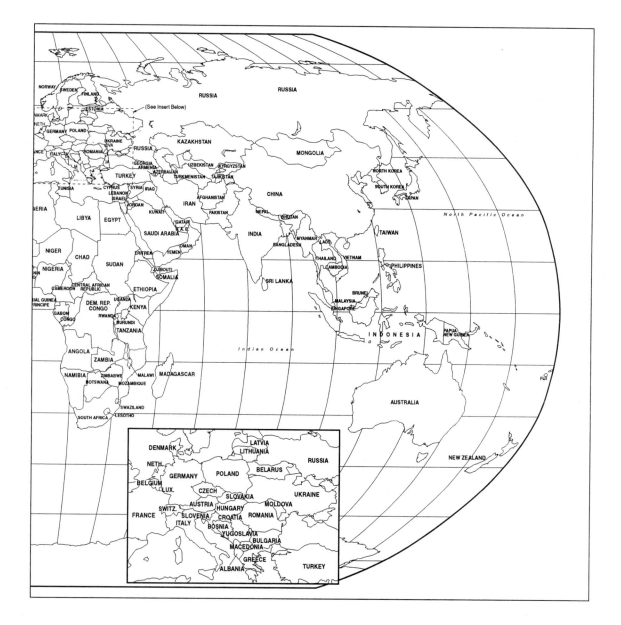

World Map

Part I

DOING COMPARATIVE POLITICS WITH EXPLORIT

CHAPTER 1

THE NATION-STATE

Without a country, I am not a man.

NAWAF AL-NASIR AL-SABAH
KUWAITI DEFENSE MINISTER, 1990

Tasks: Mapping, Univariate, Historical Trends
Data Files: GLOBAL, HISTORY

One of the great challenges associated with learning comparative politics in the post–Cold War era is the task of making some kind of order from the apparent chaos of the world in which we live. Each of the world's more than 190 countries has its own distinct political, social, and economic systems. You may have traveled abroad and done comparisons of your own. Someday you may be sent to a country you have never heard of to close a business deal or to keep the peace. You might meet an immigrant from a country different than your own or send a check to stop deforestation in a tropical country. You will be better equipped to do any of these things if you know more about our world.

The objective of comparative politics is to explain similarities and differences among nation-states. But good exploration usually begins with curiosity. For example, curious people will want to know why capital punishment (the death penalty) is used so frequently in Asia and Africa and so rarely in Europe. In a standard textbook, a statement like this might be accompanied by instructions that direct you to look at a table listing various countries according to their laws on capital punishment. In fact, as you will soon see, graphics of this type appear throughout this workbook. But the difference between this workbook and an ordinary textbook is that you can *explore* the original data yourself—not just read about what other researchers have found.

As shown in the "Getting Started" section (if you haven't yet gone through that section, do so now), the software packaged with this workbook contains numerous data sets. Many of the data sets have *variables* that can be mapped. For example, if we want to check the status of nuclear weapons development in the countries of Asia, we can use the ASIA data file to view a map showing the countries having the most (and least) developed nuclear weapons programs. If we want to look at economic growth across the countries of Africa, we can open the AFRICA file and map a variable that shows this too. To look at the number of political parties in each European country, we would select the appropriate variable from the EUROPE file, and so on. We will examine hundreds of these types of analyses throughout this workbook. To begin, we'll return to the topic of capital punishment. Using the GLOBAL data file, look at the variation in capital punishment across the world.

> *Data File:* **GLOBAL**
>> *Task:* **Mapping**
> *Variable 1:* **78) CAP PUNISH**
>> *View:* **Map**

CAP PUNISH -- The state of the death penalty in 174 nations. 1=ABOLISHED, 2=RETAINED FOR CRIMES AGAINST STATE OR SPECIAL CIRCUMSTANCES,

To reproduce this graphic on the computer screen using ExplorIt, review the instructions in the "Getting Started" section. For this example, open the GLOBAL data file, select the MAPPING task, and select 78) CAP PUNISH for Variable 1. The first view shown is the Map view. (Remember, the ➤ symbol indicates which steps you need to perform if you are doing all the examples as you follow along in the text. So, in the next example below, you only need to select a new view—that is, you don't need to repeat the first three steps because they were already done in this example.)

The nations in this map of the world appear in several colors from very dark to very light. The darker a country is, the more prevalent its use of capital punishment. The lighter a country is, the less likely it is to use capital punishment. Let's see what the different colors actually mean.

Data File: **GLOBAL**
Task: **Mapping**
Variable 1: **78) CAP PUNISH**
View: **Map**
➤ *Display:* **Legend**

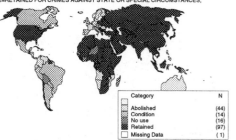

CAP PUNISH -- The state of the death penalty in 174 nations. 1=ABOLISHED, 2=RETAINED FOR CRIMES AGAINST STATE OR SPECIAL CIRCUMSTANCES,

Category	N
Abolished	(44)
Condition	(14)
No use	(16)
Retained	(97)
Missing Data	(1)

As indicated by the ➤ symbol, if you are continuing from the previous example, select the [Legend] button. (It is not necessary to reselect the MAPPING task and 78) CAP PUNISH variable.) Sometimes, as in this case, the description for a map is too long for it to fit on the screen with the map. If you want to see the complete description for a map, click on the [v |] button. A window will appear that gives you the complete description for the map.

Now you will see that the lightest colors actually mean that capital punishment has been abolished in those countries. The legend also indicates that 44 of the 174 countries in our GLOBAL file have abolished capital punishment for all crimes. The second category, colored orange, indicates that capital punishment has been abolished for all crimes except those that are treasonable or those committed during wartime. The third category, in red, indicates that the death penalty still exists in these countries but has not been used recently. The fourth category, the darkest color, indicates those countries that retain capital punishment and still use it. Ninety-seven of the 174 countries in the GLOBAL file are in this last category. Finally, you will notice that the label for the yellow box at the top of the legend is missing. The label is missing because the variable being examined has only four categories. If there were five categories, all five colors would have a label.

But what percentage of all nations has abolished the death penalty? The map legend gives you the *number* of countries that have abolished the death penalty (44) but not the proportion or percentage. If we want to find this out, we will need to approach it another way.

Data File: **GLOBAL**
➤ Task: **Univariate**
➤ Primary Variable: **78) CAP PUNISH**
➤ View: **Pie**

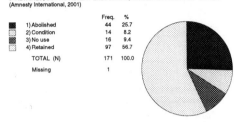

CAP PUNISH -- The state of the death penalty in 174 nations. 1=ABOLISHED, 2=RETAINED FOR CRIMES AGAINST STATE OR SPECIAL CIRCUMSTANCES, 3=RETAINED, BUT NO RECENT EXECUTIONS, 4=USED FOR ORDINARY CRIMES (Amnesty International, 2001)

	Freq.	%
1) Abolished	44	25.7
2) Condition	14	8.2
3) No use	16	9.4
4) Retained	97	56.7
TOTAL (N)	171	100.0
Missing	1	

To reproduce this new view on your screen, you will need to click the [Menu] button at the top of the screen. Then click the UNIVARIATE task, select the 78) CAP PUNISH variable, and click [OK]. (It is not necessary to reselect the GLOBAL file).

You should now see a pie chart on your screen that indicates the legal status of the death penalty in 174 nations around the world. However, this view also calculates the percentage of countries in the world that have abolished the death penalty (25.7%), the percentage of countries that permit the death penalty in exceptional cases (8.2%), the percentage of countries that allow the death penalty under law, but have not used it in more than ten years (9.4%), and finally, the number and percentage of countries that still use the death penalty (56.7%). Like the map, you will also notice that the description above the pie chart explains the variable and each category in more detail. The description also tells you where the data come from. In this case, these data come from Amnesty International's 2001 Annual Report. More detailed information on the source of the variable is always available in the bibliography of sources in the back of this workbook.

NATION-STATES

So far we have referred to countries as nations, but this term is not quite accurate for our purposes. The term *nation* is used to describe a specific ethnic group. In the United States or Canada, this use of the term is often misunderstood because in these nations there is not one dominant ethnic group. However, you may have heard someone ask you what your *nationality* is. When this question is asked in the United States or Canada, it is very likely that people reflect on the origins of their family prior to coming to North America. Perhaps they came from Ireland, Japan, or Italy, in which case one explains that his or her *nationality* is Irish, Japanese, or Italian even though the person is clearly a U.S. or Canadian citizen. If one's nationality refers to an ethnic identity, a state refers to all of the institutions of government that have sovereignty over a group of people whether they constitute a nation or not. *Nation-states*—that is, people of a particular *nationality* (or *nationalities*) governed by an autonomous state—are one of the key units we study in comparative politics.

The notion of a nation-state did not come into being until the 1648 Treaty of Westphalia, which recognized the legitimacy of the nation-state as the fundamental entity in international relations. This concept is not without its problems. One problem is that states rarely govern single ethnic groups, or nationalities.

MULTI-CULT -- MULTI-CULTURALISM:ODDS THAT ANY 2 PERSONS WILL DIFFER IN THEIR RACE, RELIGION, ETHNICITY (TRIBE),OR LANGUAGE GROUP (STARK)

Data File: **GLOBAL**
➤ Task: **Mapping**
➤ Variable 1: **15) MULTI-CULT**
➤ View: **Map**

If you are continuing from the previous example, click [Menu], and then select the MAPPING task. Select variable 15) MULTI-CULT as the new Variable 1. (Again, it is not necessary to reselect the GLOBAL file.)

This map indicates the chances out of 100 that two citizens in a nation-state will be of a different race, religion, ethnicity, or language group. The darker a nation-state, the greater the chance that a person in the nation has a chance of meeting someone of a different cultural background.

MULTI-CULT: Multi-culturalism: Odds that any 2 persons will differ in their race, religion, ethnicity (tribe), or language group

Data File: **GLOBAL**
Task: **Mapping**
Variable 1: **15) MULTI-CULT**
➤ View: **List: Rank**

RANK	CASE NAME	VALUE
1	India	91
1	Congo, Dem. Republic	91
3	Bolivia	90
4	Uganda	89
4	Cameroon	89
6	Nigeria	88
7	South Africa	87
8	Côte d'Ivoire	86
9	Bhutan	85
9	Congo, Republic	85

If you are continuing from the previous example, simply select the [List: Rank] option. The number of rows shown on your screen may be different from that shown here. Use the cursor keys and scroll bar to move through this list if necessary.

You will notice that in a nation like the Democratic Republic of Congo, one's chances of meeting someone of a different cultural background are 91 out of 100. If you scroll to the bottom of the list, you will see that in Japan one's chances of encountering someone of a different cultural background are 1 in 100. But even Japan, one of the most ethnically homogeneous countries in the world, still has within it minority ethnic groups who are not Japanese.

The definition of a nation-state itself (people governed by an autonomous government) implies that nation-states are fairly autonomous in terms of economics, politics, and culture. But in fact, nation-states are affected by factors outside their borders, such as environmental pollution and changes in the international economy. States' autonomy is also constrained by domestic particularities unique to each country, such as political conflict between ethnic groups or geographic isolation. For example, in Canada the autonomy of the state is constrained by ethnic political rivalry between French-speaking Canadians, English-speaking Canadians, and indigenous Canadians. This makes it very difficult for the nation-state to act in any particular way without considering the demands of the different peoples and their interests.

Comparative Politics

POLITICAL INDEPENDENCE

Political independence in the modern era represents the "coming of age" of a nation-state. For a very small number of countries (e.g., the United Kingdom, Russia, France, Spain, and Portugal), this coming of age occurred gradually as kings sought to consolidate their hold over peoples and territories in geographic proximity to their centers of power. Since the Treaty of Westphalia, national groups dominated by other nation-states have endeavored to form their own states in an effort to achieve national independence. This trend has accelerated from the 19th century to the present such that new nationalities seeking their own state seem to be discovered by the media almost every month of the year. Be they Québecois, Kurdish, Hutu, Chechnyan, or Pashtun, these nationalities believe that statehood guarantees them a degree of security that they should not be without. To help you better understand the history of the nation-state, the section that follows will explore comparatively the patterns of political independence worldwide.

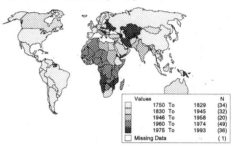

Data File:	**GLOBAL**
Task:	**Mapping**
➤ *Variable 1:*	**70) IND DATE**
➤ *View:*	**Map**
➤ *Display:*	**Legend**

If you are continuing from the previous example, return to the variable selection screen. Select variable 70) IND DATE as the new Variable 1. When the map appears, click [Legend].

As you can see, the countries shown in darker colors have become independent relatively recently. The most recent countries are in Central Asia and Eastern Europe. The next most recent group is in Africa. Let's use the rank option to see which nation-states achieved independence most recently.

IND DATE: Year of independence

Data File:	**GLOBAL**
Task:	**Mapping**
Variable 1:	**70) IND DATE**
➤ *View:*	**List: Rank**

RANK	CASE NAME	VALUE
1	Eritrea	1993
1	Slovak Republic	1993
1	Czech Republic	1993
4	Bosnia and Herzegovina	1992
4	Yugoslavia (Serbia/Montenegro)	1992
6	Lithuania	1991
6	Latvia	1991
6	Belarus	1991
6	Estonia	1991
6	Kyrgyzstan	1991

Eritrea, the Slovak Republic, and the Czech Republic all became independent in 1993. As we scroll down the list to the nation-states with the longest standing independence, we see that European countries like Russia, Spain, and France were independent by 1750, as were Asian countries such as Japan,

China, and Thailand. The GLOBAL data set contains a second version of this variable in which the dates of independence for nation-states are grouped into historically relevant periods. This map has the additional advantage of showing a clearer regional pattern to independence, particularly in South and East Asia.

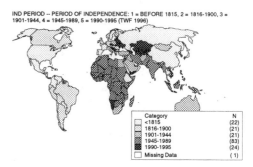

Data File: **GLOBAL**
Task: **Mapping**
➤ Variable 1: **71) IND PERIOD**
➤ View: **Map**
➤ Display: **Legend**

IND PERIOD -- PERIOD OF INDEPENDENCE: 1 = BEFORE 1815, 2 = 1816-1900, 3 = 1901-1944, 4 = 1945-1989, 5 = 1990-1995 (TWF 1996)

Category	N
<1815	(22)
1816-1900	(21)
1901-1944	(21)
1945-1989	(83)
1990-1995	(24)
Missing Data	(1)

When the mapping function displays countries by the "period" of their independence, we can see the regional patterns of independence that emerge for the individual nation-states. It makes sense to view the map in terms of periods rather than dates because the historical events that occur in different periods mark the rise and fall of the empires that gave birth to the new nations. You will notice that many countries of Western and Northern Europe, the United States, and parts of South and East Asia achieved independence or had a tradition of independence before 1815. Many of the powerful countries that were independent before 1815 had set up *colonies* throughout much of the world. A *colony* is a settlement of foreigners established and protected in a territory by the foreigners' government. The first colonizers were Portugal and Spain, which began their colonial expansion and conquest around 1450. They were followed in the 17th and 18th centuries by Britain, France, and Russia. In the 19th century, Holland, Germany, Italy, and Belgium sought the territories that were left. By 1900 every region of the world was colonized. Only a few countries in Asia (Afghanistan, China, Japan, Nepal, and Thailand) escaped colonial domination.

As you examine the map and its accompanying legend, you will probably notice that the first wave of independence after 1815 occurred in South and Central America. The Spanish and Portuguese empires collapsed in the early part of the 19th century, which precipitated a wave of independence movements throughout the former colonies of Latin America. By the beginning of the 20th century there were more than 40 independent nation-states worldwide. Around 1920 a few states in the Middle East began agitating their colonial powers to obtain independence. However, the wave of independence between 1900 and 1945 is not significant. Only 21 nation-states achieved independence during this period, and many of these acquired independence as a result of changes in the European map and Axis colonial holdings at the end of World War I.

From an examination of your map, you will notice that independence expanded at a very rapid pace at the end of World War II in 1945. Political independence since then has occurred in two distinct phases. The first phase began in 1947 as Britain and France started to recognize that they were incapable of carrying the financial burden of their colonial holdings. In addition to these peaceful withdrawals, colonial rebellion characterized independence movements between 1947 and 1975 as the number of nation-states worldwide nearly doubled during this period. The second phase of independence began in 1989 as the Soviet Union collapsed. All of the former republics of the vast Soviet empire were given their political independence. The 20th century was indeed the age of the nation-state. In 1900 there were fewer than 50 independent nation-states. At the beginning of the 21st century there are more than 190 independent nation-states, an increase of more than 400% during a single century! Our examination of the map helps us to see that there is clearly a regional pattern to independence that is strongly related to the decline of European colonial empires (Spain, Portugal, Great Britain, Germany, France, and the Soviet Union). The same general pattern can be seen historically.

➤ *Data File:* **HISTORY**
  ➤ *Task:* **Historical Trends**
➤ *Variables:* **2) IND NATION**

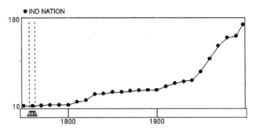

Number of independent nation-states, 1750–1998

The ➤ symbol on the Data File line indicates that you must return to the main menu and open a new data file. Now select the HISTORICAL TRENDS task and choose the variable 2) IND NATION.

As you can see, the number of countries that became independent between 1945 and 1985 more than doubled the total number of nation-states in the world. You can associate the increase in the number of independent nations with significant world events by clicking on a period that interests you or by scrolling through the world events at the bottom of your screen. Scroll up to World War II and click on it. World War II lasted for six years, so the red lines on the graph indicate the range of years in which the event occurs. You will notice that the number of independent countries increased significantly in the years following WWII. Below is a slightly different graphical representation of the same data. This variable shows the number of countries that became independent in each decade since 1750.

Data File: **HISTORY**
  Task: **Historical Trends**
➤ *Variables:* **3) IND/DECADE**

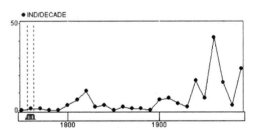

Number of countries that achieved independence in each decade

Be sure to delete the previously selected variable before selecting 3) IND/DECADE. The easiest way to do this is to click the [Clear All] button.

This graphical representation of the number of countries becoming independent in each decade helps us to see historical patterns more clearly. The last jump in the number of independent countries comes since 1989. Click on the year 1990. Notice that the scroll bar changes to display a series of events occurring in the early 1990s. It also displays a series of events that were critical during the end of the Cold War. If you scroll to 1991, you will see that the resignation of Mikhail Gorbachev and the collapse of the USSR correspond to another increase in the number of independent nations.

Now let's see how the distinct patterns of nation-state independence might be related to other phenomena. Most people are aware that some nation-states have a great deal more wealth than others. What causes such variation? Could the time at which a nation-state attains independence be a significant factor in determining its national wealth? Let's return to the GLOBAL data file and the MAPPING task to find out.

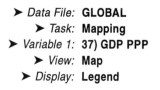

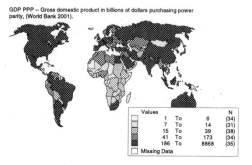

Now you can examine nation-states from the highest to the lowest gross domestic product from 1999, which is the total domestic economic output for a nation-state. Notice that the countries of Europe and North America tend to have the highest levels of wealth and that most other countries in the world have significantly lower levels. We can visualize this phenomenon more clearly by selecting the [Spot Fill] option.

> Data File: **GLOBAL**
> Task: **Mapping**
> Variable 1: **37) GDP PPP**
> View: **Map**
> Display: **Legend**
>   **Spot**

If you are continuing from the previous example, select the [Spot Fill] display option.

The size of each spot is proportional to the value of each state on the variable being mapped. Thus the United States, Japan, and several countries in Europe have the largest spots. The color keys remain as they were when the whole country was colored in, but these are difficult to see because the level of GDP in the wealthiest countries is so much larger than it is in the poorer countries.

One problem with using GDP is that it is very closely linked to the population of a country. You can see this by ranking the nations by GDP.

GDP PPP: Gross domestic product in billions of U.S. dollars

Data File: **GLOBAL**
Task: **Mapping**
Variable 1: **37) GDP PPP**
➤ View: **List: Rank**

RANK	CASE NAME	VALUE
1	United States	8868
2	China	4535
3	Japan	3151
4	India	2242
5	Germany	1949
6	France	1342
7	United Kingdom	1315
8	Italy	1278
9	Brazil	1182
10	Russia	1093

You will notice that China, which has the largest population in the world (1.2 billion), has the second largest GDP in the world. If you scroll down the ranking, you will also see that the country of Luxembourg has a GDP ranking of 98 out of 163 nations. Analysis of this result alone indicates that China may be wealthier than Luxembourg, but this interpretation is misleading. A better measure of national wealth is GDP per capita.

GDPCAP PPP: Gross domestic product per capita

Data File: **GLOBAL**
Task: **Mapping**
➤ Variable 1: **38) GDPCAP PPP**
➤ View: **List: Rank**

RANK	CASE NAME	VALUE
1	Luxembourg	42769
2	United States	31872
3	Norway	28433
4	Iceland	27835
5	Switzerland	27171
6	Canada	26251
7	Ireland	25918
8	Denmark	25869
9	Belgium	25443
10	Austria	25089

We use per capita (or "per person") figures instead of the actual GDP because it adjusts for nations having large or small populations. In this instance you will see that Luxembourg's GDP per capita is $42,769 (in U.S. dollars), which ranks it 1st among all nation-states. China is an example of the other extreme. China's GDP per capita of $3,617 (again, in U.S. dollars) puts it at 92nd in the ranked list. Since we are more interested in the average amount of economic output a person generates within a nation-state, the GDP per capita figure is the better measure for our purposes.

If you want to see where a particular country stands in terms of its ranking on GDP per capita, you can identify it by selecting the [Find case] option that appears on the mapping screen. An alphabetical list of all countries will appear, and you can select the country you're interested in. Select the box next to Canada and click [OK]. The map now highlights the country you selected (Canada) and shows its value and rank on the variable at the bottom of the screen. If you know the location of the country you're interested in, you can also click on the country. For example, click on the United States and you will see its value and rank on the GDP per capita variable.

ExplorIt's MAPPING task allows you to examine two maps at once. This is extremely useful if you are trying to determine if regional patterns for one variable are similar to regional patterns of another variable. Let's continue to use GDPCAP PPP as Variable 1, but add IND DATE as our second variable.

Data File: **GLOBAL**
Task: **Mapping**
Variable 1: **38) GDPCAP PPP**
➤ *Variable 2:* **70) IND DATE**
➤ *Views:* **Map**
➤ *Display:* **Legend**

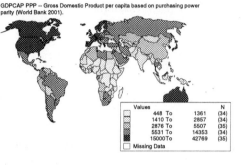

GDPCAP PPP -- Gross Domestic Product per capita based on purchasing power parity (World Bank 2001).

Values		N
448 To	1361	(34)
1410 To	2857	(34)
2876 To	5507	(35)
5531 To	14353	(34)
15000 To	42769	(35)
☐ Missing Data		

r = −0.365**

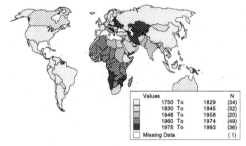

IND DATE -- YEAR OF INDEPENDENCE (TWF 1996)

Values		N
1750 To	1829	(34)
1830 To	1945	(32)
1946 To	1958	(20)
1960 To	1974	(49)
1975 To	1993	(36)
☐ Missing Data		(1)

If you are continuing from the previous example, return to the variable selection screen. Select the variable 70) IND DATE for Variable 2.

If you are continuing from the previous example, return to the variable selection screen. Select the variable 70) IND DATE for Variable 2.

We saw the lower map showing independence dates earlier. As you'll recall, the darker countries in the IND DATE map are those that achieved independence most recently; the lighter countries have been independent the longest. Now, compare the top map (GDP per capita) to the independence date map. Although the pattern is not perfect, the maps are almost mirror opposites of one another. That means the more established a country is, the more likely it is to have generated significant wealth per capita. Conversely, countries that have been independent a shorter period of time have less wealth per capita. Indeed, there appears to be a relationship between the year a country became independent and the relative degree of wealth a country has.

You can also use the [List: Rank] option to show the distributions for both of these variables.

GDPCAP PPP: Gross domestic product per capita

RANK	CASE NAME	VALUE
1	Luxembourg	42769
2	United States	31872
3	Norway	28433
4	Iceland	27835
5	Switzerland	27171

Data File: **GLOBAL**
Task: **Mapping**
Variable 1: **38) GDPCAP PPP**
Variable 2: **70) IND DATE**
➤ *Views:* **List: Rank**

IND DATE: Year of independence

RANK	CASE NAME	VALUE
1	Eritrea	1993
1	Slovak Republic	1993
1	Czech Republic	1993
4	Bosnia and Herzegovina	1992
4	Yugoslavia (Serbia/Montenegro)	1992

If you do some tallying for the 174 countries in our GLOBAL file, you'll see that 13 of the 20 countries ranked highest on GDP per capita were independent nation-states before 1900. Seventeen of the top 20 were independent by the early 1940s, and two of the remaining three (United Arab Emirates, Qatar) are wealthy because of their enormous oil reserves. Looking at the bottom of the GDP per capita list, the opposite trend is clearly visible. Of the 20 countries ranked lowest in terms of GDP per capita, 16 obtained their independence since 1960.

Sometimes people who are trying to understand the underlying reasons for social problems in certain countries, such as overpopulation, child poverty, or unemployment, may wish to compare variables to understand these problems better. In addition to national wealth, we can compare the map of national independence with other social factors, such as the fertility rate, across nations.

Data File: **GLOBAL**
Task: **Mapping**
➤ *Variable 1:* **71) IND PERIOD**
➤ *Variable 2:* **25) FERTILITY**
➤ *Views:* **Map**
➤ *Display:* **Legend**

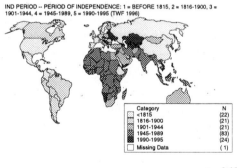

IND PERIOD -- PERIOD OF INDEPENDENCE: 1 = BEFORE 1815, 2 = 1816-1900, 3 = 1901-1944, 4 = 1945-1989, 5 = 1990-1995 (TWF 1996)

Category	N
<1815	(22)
1816-1900	(21)
1901-1944	(21)
1945-1989	(83)
1990-1995	(24)
Missing Data	(1)

r = 0.197**

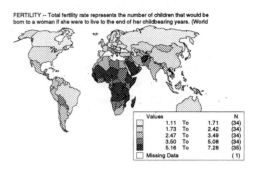

FERTILITY -- Total fertility rate represents the number of children that would be born to a woman if she were to live to the end of her childbearing years. (World

Values			N
1.11	To	1.71	(34)
1.73	To	2.42	(34)
2.47	To	3.49	(34)
3.50	To	5.08	(34)
5.16	To	7.28	(35)
Missing Data			(1)

Once again, the darkest countries in the top map are the nation-states that have become independent most recently. The second map shows the average number of children born per woman in her lifetime for each country. These maps are very similar, which indicates that younger countries tend to have much higher rates of fertility than older countries.

The modern nation-state has clearly matured in the 20th century. Our examination of patterns of independence revealed that nation-states have proliferated at an accelerating pace since 1900. We have also witnessed that the year a country became independent may have a lot to do with its national characteristics such as wealth and fertility.

Before you start on the worksheet section that follows, I'd like to show you another feature in ExplorIt that you will find very useful. Return to the variable selection screen for the MAPPING task and click the [Search] button. If you want to find a variable in the data set but don't know its number or location (or even if such a variable exists), this option lets you search variable names and descriptions for key words. Type in the word REGION and click [OK]. An abbreviated list of variables is now shown and each variable having the word REGION in either its variable name or description is listed. It is obvious why the variables 10) REGION and 11) REGION2 were found in this search, but it is not immediately clear why the variable 73) WAR is listed. Click once on the variable WAR and examine the variable description in the window at the lower right. Sure enough, a variant of the word region ("regional") appears in the variable description. Had we typed in only the first three letters REG, we would have additionally located variables that had the word REGIME in the variable description. If you wanted to conduct another search, you would click on the [Full List] button to return to the full list of variables. But instead, select the variable REGION and click [OK] to view the map. (Remember to clear all of your previously selected variables.) Then click the [Legend] option.

REGION -- REGION (HDR, 1998)

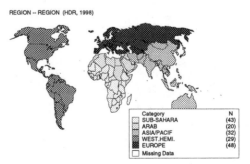

Category	N
SUB-SAHARA	(43)
ARAB	(20)
ASIA/PACIF.	(32)
WEST.HEMI.	(29)
EUROPE	(48)
Missing Data	

This map shows the regions of the world broken down into five categories: sub-Saharan Africa, Arab nation-states, Asia/Pacific, the Western Hemisphere, and Europe. There are many different ways to classify the regions of the world, but we will often use this particular grouping to keep things simple. Likewise, if you encounter a question in the workbook that requires you to refer to a particular region of the world, you can use this region variable for guidance.

Speaking of workbook questions, you are now ready for the first worksheet section in this book.

WORSHEET

NAME: _____

COURSE: _____

DATE: _____

If you have not already done so, review the instructions in the "Getting Started" section.

REVIEW QUESTIONS

Based on the first part of this chapter, answer the following questions:

1. A(n) _____ is a term used to describe a specific ethnic group.   _____

2. However, a(n) _____ is one of the key units we study in comparative politics.   _____

3. Is a nation with a multicultural rating of 2 (out of 100) very homogeneous or heterogeneous?   _____

4. For the most part, nation-states in Central Asia and Eastern Europe are relatively recent independent states.   T   F

5. Compared to other nation-states, the United States is a fairly new independent state.   T   F

6. Japan, China, and Thailand were colonies until the late 1800s, at which time they obtained their independence.   T   F

7. The number of nation-states more than doubled in the last half of the 20th century.   T   F

8. For our purposes, the GDP *per capita* is a better measure than the actual GDP because it adjusts for variations in national population.   T   F

9. A key advantage of ExplorIt's MAPPING task is that you can see how political boundaries were formed by natural terrain, such as mountains and rivers.   T   F

10. According to the preliminary section of this chapter, nation-states that have early dates of independence generally tend to be _____ than nation-states with later dates of independence. (circle one of the following)
    a. larger
    b. wealthier
    c. poorer
    d. more ethnically diverse

11. According to the preliminary section, nation-states that have early dates of independence generally have lower rates of _____ than nation-states with later dates of independence. (circle one of the following)

    a. crime

    b. diversity

    c. war

    d. fertility

EXPLORIT QUESTIONS

> **You will need to use the ExplorIt software for the following questions. Make sure you have already gone through the "Getting Started" section that is located prior to the first chapter. If you have any difficulties using the software to obtain the appropriate informa-tion, or if you want to learn about additional features of ExplorIt's MAPPING task, refer to the on-line help topics on MAPPING under the Help menu.**

I. Earlier in this chapter we looked at the relationship between a country's date of independence and its GDP per capita and fertility rate. Let's pursue this analysis to see if the independence date of a coun-try is related to other important social factors. We might theorize that the longer a nation-state has been an independent and sovereign entity, the more likely it is able to pursue the benefits of a good society (i.e., higher levels of education, health, and wealth). A statement such as this is known as a hypothesis. A hypothesis is a statement of probability. It does not seek to determine whether some-thing is "true" or "false" but, rather, whether a relationship is likely to exist based on the evidence. In the first few analyses below, we will study the relationship between the length of time a nation-state has been independent and other social factors that might evidence a good society. Variable 16) EDUC INDEX combines a country's literacy rate and school enrollment rates to come up with an index between 0 and 1.00 for the level of education in a country. A number like .15 (Niger) would mean that there is a relatively low level of education in a nation-state while a number like .99 (New Zealand) means that there is relatively high education.

        ➤ *Data File:* **GLOBAL**
           ➤ *Task:* **Mapping**
     ➤ *Variable 1:* **16) EDUC INDEX**
     ➤ *Variable 2:* **70) IND DATE**
          ➤ *View:* **Map**

12. Do these two maps look quite similar, nearly opposite, or neither? [By opposite, we mean that countries that are light on one map appear in a darker color on the other map, and vice versa.] (circle one)

    a. Similar

    b. Opposite

    c. Neither

II.   In the first column below, list the top five nation-states in terms of the education index. In the second column, indicate the year in which each country became independent. (Hint: Use the [List: Alpha] option for the bottom map to list the countries in alphabetical order.)

EDUCATION INDEX   **INDEPENDENCE DATE**

_____   _____

_____   _____

_____   _____

_____   _____

_____   _____

Now list the lowest ranked nation-states in terms of the education index. Also list their independence date. (Exclude nation-states that don't have any data listed for them.)

EDUCATION INDEX   **INDEPENDENCE DATE**

_____   _____

_____   _____

_____   _____

_____   _____

_____   _____

13.   Which of the following statements most closely resembles the patterns that you have examined above?

  a.   Nation-states with earlier independence dates tend to have a lower education index rating.

  b.   Nation-states with later independence dates tend to have a lower education index rating.

  c.   Nation-states with earlier independence dates tend to have a higher education index rating.

  d.   Nation-states with later independence dates tend to have a higher education index rating.

  e.   Both b and c are correct.

III.   The variable 36) QUAL. LIFE is a composite measure of the physical quality of life for a nation. It combines child mortality rates, literacy, and life expectancy, and it ranges from 25 (low) to 100 (high).

14. Based on our earlier findings, do you predict that nations that achieved early independence will be ranked low or high on this measure?

    a. Low

    b. High

Let's test your prediction.

> Data File: **GLOBAL**
> Task: **Mapping**
> ➤ Variable 1: **36) QUAL. LIFE**
> ➤ Variable 2: **70) IND DATE**
> ➤ View: **Map**

15. Do these two maps look quite similar, nearly opposite, or neither? (circle one)

    a. Similar

    b. Opposite

    c. Neither

16. In terms of quality of life, how many of the 14 highest ranked nation-states obtained independence prior to the end of World War II (1945)? _____

17. In terms of quality of life, how many of the 10 lowest ranked nation-states obtained independence after the end of World War II? _____

IV. A basic goal of a society is to ensure that there is sufficient food for its people. Use ExplorIt's search function to locate a variable that measures the amount of food or calories that is available to members of a society.

18. Which variable did you select? _____

19. Based on our earlier findings, do you predict that nations that achieved early independence will be ranked low or high on this measure? _____

Use the MAPPING task to compare the variable you selected with the map of independence date.

20. Do these two maps look quite similar, nearly opposite, or neither? (circle one)

    a. Similar

    b. Opposite

    c. Neither

21. Does your prediction seem to be supported by the analysis? (circle one)

    a. Yes

    b. No

V. So far in this chapter we've looked at the relationship between a nation-state's date of independence and its quality of life, GDP per capita, education levels, and food availability. Let's look at an aspect of employment. Do you think there is a relationship between the independence date of a nation and the percentage of women (relative to men) who are part of the workforce? Since we know nation-states that recently achieved independence are poorer, we might predict that women in these countries enter the workforce out of sheer necessity because dual incomes are needed to survive.

> Data File: **GLOBAL**
> Task: **Mapping**
> ➤ Variable 1: **99) F/M EMPLOY**
> ➤ Variable 2: **70) IND DATE**
> ➤ View: **Map**

22. Do these two maps look quite similar, nearly opposite, or neither? (circle one)

a. Similar

b. Opposite

c. Neither

23. According to the map legend, 31 nation-states have female employment rates (as a percentage of male employment) that are between 10% and 30%.   T   F

24. According to the map legend, 35 nation-states have female employment rates that are between 73% and 88%.   T   F

25. Of the 10 nation-states ranked lowest in terms of female employment, more than half were independent before World War II.   T   F

26. There is strong support for our prediction that newly independent nations will likely have higher levels of female employment.   T   F

VI. Now compare the region map we examined in the preliminary part of this chapter to the map for female employment.

> Data File: **GLOBAL**
> Task: **Mapping**
> Variable 1: **99) F/M EMPLOY**
> ➤ Variable 2: **10) REGION**
> ➤ View: **Map**
> ➤ Display: **Legend**

27. On the female employment map, locate the region having the lowest rates of female employment. What is the name of this region (according to the region map)?   _____

VII. Earlier in this chapter we examined a map showing the level of multiculturalism for each nation of the world. As you will recall, the variable 15) MULTI-CULT indicates the odds that any two persons in a nation-state will differ in their race, religion, ethnicity, or language group. Let's take a brief look at how the level of multiculturalism in a nation-state might be related to internal cultural conflict.

Before mapping 58) C.CONFLICT, write down its complete variable description.

_____

_____

> Data File: **GLOBAL**
> Task: **Mapping**
> ➤ Variable 1: **15) MULTI-CULT**
> ➤ Variable 2: **58) C.CONFLICT**
> ➤ Views: **Map**

28. Do these two maps look quite similar, nearly opposite, or neither? (circle one)

 a. Similar

 b. Opposite

 c. Neither

VIII. Civil liberties are basic freedoms that include such things as freedom of speech, press, religion, and assembly. An international organization known as Freedom House has created an index that scores every nation in terms of civil liberties from 1 (most free) to 7 (least free). Let's use this index to look at the relationship between multiculturalism and civil liberties. Since nations having high levels of multiculturalism tend to have more internal struggles, let's predict civil liberties will be lowest in nation-states having high levels of multiculturalism.

> Data File: **GLOBAL**
> Task: **Mapping**
> Variable 1: **15) MULTI-CULT**
> ➤ Variable 2: **59) CIV LIBS**
> ➤ View 1: **List: Rank**
> ➤ View 2: **List: Alpha**

29. Less than half of the 10 nation-states having the highest level of multiculturalism scored less than a 4 on civil liberties.   T   F

30. More than half of the 10 nation-states having the lowest levels of multiculturalism scored a 1 or 2 on the civil liberties index.   T   F

IN YOUR OWN WORDS

In your own words, please answer the following questions.

1. Summarize the relationship between the age of the nation-state and its quality of life.

2. Summarize the relationship between the level of multiculturalism in nation-states and their level of cultural conflict.

3. In a brief paragraph, explain why you think the relationship between civil liberties and multiculturalism exists (or does not exist).

CHAPTER 2

PEOPLE, POPULATIONS, AND STATE CAPACITY

An empty stomach is not a good political advisor.
ALBERT EINSTEIN

Tasks: Mapping, Scatterplot
Data Files: GLOBAL

I n the previous chapter we learned to compare maps to identify similarities and differences between nation-states. As you'll recall, we looked briefly at several basic economic and political indicators such as gross domestic product per capita, capital punishment, and political independence. When political scientists or, broadly speaking, social scientists consider the overall concept of "development," the examination extends well beyond the general wealth and democracy of nation-states. Development includes the entire realm of social factors such as population growth, infant mortality rates, employment, health care, education, and nutrition. In a basic sense, these are problems that all governments must address in one way or another. State capacity refers to a state's ability to use resources to achieve social and economic change. States with a high capacity are relatively more effective in achieving policy goals than those states with low capacity. Human development and state capacity will be the focus of this chapter.

Let's begin by looking at a common, albeit important, social indicator: population growth rates.

> *Data File:* **GLOBAL**
> *Task:* **Mapping**
> *Variable 1:* **13) POP GROWTH**
> *View:* **Map**
> *Display:* **Legend**

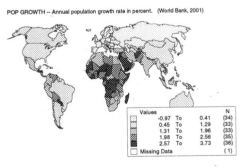

POP GROWTH -- Annual population growth rate in percent. (World Bank, 2001)

This map shows the annual population growth for nation-states across the world. With the exception of Belize, sub-Saharan Africa and the Islamic nation-states have the highest population growth rates. Population growth rates in some countries pose a very serious problem to developing nations. For example, an annual population growth rate of 3% per year means that a nation's population will double every 23 years. This poses serious problems for governments in the developing world that would be challenged to keep order and encourage development under conditions of zero population growth. In the chapter that follows, we will examine population growth as an example of one problem that states must manage.

Data File: **GLOBAL**
Task: **Mapping**
Variable 1: **13) POP GROWTH**
➤ View: **List: Rank**

POP GROWTH: Current annual population growth rate

RANK	CASE NAME	VALUE
1	Palestinian Authority	3.73
2	Bahrain	3.58
3	Belize	3.44
3	Qatar	3.44
5	Niger	3.39
6	Somalia	3.38
7	United Arab Emirates	3.29
8	Afghanistan	3.21
9	Congo, Dem. Republic	3.18
10	Madagascar	3.09

The Palestinian Authority (3.73%) and Bahrain (3.58%) have the first and second highest annual growth rates. At the bottom of the list we see that 14 nations are actually declining in population. In 1999, Kazakhstan had the greatest decline (–0.97%), followed by Belarus (–0.92%), Croatia (–0.83), Latvia (–0.72%), Ukraine (–0.69%), and Bulgaria (–0.60). Most liberal democracies fall in the 0% to 1% range for annual growth.

What causes the variation in population growth across nation-states? The most obvious answer is the birth rate. As the birth rate increases, so does the population. Notice that almost all the nation-states at the bottom of the list were from the former Soviet Union or its satellite states. Was there something about the breakup of the Soviet Union that led to these declines, or did the pattern of low population growth exist before this time? Perhaps nation-states having people with higher life expectancies experience higher levels of population growth. Along this line of thinking, we might attribute the level of health care for a country as an indirect contributor to population growth. Perhaps nations with high infant mortality rates have lower population growth. We can investigate many of these questions with ExplorIt.

The most obvious answer to our population growth question is birth rates. Let's start there.

Data File: **GLOBAL**
Task: **Mapping**
Variable 1: **13) POP GROWTH**
➤ Variable 2: **24) BIRTHRATE**
➤ Views: **Map**
➤ Display: **Legend**

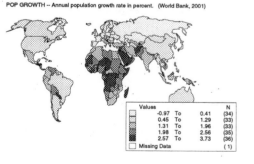

POP GROWTH -- Annual population growth rate in percent. (World Bank, 2001)

Values			N
	-0.97 To	0.41	(34)
	0.45 To	1.29	(33)
	1.31 To	1.96	(33)
	1.98 To	2.56	(35)
	2.57 To	3.73	(36)
Missing Data			(1)

r = 0.813**

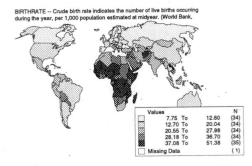

Values			N
7.75	To	12.60	(34)
12.70	To	20.04	(34)
20.55	To	27.98	(34)
28.18	To	36.70	(34)
37.08	To	51.38	(35)
Missing Data			(1)

These two maps are clearly similar. We see that sub-Saharan Africa and the Arab nation-states are also the highest in terms of birth rate. Use the [List: Rank] option to list the results for the BIRTHRATE variable. In terms of birth rates, Somalia is the highest with 51.38 births per 1,000 population, followed by Niger (51.20) and Angola (47.80). At the bottom of the birth rate list we find Latvia (7.75), Bulgaria (8.05), the Czech Republic (8.70), and Estonia (8.70). Again, the Eastern European nations are at the bottom of the list.

In the previous chapter you used comparison maps to determine whether one variable is similar to another. If two maps are very similar to (or mirror opposites of) one another, it is fairly easy to determine the relationship. But, as you examine maps that are less alike, it is more difficult to identify the patterns. Comparing ranked lists of nation-states is also cumbersome, especially when you have to keep track of 172 nations. While comparison maps are helpful, there is another method that is more precise and informative in describing the similarity of two maps. The method was invented about 100 years ago in England by Karl Pearson. Once you see how he did it, you will find it very easy to apply to your own analysis. To understand Pearson's method, we draw a horizontal line to represent the BIRTHRATE map. On the left end of the line we write 7.75 to represent the nation-state with the lowest birth rate (Latvia); on the right end of the line we write 51.38 to represent the nation-state with the highest birth rate (Somalia).

7.75   BIRTHRATE   51.38

Starting at the left end of the horizontal line, we now draw a vertical line of equal length up the left side of the paper to represent the population growth. At the bottom of this line we write –0.97 to represent Kazakhstan's population growth rate, and at the top of the line we write 3.73 to represent the population growth rate for the Palestinian Authority.

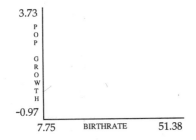

What we end up with are two lines having an appropriate scale to represent each map. The bottom line representing the birth rate is called the x-axis; the vertical line representing growth rate is called the y-axis. The next step is to obtain the value for each nation-state and locate it on each line according to its score. Let's start with Somalia. Since it has the highest birth rate of 51.38 per 1,000 population, it's easy to locate its place on the horizontal line. Place a small mark on the horizontal line to indicate Somalia's location. Next, we need to find Somalia's location on the vertical line. Somalia's annual growth rate is 3.38% so we place a mark on the vertical line at its approximate location. Now, we draw a line up from the mark for Somalia on the horizontal line and draw another line out from its mark on the vertical line. Where these two lines intersect we place a dot. This dot represents the combined values for the population growth rate and the birth rate for Somalia.

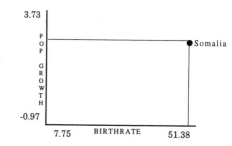

Let's also locate the Palestinian Authority. To find the Palestinian Authority on the line representing birth rates, estimate where 40.98 is located and make a mark on the horizontal line. The Palestinian Authority is easy to locate on the vertical line because its value of 3.73% is the highest of all nation-states. So make a mark at the top of the vertical line. Again, draw a line up from the horizontal line and out from the vertical line. Where these two lines meet is the combined location for the Palestinian Authority. Don't worry, you'll never have to complete this process for all 172 nations in the data set— ExplorIt can do this for you. But do recognize that if we followed this procedure for all nations, we would have all 172 nations located within the space defined by the vertical and horizontal lines representing the two maps. What you would have created is known as a scatterplot. Use ExplorIt to create a complete scatterplot using these same two variables.

Data File: **GLOBAL**
➤ Task: **Scatterplot**
➤ Dependent Variable: **13) POP GROWTH**
➤ Independent Variable: **24) BIRTHRATE**

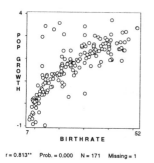

r = 0.813**   Prob. = 0.000   N = 171   Missing = 1

Special Feature: When the scatterplot is showing, you may obtain information on any dot by clicking on it. A little box will appear around the dot, and the values of 13) POP GROWTH (or the y-axis variable) and 24) BIRTHRATE (or the x-axis variable) will be shown. To deselect the case, click the [Find case] box.

Each of the dots shown here represents a nation-state. To identify a dot, just point at it with your mouse and click. Start by clicking on the dot at the top of the scatterplot. As expected, ExplorIt will identify it as the Palestinian Authority, which had the highest population growth rate in 1999. When you click on a dot, information about its exact coordinates on the x-axis and y-axis appears to the left of the scatterplot. Here we see that the Palestinian Authority's X value (birth rate) is 40.98 per 1,000 population; its Y value (population growth) is 3.73%. Now, click on the dot located farthest to the right on the graph. Somalia is identified as the case, and its values on both variables are shown on the left side of the screen.

Once Pearson created a scatterplot, his next step was to calculate what he called the regression line.

> Data File: **GLOBAL**
> Task: **Scatterplot**
> Dependent Variable: **13) POP GROWTH**
> Independent Variable: **24) BIRTHRATE**
> ➤ View: **Reg. Line**

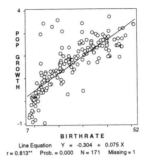

To show the regression line, select the [Reg. Line] option from the menu.

The regression line represents the best effort to draw a straight line that minimizes the distance between all of the dots. It is unnecessary for you to know how to calculate the regression line since the program does it for you. The line alerts us to a pattern in the data. In our comparison of the birth rate and population growth, the line slopes upward. The regression line tells us that as the birth rate increases, population growth also increases. If you would like to see how the regression line looks if the maps are identical, then all you need to do is examine a scatterplot of identical maps. So, if you create a scatterplot using POP GROWTH as both the dependent and independent variables, you will be comparing identical maps and the dots representing countries on the regression line will look like a string of beads. However, since the maps for POP GROWTH and BIRTHRATE are only very similar, but not identical, most of the dots are scattered near, but not on, the regression line. Pearson's method for calculating how much alike are any two maps or lists is very easy once the regression line has been drawn. What it amounts to is measuring the distance out from the regression line to every dot. To do this, simply click on [Residuals].

> Data File: **GLOBAL**
> Task: **Scatterplot**
> Dependent Variable: **13) POP GROWTH**
> ➤ Independent Variable: **24) BIRTHRATE**
> ➤ View: **Reg. Line/Residuals**

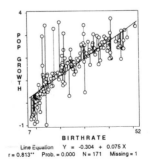

To show the residuals, select the [Residuals] option. Keep the [Reg. Line] option selected too.

See all of the little lines. If you added them all together, you would have a sum of the deviation of all the dots from the regression line. The smaller this sum is, the more alike are the two maps. For example, when the maps are identical and all the dots are on the regression line, the sum of the deviations is 0. In order to make it simple to interpret results, Pearson invented a procedure to convert the sums into a number called the correlation coefficient. The correlation coefficient varies from 0.0 to 1.0. When maps are identical, the correlation coefficient will be 1.0. When they are completely unalike, the correlation coefficient will be 0.0. Thus, the closer the correlation coefficient is to 1.0, the more alike the two maps or lists. Pearson used the letter r as the symbol for his correlation coefficient. Look at the lower left of the screen and you will see r = 0.813**. The number indicates that the maps are quite similar and that the relationship between the two variables is strong. The meaning of the asterisks will be discussed later in this chapter.

Correlation coefficients can be either positive or negative. This correlation is positive: where birth rates are higher, the population growth rate is higher. That is, as one rises so does the other; they tend to rise or fall in unison. If nation-states are trying to reduce their population growth rates, they might first attempt to reduce their birth rates. A successful solution for reducing the birth rate should be negatively correlated with the birth rate. For example, we might expect that as the percentage of women in the population who use contraception increases, the birth rate would decrease. Hence, we are looking for a negative correlation between contraception use and birth rates. We expect that as contraception use increases, birth rates will fall.

Data File:	**GLOBAL**
Task:	**Scatterplot**
➤ *Dependent Variable:*	**24) BIRTHRATE**
➤ *Independent Variable:*	**28) CONTRACEPT**
➤ *View:*	**Reg. Line**

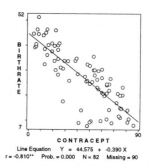

Line Equation   Y = 44.575 + -0.390 X
r = -0.810**   Prob. = 0.000   N = 82   Missing = 90

Here we see a very clear relationship between the use of contraception and the birth rates in nation-states. As the percentage of women using contraception increases, the birth rate decreases. Notice that in this case, the regression line slopes downward from left to right, rather than upward. That always indicates a negative correlation. Also notice that a minus sign now precedes the correlation coefficient (r = −0.810**). Incidentally, you will rarely see a correlation coefficient this high. It suggests that the negative correlation between these two variables is very close to the perfect value of 1.0.

The purpose of calculating correlation coefficients isn't simply to say how alike or unalike two maps are. The point of comparing two maps or creating a scatterplot is to search for links, or connections, between variables. Ultimately, we are looking for causal relationships. Only when such links exist can we propose that there is a causal relationship between them. Thus, implicit in our first two uses of the scatterplot is the assumption that one variable might be the cause of the other. Whenever social scientists become interested in a variable, the first thing they do is ask what causes it to vary. And the *first* test of any proposed answer to the question is to demonstrate the existence of a correlation between the variable to be explained and its proposed cause. In this instance we have demonstrated that contraception use in a society may be the cause of the birth rate in a society since the two are highly correlated. By itself, correlation does not establish that a causal relationship exists. But without a correlation there can be no causal relationship. That helps us explain the distinction between independent and dependent variables. In the SCATTERPLOT task, the software asks for the dependent variable and then asks for the independent variable. If we think something might be the cause of something else, we say that the cause is the independent variable and that the consequence (or the thing that is being caused) is the dependent variable. Put another way, the dependent variable depends on the independent variable.

Suppose a researcher thought that population growth rates might be related to the death rates in countries. If population growth is high, perhaps it's related to the fact that not enough people are dying to offset other factors that contribute to population growth. Let's create a scatterplot using annual population growth and the number of deaths per 1,000 population per year.

           Data File: **GLOBAL**
               Task: **Scatterplot**
➤ *Dependent Variable:* **13) POP GROWTH**
➤ *Independent Variable:* **29) DEATHRATE**
            ➤ *View:* **Reg. Line**

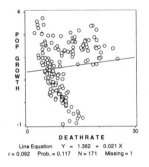

The correlation is positive, but it's not very strong (r = 0.092). Also notice that the result is not significant (there are no asterisks). According to this analysis, there is no relationship between population growth and the death rate. While this is certainly the case for all 171 countries in our analysis, it is also possible that there is a pattern that is not at first apparent. Click on two or three of the countries in the far upper-left corner of the scatterplot. These countries have very high population growth rates and low death rates. You should notice that most of these countries are Islamic oil-producing countries in the Middle East and South Asia. These are unique cases because they are wealthy societies that are able to promote public health (and have a low death rate), but they are also Islamic societies that have a high birth rate for religious reasons. For these reasons we might consider that these societies are what are called outliers in our analysis. When doing comparative analysis, it is sometimes necessary to exclude outliers from the analysis so that they don't substantially exaggerate (or dampen) the overall results. If there is a reasonable explanation for removing an outlier, it is often justified for these reasons. Click on the option labeled [Outlier] and notice that the case located far above the rest in terms of population growth is highlighted. This is the nation of Bahrain, located off the coast of Saudi Arabia. Because of this special situation, let's remove Bahrain from the analysis. To do this, simply click the [Remove] button located to the left of the scatterplot. Bahrain is now removed and the scatterplot is rescaled to adjust the new range of values. Notice too that the correlation coefficient (r) has risen to 0.109.

Notice that there is very little slope to the regression line. Moreover, the dots are not located very close to the regression line. This is what it looks like when two variables have almost no correlation. So population growth does not seem to be related to the death rate. Notice, however, that the value is not at absolute zero (with the outlier removed, r = 0.109). So, how are we able to say that these two variables aren't correlated? We can say it because the odds are very high that this correlation is nothing but a random occurrence—in short, an accident.

Now let's see if removing Islamic nations from this analysis makes a difference in the relationship between population growth and death rate.

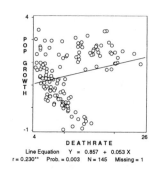

Data File: **GLOBAL**
Task: **Scatterplot**
Dependent Variable: **13) POP GROWTH**
Independent Variable: **29) DEATHRATE**
➤ Subset Variable: **80) WORLDS.7**
➤ Subset Category: **Exclude: 5) Islamic**
➤ View: **Reg. Line**

> **If you are working from the previous example, click the arrow button [↻] and add the subset variable called 80) WORLDS.7. Select 5) Islamic from the list. Also check the option "Exclude selected categories."**

This will give you the same scatterplot as before, but without Islamic countries, which seem to be unique. You will notice that the new correlation coefficient is 0.230**. This result is not very strong, but it is significant. This suggests that there is a weak and significant relationship between population growth and the death rate in non-Islamic countries.

Many correlations are so small that we treat them as if they were zero. The software automatically does the calculation for you and gives you the results. If you look back at the correlation between birth rate and contraception use, you will see that there are two asterisks following the value of r ($r = -0.810^{**}$). Two asterisks mean that there is less than 1 chance in 100 that this correlation is a random accident. One asterisk means that the odds against a correlation being random are 1 in 20 (or 5 out of 100). Whenever there are no asterisks following a correlation, the odds are too high that it could be random. Thus, the result is not significant.

That's how we know that the original correlation between the population growth and death rate (before we exclude Islamic countries) is too small to matter: there are no asterisks. Treat all correlations without asterisks as if they were zero correlations.

When r has at least one asterisk, it indicates a statistically significant relationship. In assessing the strength of a correlation coefficient, treat an r smaller than .30 as a weak relationship, an r between .30 and .60 as a moderate relationship, and an r greater than .60 as a strong relationship. Also remember to examine whether the relationship is positive or negative.

As you will find in Chapter 4, statistical significance in survey data helps us to assess whether or not a relationship exists in the population from which the survey sample was drawn. In ecological data sets, such as the GLOBAL file, statistical significance helps us determine whether the existing relationship is a result of chance factors. This rule of thumb does not apply in the use of survey data. A rule of thumb for interpreting correlation coefficients in survey data is discussed in Chapter 4.

Finally, keep in mind that correlation and causation are *not* the same thing. It is true that without correlation there can be no causation, but correlations often occur between two variables without one being a cause of the other. And we are often interested in correlations between two variables even when we don't think that one causes the other. For example, we might wonder if nation-states that have more cars might also have higher rates of education for women.

To see if these two variables are correlated, we will go back to the MAPPING task.

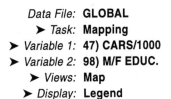

Data File: **GLOBAL**
➤ Task: **Mapping**
➤ Variable 1: **47) CARS/1000**
➤ Variable 2: **98) M/F EDUC.**
➤ Views: **Map**
➤ Display: **Legend**

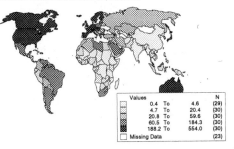

CARS/1000 -- CARS PER 1000 PERSONS (WABF, 1995)

Values			N
0.4 To	4.6		(29)
4.7 To	20.4		(30)
20.8 To	59.6		(30)
60.5 To	184.3		(30)
188.2 To	554.0		(30)
Missing Data			(23)

r = 0.528**

M/F EDUC. -- AVERAGE FEMALE YEARS OF SCHOOLING AS A PERCENTAGE OF AVERAGE MALE YEARS (CALCULATED)

Values			N
14.3 To	32.0		(24)
33.3 To	60.0		(34)
60.9 To	87.0		(30)
88.5 To	96.7		(29)
96.9 To	148.1		(30)
Missing Data			(25)

The maps look very similar. CARS/1000 is high in the Northern Hemisphere and low in the Southern Hemisphere, and the ratio of educated women to educated men is low in the Southern Hemisphere and higher in the Northern Hemisphere. Pearson's r (r = 0.528**) is already calculated for you in the map comparison. This calculation is the same in both the MAPPING task and the SCATTERPLOT task. The two asterisks show that this is a significant correlation, but it does not show that one variable is causing another. Women are not more educated because there are more cars in a society. Nor are there more cars in a society because women are more educated. This could still be interesting to social scientists, though, because both of these phenomena might be the result of another variable, such as the level of economic development.

The SCATTERPLOT task and Pearson's correlation coefficient are powerful tools. In the worksheet section that follows, you'll use these tools to examine a number of issues related to social development and state capacity.

WORKSHEET

CHAPTER
2

NAME: _____

COURSE: _____

DATE: _____

REVIEW QUESTIONS

Based on the first part of this chapter, answer the following questions:

1. Sub-Saharan Africa and the Arab nation-states have the highest population growth rates.   T   F

2. The Palestinian Authority's population growth rate is high because of an exceptionally high birth rate.   T   F

3. The correlation coefficient produced by the scatterplot is more accurate than the one produced by the compare map function.   T   F

4. If one variable causes another, then they must be correlated.   T   F

5. When a correlation is followed by asterisks, we treat the results as statistically significant.   T   F

6. State capacity refers to a state's ability to use resources to achieve social and economic change.   T   F

7. The last two maps in the preliminary section of the chapter tell us that women who drive cars are more educated.   T   F

8. A key advantage of the SCATTERPLOT task is that it allows us to examine three variables at once.   T   F

9. In a causal relationship, the _____ variable is said to be the cause of something and the consequence is the _____ variable.   _____

    _____

10. The _____ represents the best effort to draw a straight line that connects all the dots in a scatterplot.   _____

11. A(n) _____ is an oddball case in a scatterplot that is located far from all other cases.   _____

<u>EXPLORIT QUESTIONS</u>

> **If you have any difficulties using the software to obtain the appropriate information, or if you want to learn about additional features of ExplorIt's SCATTERPLOT task, refer to the on-line help under the Help menu.**

I. In the preliminary part of this chapter, we examined several factors that were related to population growth. One way that we can begin to understand state capacity is to analyze the relationship between basic government-sponsored programs and public health. Let's pursue this analysis by looking at the issue of child health worldwide. The hypothesis is: Countries with higher government commitment to health care will have better public health. First let's look at the effect of immunization programs on child health. In the analysis below we will use the following variables: 27) MORTAL<5; 30) IM:DPT; 31) IM:MEASLES. We assume that a state's child vaccination rate is an indicator of state capacity. In other words, states with high vaccination coverage for children have higher state capacity than those without high rates of child vaccination.

> ➤ *Data File:* **GLOBAL**
> ➤ *Task:* **Scatterplot**
> ➤ *Dependent Variable:* **27) MORTAL<5**
> ➤ *Independent Variable:* **30) IM:DPT**
> ➤ *View:* **Reg. Line**

12. From the variable description for 27) MORTAL<5, we see that this variable is a measurement of (circle one of the following)
    a. the probability that a newborn baby will live past his/her fifth birthday.
    b. the probability that a newborn baby will die before his/her fifth birthday.
    c. the death of fewer than five people for every 1,000.
    d. It's not possible to tell from the graph.

13. From the variable description for 30) IM:DPT, we see that this variable is a measurement of
    a. the probability that a child will be immunized against diphtheria, pertussis, and tetanus.
    b. the rate of vaccination coverage for diphtheria, pertussis, and tetanus for children under one year of age.
    c. the immortality rate of people exposed to DPT.
    d. It's not possible to tell from the graph.

14. The countries that are the highest on 27) MORTAL<5 should appear as dots at the
    a. right of the scatterplot.
    b. left of the scatterplot.
    c. top of the scatterplot.
    d. bottom of the scatterplot.
    e. It's not possible to tell without looking at the values.

15. The dots that appear farthest to the right side of the scatterplot represent those countries that have the (circle one of the following)

    a.   highest rates of mortality under age 5.

    b.   the highest rates of vaccination coverage for DPT.

    c.   the lowest rates of mortality under age 5.

    d.   the lowest rates of coverage for DPT.

    e.   The location of the dots tells us nothing about the values of the cases or these variables.

16. What is the correlation coefficient for these results?   r = _____

17. Is the relationship positive or negative?   _____

18. Are these results statistically significant?   Yes   No

19. What is the name of the outlier in this scatterplot?   _____

20. Remove the outlier and indicate the new correlation coefficient.   r = _____

21. Are these new results statistically significant?   Yes   No

22. Do these results support the hypothesis that countries with higher levels of immunization for DPT have lower rates of child mortality for children under age 5?   Yes   No

Now analyze the relationship between 31) IM:MEASLES and 27) MORTAL<5.

> Data File: **GLOBAL**
> Task: **Scatterplot**
> Dependent Variable: **27) MORTAL<5**
> ➤ Independent Variable: **31) IM:MEASLES**
> ➤ View: **Reg. Line**

23. What is the correlation coefficient for these results?   r = _____

24. Is the relationship positive or negative?   _____

25. Are these results statistically significant?   Yes   No

26. What is the name of the outlier in this scatterplot?   _____

27. Remove the outlier and indicate the new correlation coefficient.   r = _____

28. Are these new results statistically significant?   Yes   No

29. Do these results support the hypothesis that countries with higher levels of immunization for measles have lower rates of child mortality for children under age 5?   Yes   No

II. The state's use of the education system is another way to achieve significant change in a society. In the following analysis, we assume that high capacity states have stronger education systems than low capacity states. In the preliminary part of the chapter, we saw that birthrates were substantially lower in countries with higher percentages of women using contraception. For contraceptives to be effective, people must first learn how to use them. So, it would seem that nations that have a strong education infrastructure would be best equipped for distributing information about contraceptives. So our hypothesis is: Citizens in nation-states with higher levels of education will be more likely to use contraceptives. In the analysis that follows, we will assess the relationship between the variables 28) CONTRACEPT and 16) EDUC INDEX.

> Data File: **GLOBAL**
> Task: **Scatterplot**
> ➤ Dependent Variable: **28) CONTRACEPT**
> ➤ Independent Variable: **16) EDUC INDEX**
> ➤ View: **Reg. Line**

30. Identify the country that is highest on 28) CONTRACEPT.   _____

31. What percentage of married women of childbearing age use contraception in the above listed country?   _____%

32. Identify the country that is the highest on 16) EDUC INDEX.   _____

33. What is the education index number for the above listed country?   _____

34. What is the correlation coefficient for this scatterplot? $r =$ _____

35. Are the results statistically significant?   Yes   No

36. Do these results offer support to our hypothesis?   Yes   No

Let's see if there are other variables that might be related to contraception rates. Create a scatterplot between 28) CONTRACEPT and each variable listed below. For each analysis, fill in the correlation coefficient and indicate whether the results are statistically significant. Then answer the series of questions that follow. (Note: Be sure to examine each variable description before you select it for analysis.)

DEPENDENT   INDEPENDENT

37. 28) CONTRACEPT and 35) CALORIES $r =$ _____   Significant?   Yes   No

38. 28) CONTRACEPT and 112) URBAN % $r =$ _____   Significant?   Yes   No

39. 28) CONTRACEPT and 98) M/F EDUC. $r =$ _____   Significant?   Yes   No

40. 28) CONTRACEPT and 99) F/M EMPLOY $r =$ _____   Significant?   Yes   No

41. Nation-states with higher percentages of women using contraception are likely to have greater amounts of calories (food) available per person. T F

42. There is a strong relationship between contraceptive use and the percentage of the population who live in urban areas. T F

43. Countries with higher percentages of contraceptive use are likely to have greater proportions of women who are educated. T F

44. Countries with higher percentages of contraceptive use are likely to have greater levels of female unemployment. T F

45. Each of the results in the analysis of contraception is statistically significant. T F

III. Does religion play a role in development? Is development affected by the predominant religion in a nation-state? Let's compare nation-states having high percentages of Muslims with those having high percentages of Christians. The first variable listed is dependent.

46.	28) CONTRACEPT and 83) %MUSLIM	r = _____	Significant?	Yes	No
47.	24) BIRTHRATE and 83) %MUSLIM	r = _____	Significant?	Yes	No
48.	16) EDUC INDEX and 83) %MUSLIM	r = _____	Significant?	Yes	No
49.	98) M/F/ EDUC. and 83) %MUSLIM	r = _____	Significant?	Yes	No
50.	99) F/M EMPLOY and 83) %MUSLIM	r = _____	Significant?	Yes	No
51.	28) CONTRACEPT and 84) %CHRISTIAN	r = _____	Significant?	Yes	No
52.	24) BIRTHRATE and 84) %CHRISTIAN	r = _____	Significant?	Yes	No
53.	16) EDUC INDEX and 84) %CHRISTIAN	r = _____	Significant?	Yes	No
54.	98) M/F/ EDUC. and 84) %CHRISTIAN	r = _____	Significant?	Yes	No
55.	99) F/M EMPLOY and 84) %CHRISTIAN	r = _____	Significant?	Yes	No

IN YOUR OWN WORDS

In your own words, please answer the following questions.

1. From the results of your analysis in Questions 46–55, how does religion relate to patterns of social development? Be sure to support your response with evidence. From this analysis, can you conclude that variations in social development are caused by religious differences?

2. Using the GLOBAL file, analyze the relationship between the dependent variable 27) MORTAL<5 and the independent variables 56) ARMY/DOCTR, 53) MIL/BUDGET, and 54) MIL/GNI. Be sure to carefully examine both variable descriptions carefully before you answer. Remove one outlier from each analysis and consider the following: Often a country chooses between building up a large army and promoting the health of its citizens. Based on this analysis (without the outlier), is there a relationship between a state's support for the military and the health of citizens? Be sure to support your answer with evidence.

ORGANIZING POLITICAL SYSTEMS: FIRST, SECOND, AND THIRD WORLDS?

As the long forgotten peoples of the respective continents rise and begin to reclaim their ancient heritage, they will discover the meaning of the lands of the ancestors.

VINE VICTOR DELORIA, JR.
NATIVE AMERICAN HISTORIAN
AND ACTIVIST

Tasks: Mapping, Univariate, Cross-tabulation
Data Files: GLOBAL

I f one of the primary objectives of comparative politics is to study the differences and similarities of countries, then how do we make order out of the apparent chaos of all the nation-states in the world? Political philosophers throughout Western history have sought to organize political systems into categories to aid in the understanding of the most basic questions of political organization: Why do some governments fail while others do not? Why are some nations democratic while others are not? Why have some states been easier to conquer than others? Aristotle collected the constitutions of about 150 city-states in an attempt to answer the question of which government system was most stable. From his analysis he generated a classification scheme to organize the various political models that were operative in ancient Greece (Table 3.1).

Table 3.1. Aristotle's Classification of Regimes

Rule by	Virtuous Form	Degenerative Form
One	Monarchy	Tyranny
Few	Aristocracy	Oligarchy
Many	Polity	Democracy

The key variable that Aristotle identified in his attempt to explain or understand government instability was the number of people involved in governing the state or regime. In addition, he recognized that these governments were sometimes capable of governing virtuously, and thus have just, fair, and efficient forms, and that they were also capable of governing selfishly, which produced degenerative forms.

In his quest to understand the cause of political instability, or a state's movement from the virtuous form to the degenerative form, he examined the effects of social and economic factors that supported or undermined the stability of the regimes. Based on this examination of real cases in ancient Greece, Aristotle concluded that democracy and oligarchy were the least stable forms of political organization, whereas systems that combined these two forms tended to be the most stable.

Those who study comparative politics are still in pursuit of answers to the same questions Aristotle asked in ancient Greece. We also must have the means to classify nation-states into groups with similar characteristics so that we might better understand the factors that are responsible for the similarities and differences of the various groups. From the end of World War II until 1989, it was commonplace for teachers and students of comparative politics to classify nation-states according to the Three Worlds classification schema. To see how these categories appear geographically, map the following procedure:

➤ *Data File:* **GLOBAL**
  ➤ *Task:* **Mapping**
➤ *Variable 1:* **79) THREEWORLD**
  ➤ *View:* **Map**

THREEWORLD -- CLASSIFICATION OF COUNTRIES INTO THREE WORLDS MODEL: 1 = FIRST WORLD, 2 = SECOND WORLD, 3 = THIRD WORLD (LE ROY, 1998)

You will notice that this categorization of nation-states is most useful for geographers. With the exception of Japan, Australia, and New Zealand, this classification locates all First World countries in Europe and North America. Almost all Second World countries are located in Eastern Europe and Asia, and all Third World nation-states are located to the south of the First and Second Worlds.

Political scientists have found it very useful to organize or classify countries according to their political system, economic system, size, geopolitical power, wealth, and region. The Three Worlds was the dominant classification method used during the Cold War. This system of organization classified countries according to their political and economic systems. People classified First World countries according to their form of political organization (i.e., democratic) and their economic system (i.e., free-market capitalist). In contrast, Second World countries were organized according to a totalitarian form of government (i.e., communist) and their centrally planned, state-dominated economies. The classification was a little broader for Third World countries because this tended to include almost all countries that were former colonies of First World nations that were not easily classified in either of the other two categories.

Politically speaking, Third World countries tended to be authoritarian rather than totalitarian. The difference between authoritarianism and totalitarianism is that in totalitarian systems the leadership seeks to extend its authority to all domains, such as religion, family life, and economic activity. Authoritarian regimes are usually concerned only with controlling those domains specifically related to political activity. Economically, Third World nation-states were characterized by a wide variety of economic systems. Some, such as Cuba and Vietnam, have a state-dominant economy, whereas others, including Chile and Brazil, chose a capitalist economy. A large number of countries, such as India, Egypt, and Tunisia, also tried to experiment with a "mixed economy." That is, they sought to draw from both economic traditions. Table 3.2 shows that First World and Second World countries have very distinct political and economic systems, but Third World countries tend to vary a great deal.

Table 3.2. Three Worlds by Economic and Political System

	Democratic	Totalitarian	Authoritarian
Capitalist	First World Great Britain	N/A	Third World Chile
State-Dominant	N/A	Second World U.S.S.R.	Third World Iraq
Mixed	Third World India	Third World China	Third World Egypt

As you can see in the table, there were five types of nations that were classified as Third World and only one type classified as either First or Second World. This means that a large number of nation-states were bound to be classified in the third category and relatively few would be classified in the other two groups.

No classification system is perfect, but the Three Worlds approach worked well during the Cold War because it highlighted the differences between the two major superpowers. However, in the 1970s, this classification system came under attack by scholars who thought it was important to more carefully classify the countries of the Third World. We can see the reason for this when we examine the number of countries in each of these categories in the map legend below.

Data File: **GLOBAL**
Task: **Mapping**
Variable 1: **79) THREEWORLD**
View: **Map**
➤ Display: **Legend**

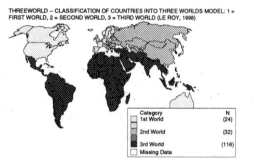

With the legend showing on the screen, notice the numbers that appear to the right side of the legend window. The "N" is a symbol that represents the number of cases for each category. We see that there are 24 nation-states categorized as First World, 32 categorized as Second World, and 116 categorized as Third World.

Remember that we can also examine the number of countries in each of these categories through a procedure called univariate analysis, which allows us to view these same numbers in the form of a pie chart or bar graph.

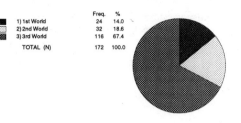

Data File: **GLOBAL**
➤ *Task:* **Univariate**
➤ *Primary Variable:* **79) THREEWORLD**
➤ *View:* **Pie**

THREEWORLD -- CLASSIFICATION OF COUNTRIES INTO THREE WORLDS MODEL: 1 = FIRST WORLD, 2 = SECOND WORLD, 3 = THIRD WORLD (LE ROY, 1998)

	Freq.	%
■ 1) 1st World	24	14.0
▨ 2) 2nd World	32	18.6
▨ 3) 3rd World	116	67.4
TOTAL (N)	172	100.0

Return to the main menu of ExplorIt and select the UNIVARIATE task. Select 79) THREE-WORLD as your variable.

Using the UNIVARIATE task, you get a pie chart that shows you the distribution of countries according to their classification in the Three Worlds schema. Notice that the numbers to the right of the pie chart match those provided by the map legend. Additional information is also provided, such as the percentage of nation-states that fall into each category. Here we see that 14.0% of countries are categorized as First World countries, 18.6% are Second World, and 67.4% are Third World countries. While this classification schema may provide some insight to the economic and political characteristics of First World and Second World nation-states, it is problematic when you consider that over two-thirds of all countries fit into one category (Third World). Are two-thirds of the nation-states really that similar?

With the ExplorIt software, we can test the validity of the Three Worlds classification method. To do this, we will use a variable that places all the countries of the world into one of three categories, according to their gross domestic product per capita.

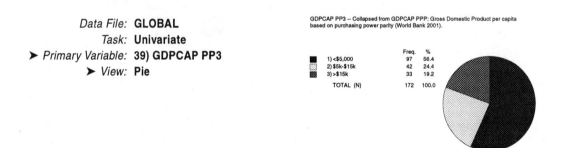

Data File: **GLOBAL**
Task: **Univariate**
➤ *Primary Variable:* **39) GDPCAP PP3**
➤ *View:* **Pie**

GDPCAP PP3 -- Collapsed from GDPCAP PPP: Gross Domestic Product per capita based on purchasing power parity (World Bank 2001).

	Freq.	%
■ 1) <$5,000	97	56.4
▨ 2) $5k-$15k	42	24.4
▨ 3) >$15k	33	19.2
TOTAL (N)	172	100.0

Here we see that 56.4% of nations have a GDP per capita of less than $5,000. 24.4% are located in the $5,000 to $15,000 range, and another 19.2% of nations have a GDP per capita of over $15,000. Notice that the percentage distributions of these categories are fairly equal to those for the Three Worlds variable. Hence, if the Three Worlds classification works for the purpose of economic differentiation, we would expect First World nations to be concentrated in the highest GDP per capita category, Second World nations to be found mainly in the middle GDP category, and Third World nations to be located primarily in the lowest GDP category.

Let's use ExplorIt's subset feature to see how the nation-states of the First World are distributed according to their wealth per capita.

Data File: **GLOBAL**
Task: **Univariate**
Primary Variable: **39) GDPCAP PP3**
➤ *Subset Variable:* **79) THREEWORLD**
➤ *Subset Category:* **Include: 1) 1st World**
➤ *View:* **Pie**

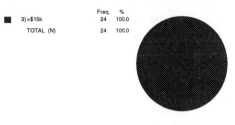

GDPCAP PP3 -- Collapsed from GDPCAP PPP: Gross Domestic Product per capita based on purchasing power parity (World Bank 2001).

		Freq.	%
■	3) >$15k	24	100.0
	TOTAL (N)	24	100.0

[Subset]

The option for selecting a subset variable is located on the same screen you use to select other variables. For this example, select 79) THREEWORLD as a subset variable. A window will appear that shows the categories of the subset variable. Select 1) 1st World as your subset category and choose the [Include] option. Then click [OK] and continue as usual.

With this particular subset, the results will be limited to the First World countries in the data file. Note that the subset selection continues until you delete the subset variable, or use the [Clear All] button to remove all variable selections, or exit the task completely.

The subset category we selected limits the analysis to countries categorized as First World. All of the nations classified as First World fall into the top wealth category.

We could repeat this analysis using the subset option to limit analyses to countries categorized as Second World, and then do a third analysis including only Third World countries. But this is a time-consuming process and there is, in fact, an easier way to obtain the same results in one step by using ExplorIt's CROSS-TABULATION task.

Data File: **GLOBAL**
➤ *Task:* **Cross-tabulation**
➤ *Row Variable:* **39) GDPCAP PP3**
➤ *Column Variable:* **79) THREEWORLD**
➤ *View:* **Tables**
➤ *Display:* **Column %**

GDPCAP PP3   by   THREEWORLD
Cramer's V: 0.589 **

		THREEWORLD			
		1st World	2nd World	3rd World	TOTAL
GDPCAP PP3	<$5,000	0	19	78	97
		0.0%	59.4%	67.2%	56.4%
	$5k-$15k	0	12	30	42
		0.0%	37.5%	25.9%	24.4%
	>$15k	24	1	8	33
		100.0%	3.1%	6.9%	19.2%
	TOTAL	24	32	116	172
		100.0%	100.0%	100.0%	

To construct this table, return to the main menu and select the CROSS-TABULATION task. Then select 39) GDPCAP PP3 as the row variable and 79) THREEWORLD as the column variable. When the table appears, select the [Column %] option.

Focus on the bottom row of the table (the one representing nations having GDP per capita of greater than $15,000). As we saw in the previous analysis, 100% of First World countries fall into the highest category for GDP per capita. Reading across this row we see that only one (3.1%) of the Second World nations falls into this category, while 6.9% of Third World nations are located in the highest GDP per capita category. The First World classification does seem to work fairly well.

But look at the row for $5,000 to $15,000 GDP per capita. Here we see that none of the First World nations fall into this category, compared to 37.5% of Second World nations and 25.9% of Third World nations. The pattern of the results is somewhat along the line of what we might expect, but there is not a clear-cut distinction between Second World and Third World nations in terms of GDP per capita.

As we move to the top row (less than $5,000 GDP per capita), a similarly muddled picture appears. Second World and Third World nations have similar percentages across this category (both are around 60%). As it turns out, there is not a clear economic distinction between Second World and Third World nation-states.

These same results can be viewed graphically by selecting the [Bar] option shown on your screen.

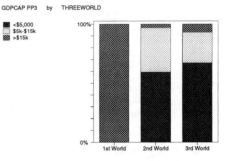

Data File: **GLOBAL**
Task: **Cross-tabulation**
Row Variable: **39) GDPCAP PP3**
Column Variable: **79) THREEWORLD**
➤ View: **Bar**

This graph helps illustrate what we've been analyzing on the table. The First World category is characterized by nation-states having a high GDP per capita. When we examine the Second World and Third World classifications, we again see that a clear economic distinction between these two categories does not exist.

In addition to economic classification, the Three Worlds approach was used to describe the political makeup of a nation-state. In the 1960s, during the Cold War, the Three Worlds classification worked well because it illuminated the conflict between democratic capitalism (the First World) and communism (the Second World) and the attempt of both groups to win over the other countries (the Third World). Some countries, like China, Vietnam, Cuba, and Angola, were clearly in the communist camp due to their Marxist-Leninist commitments and one-party political systems. So they were classified as Second World nations, even though many were preindustrial and very poor. There were also a number of nation-states, such as Saudi Arabia, Kuwait, and Oman, that were neither democratic nor communist (hence, classified Third World) although they had relatively high GDP per capita due to oil income. As the Cold War wound down in the late 1980s and many communist countries became "postcommunist," it became increasingly apparent that making political distinctions based on the Three Worlds categories was not very useful.

The Three Worlds classification is clearly problematic. But what can we use to place nation-states into groups? Aristotle would agree with most contemporary political scientists that it's essential to place nation-states into groupings that allow systematic study. This need is made even more clear by the fact that institutions like the United Nations, the World Bank, the International Monetary Fund, governments of wealthy nations, and nongovernmental organizations (NGOs) must decide how to focus their efforts to serve less developed countries based on some type of criteria. Which groups of nations are the most in need of economic assistance? Which nations are successfully developing? What factors have led to development failures? Leaders from one country may wish to give aid only to stable, democratic governments. How do they do this without a means of identifying the groups of countries that fit this criterion? All of these questions demand methods of classification to organize nation-states in an intellectually coherent manner.

In order to develop a proper classification schema, social scientists must consider at least three major forces that shape a nation-state: political factors, economic factors, and social factors. (By social factors, we are referring to the ethnic, linguistic, and cultural factors that characterize a society.) If you emphasize just one of the three factors, you overlook the important role the other two play in shaping the nation-state.

A political scientist by the name of John McCormick has argued for an alternative classification scheme that attempts to incorporate political, social, and economic factors.[1] Nation-states are categorized as follows: (1) liberal democracies (very similar to the First World category of countries that emphasizes democracy and capitalism), (2) communist or postcommunist, (3) newly industrialized countries (NICs), (4) less developed countries (LDCs), (5) Islamic countries, (6) marginal countries (so underdeveloped and devastated by warfare, they are hardly nation-states at all), and (7) micro countries (those that stand out because they are so small). Let's examine this Seven Worlds classification using the UNIVARIATE task.

Data File: **GLOBAL**
➤ Task: **Univariate**
➤ Primary Variable: **80) WORLDS.7**
➤ View: **Pie**

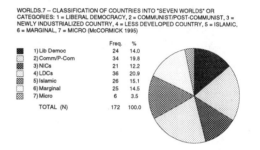

WORLDS.7 -- CLASSIFICATION OF COUNTRIES INTO "SEVEN WORLDS" OR CATEGORIES: 1 = LIBERAL DEMOCRACY, 2 = COMMUNIST/POST-COMMUNIST, 3 = NEWLY INDUSTRIALIZED COUNTRY, 4 = LESS DEVELOPED COUNTRY, 5 = ISLAMIC, 6 = MARGINAL, 7 = MICRO (McCORMICK 1995)

	Freq.	%
1) Lib Democ	24	14.0
2) Comm/P-Com	34	19.8
3) NICs	21	12.2
4) LDCs	36	20.9
5) Islamic	26	15.1
6) Marginal	25	14.5
7) Micro	6	3.5
TOTAL (N)	172	100.0

Look at the distribution of these countries. Communist /postcommunist nation-states and the LDCs are the largest categories with around 20% each. Liberal democracies, NICs, Islamic countries, and marginal countries each make up about 15%. The smallest group is those countries classified as micro (3.5%).

Let's return to the CROSS-TABULATION task and repeat the earlier analysis using GDP per capita. This time, however, we'll use the Seven Worlds variable.[2]

Data File: **GLOBAL**
➤ Task: **Cross-tabulation**
➤ Row Variable: **39) GDPCAP PP3**
➤ Column Variable: **80) WORLDS.7**
➤ View: **Tables**
➤ Display: **Column %**

GDPCAP PP3   by   WORLDS.7
Cramer's V: 0.672 **
Warning: Potential significance problem. Check row and column totals.

		WORLDS.7								
		Lib Democ	Comm/P-Com	NICs	LDCs	Islamic	Marginal	Micro	Missing	TOTAL
GDPCAP PP3	<$5,000	0	21	4	30	15	23	4	1	97
		0.0%	61.8%	19.0%	83.3%	57.7%	92.0%	66.7%		56.4%
	$5k-$15k	0	12	14	6	7	1	2	0	42
		0.0%	35.3%	66.7%	16.7%	26.9%	4.0%	33.3%		24.4%
	>$15k	24	1	3	0	4	1	0	0	33
		100.0%	2.9%	14.3%	0.0%	15.4%	4.0%	0.0%		19.2%
	Missing	0	0	0	0	0	1	0	0	1
	TOTAL	24	34	21	36	26	25	6	1	172
		100.0%	100.0%	100.0%	100.0%	100.0%	100.0%	100.0%		

---

[1] John McCormick, *Comparative Politics in Transition* (New York: Wadsworth, 1995), pp. 5–17.

[2] There are some instances in this chapter (and in the worksheet section that follows) where the cross-tabulation results using the GLOBAL file produce the statement "Warning: Potential significance problem." This is to alert you that the statistical significance value may not be reliable due to the small number of nations used in the analysis. This is not a problem for the type of analysis that we are currently conducting. For our purposes in this chapter, we will often ignore this warning.

Although the 21 cells of this table can be overwhelming at first, it provides more useful information than the earlier table that used the Three Worlds variable. Let's start with the bottom row (>$15,000). Again, 100% of liberal democracies fall into this category, compared to 14.3% of NICs and 15.4% of Islamic nation-states. There is only one communist/postcommunist country in this category, no LDCs and only one marginal country.

Skipping to the top row (>$5,000), we see that all but two marginal countries (or 92%) fall into this category, followed by LDCs (83.3%), communist/postcommunist (61.8%), micro countries (66.7%), and Islamic countries (57.7%). In the center row ($5,000–$15,000), the most notable result is that for newly industrialized countries. Nearly 66.7% of all NICs are in this category.

Let's look at a bar graph of these results.

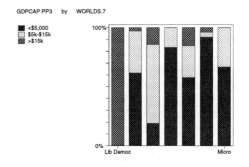

Data File: **GLOBAL**
Task: **Cross-tabulation**
Row Variable: **39) GDPCAP PP3**
Column Variable: **80) WORLDS.7**
➤ View: **Bar**

You'll recall that one of the problems with the Three Worlds variable was that there wasn't much differentiation between Second World and Third World countries in terms of GDP per capita (and many other variables, as it turns out). But the Seven Worlds variable provides substantially more information. Marginal societies are clearly different from both communist/postcommunist societies and NICs. Islamic countries and NICs have fairly sizable numbers in each GDP category, whereas several of the other types of nation-states do not.

We will use the Seven Worlds variable often throughout this workbook. Although this classification is not perfect, it does provide better insight to the social, political, and economic differences among nation-states than does the Three Worlds system.

Now it's your turn to test the Seven Worlds variable in the worksheet section that follows.

WORKSHEET

CHAPTER

3

REVIEW QUESTIONS

Based on the first part of this chapter, answer True or False to the following items:

1. Aristotle's reason for studying types of governments was to understand how war could be avoided. T F

2. One of the most important objectives of comparative politics is to understand what accounts for the differences and similarities between nation-states. T F

3. The Three Worlds classification is based on the Old World of Europe (e.g., Great Britain, France), the New World (e.g., United States, Canada, Australia), and the developing world (e.g., Africa, Asia, South America). T F

4. The Three Worlds classification seemed to have its greatest validity during the Cold War era. T F

5. The First World classification holds up rather well in an analysis of GDP per capita because most of these nation-states are concentrated in the highest levels of GDP. T F

6. The Second World and Third World classifications don't hold up well in an analysis of GDP per capita because there is not much differentiation between the two types of nation-states. T F

7. The subset feature of ExplorIt's UNIVARIATE task allows you to limit analysis to a particular category of a second variable. T F

8. ExplorIt's CROSS-TABULATION task allows you to create pie charts and maps. T F

EXPLORIT QUESTIONS

> **If you have any difficulties using the software to obtain the appropriate information, or if you want to learn about additional features of ExplorIt's CROSS-TABULATION task, refer to the ExplorIt help topics under the Help menu.**

I. The GLOBAL file contains a variable named 61) POL RIGHTS that measures the level of political freedom individuals have within a given nation. The political organization, Freedom House, surveys each country and compiles a set of scores on a number of criteria, such as the right of all adults to vote, the right to compete for public office, and the right for elected representatives to have a decisive vote on public policies. Nation-states that meet all the criteria are given a score of 1 (most free), whereas those that meet none of the criteria are given a score of 7 (least free). The POL RIGHTS variable contains a complete set of scores for the nations in the GLOBAL data file.

> ➤ Data File: **GLOBAL**
> ➤ Task: **Univariate**
> ➤ Primary Variable: **61) POL RIGHTS**
> ➤ View: **Pie**

9.   Freedom House gave a score of 1 or 2 to more than a third of all nations.   T   F

10. More nation-states received a score of 7 than any other score.   T   F

To simplify things a bit, it's possible to create a second variable that places all nation-states with a score of 1 or 2 in a "free" category; nation-states that scored a 3, 4, or 5 in a "partially free" category, and nation-states that scored a 6 or 7 in a category called "not free." We'll use this second version of the variable, 62) POL RIGHT2, to examine the Seven Worlds classification.

> Data File: **GLOBAL**
> ➤ Task: **Cross-tabulation**
> ➤ Row Variable: **62) POL RIGHT2**
> ➤ Column Variable: **80) WORLDS.7**
> ➤ View: **Tables**
> ➤ Display: **Column %**

11. In terms of political rights, which nation-state categories had less than half of their countries scored as "free"? (circle all that apply)

    a.   Liberal democracies

    b.   Comm/P-Com

    c.   NICs

    d.   LDCs

    e.   Islamic

    f.   Marginal

    g.   Micro

12. Which nation-state grouping has the lowest percentage of its countries in the free category?   _____

13. Which nation-state grouping has the highest percentage of its countries in the free category?   _____

14. In terms of political rights, newly industrialized countries are more similar to

    a.   liberal democracies.

    b.   less developed countries.

II. In the first chapter we examined another Freedom House measure for civil liberties. As a reminder, civil liberties include such things as freedom of speech, press, religion, and assembly. Freedom House also scored nation-states on a scale of 1 (high protection of civil liberties, or most free) to 7 (no protection of civil liberties, or least free). However, for the following analysis, we will use a second version of the variable that combines categories 1–2 (for "free"), 3–5 (for "partially free"), and categories 6–7 (for "not free").

> Data File: **GLOBAL**
> Task: **Cross-tabulation**
> ➤ Row Variable: **60) CIV LIBS2**
> ➤ Column Variable: **80) WORLDS.7**
> ➤ View: **Tables**
> ➤ Display: **Column %**

15. In terms of civil liberties, which nation-state categories had less than half of their countries scored as "free"? (circle all that apply)

   a. Liberal democracies

   b. Comm/P. Comm

   c. NICs

   d. LDCs

   e. Islamic

   f. Marginal

   g. Micro

16. Which nation-state grouping had the lowest percentage of its countries in the free category? _____

17. Which nation-state grouping had the highest percentage of its countries in the free category? _____

18. In terms of civil liberties, are communist/postcommunist countries more similar to liberal democracies or less developed countries? _____

III. Is there a geographic pattern to the Seven Worlds classification of nation-states? For example, do liberal democracies tend to be located in a particular region? What about other regions of the world? The variable 10)REGION shows you the five key regions used by the United Nations Development Program (UNDP). If you map this variable, you can see them: 1. sub-Saharan Africa, 2. Arab states, 3. Asia and the Pacific, 4. the Western Hemisphere, and 5. Europe. Now let's try to see if our nation-state categories are concentrated in a specific region.

> Data File: **GLOBAL**
> Task: **Cross-tabulation**
> ➤ Row Variable: **10) REGION**
> ➤ Column Variable: **80) WORLDS.7**
> ➤ View: **Tables**
> ➤ Display: **Column %**

Fill in the percentaged results for the *first, second, and fifth* rows of the table.

	LIB.DEM	COMM/ P-COM	NIC	LDC	ISLAMIC	MARGINAL	MICRO
SUB-SAHARAN AFRICA	____%	____%	____%	____%	____%	____%	____%
ARAB	____%	____%	____%	____%	____%	____%	____%
EUROPE	____%	____%	____%	____%	____%	____%	____%

19. What percentage of liberal democracies are in Europe?   _____

20. Over half of liberal democracies are in Europe.   T   F

21. Most communist or postcommunist nations are located in sub-Saharan Africa
     and the Arab regions.   T   F

22. A majority of the LDCs and marginal states are located in sub-Saharan Africa.   T   F

23. Most Islamic nations are in the Arab region.   T   F

Now that we understand where each type of nation-state is concentrated, let's see if these regions tend to be dominated by certain types of regimes. For example, does Europe tend to be dominated by a particular type of nation-state? To do this, we just reverse the variables in our analysis.

> Data File: **GLOBAL**
> Task: **Cross-tabulation**
> ➤ Row Variable: **80) WORLDS.7**
> ➤ Column Variable: **10) REGION**
> ➤ View: **Tables**
> ➤ Display: **Column %**

24. What percentage of European countries are communist or postcommunist?   _____

Use either the bar graph or the table (with column percentaging) to answer the following questions:

25. Nation-states in the Asia and Pacific regions have the greatest variety in terms of
     the Seven Worlds classification.   T   F

26. Europe tends to have the least variety of nation-states in the Seven Worlds
     classification.   T   F

27. The two most common types of nation-state types in the Western Hemisphere are the
     less developed countries and the newly industrialized countries.   T   F

28. In Europe there are more liberal democracies than communist/postcommunist nation-states.   T   F

IV. In the first chapter of this book, we examined the independence date of nation-states in terms of numerous social and political factors. Let's see if there is a connection between the period in which a nation-state became independent and its Seven Worlds classification.

> *Data File:*   **GLOBAL**
> *Task:*   **Cross-tabulation**
> *Row Variable:*   **80) WORLDS.7**
> ➤ *Column Variable:*   **71) IND PERIOD**
> ➤ *View:*   **Tables**
> ➤ *Display:*   **Column %**

Fill in the percentaged results for the *top* row of the table.

	<1815	1816–1900	1901–1944	1945–1989	1990–1995
LIBERAL DEMOC.	_____%	_____%	_____%	_____%	_____%

29. What percentage of those countries that achieved independence between 1901 and 1944 are liberal democracies?   _____

30. Around 40 percent of nation-states that achieved independence before 1815 are now liberal democracies.   T   F

31. Only one of the nation-states that achieved independence since 1945 is categorized as a liberal democracy.   T   F

Use either the bar graph or the table (with column percentaging) to answer the following questions:

32. The period 1945–89 witnessed the independence of mainly one type of nation-state.   T   F

33. Most Islamic nation-states became independent between 1900 and 1989.   T   F

34. All micro nation-states became independent between 1945 and 1989.   T   F

V. Warfare is the most violent and costly interaction among nation-states. Civil wars are also prevalent within many nation-states. Are certain types of nation-states more likely to experience warfare?

> *Data File:*   **GLOBAL**
> *Task:*   **Cross-tabulation**
> ➤ *Row Variable:*   **73) WAR**
> ➤ *Column Variable:*   **80) WORLDS.7**
> ➤ *View:*   **Tables**
> ➤ *Display:*   **Column %**

Use both the [Column %] and the [Bar] option to answer the following questions.

35. Liberal democracies and micro nation-states are the least likely to have warfare.   T   F

36. Marginal nation-states are the most likely to have civil wars.   T   F

37. Islamic nation-states are the least likely to have interstate wars.   T   F

38. Overall, marginal nation-states have experienced the most warfare.   T   F

39. Micro nation-states have experienced the least warfare.   T   F

IN YOUR OWN WORDS

In your own words, please answer the following questions.

1. Imagine that you are a representative of a human rights organization concerned with political rights and civil liberties. Which category of countries shows the most promise for improving political rights and civil liberties to the level of liberal democracies and microstates? In a brief paragraph, describe the similarities and/or differences between the results you found in the political rights analysis and the civil liberties analysis. Be sure to support your claims with evidence.

2. In the Three Worlds classification, NICs and LDCs would be placed in the same Third World category. What are the differences between these two groups of countries with respect to per capita wealth (use GDPCAP PP3), war, civil liberties, and political rights? Are they different enough to warrant separate categories?

Part II

POLITICS AND GOVERNMENT IN LIBERAL DEMOCRACIES

CHAPTER 4

POLITICAL CULTURE IN LIBERAL DEMOCRACIES

The ruling ideas of each age have ever been the ideas of its ruling class.

KARL MARX AND FRIEDRICH
ENGELS, 1848

Tasks: Mapping, Cross-Tabulation, Univariate
Data Files: GLOBAL, WVS97all, WVS97–AUSTRALIA, WVS97–GERMANY, WVS97–JAPAN,
WVS97–SWEDEN, WVS97–USA

In Chapter 3 we learned that there are different types of nation-states in the international system. Some scholars refer to these differences according to the traditional Three Worlds classification, while others are more specific in their characterization of these nation-states. We also learned that these differences in classification are most pronounced when we are trying to characterize the differences in developing nations. But both characterizations seem to agree that liberal democracies have very distinct characteristics *vis-à-vis* other nation-states throughout the world: they are all democratic, they are relatively wealthy, and they are relatively stable compared to most other categories of nation-states.

In the previous chapter, we looked at the factors that distinguish countries from each other at the nation-state level. Most of us would agree that liberal democracies have different levels of wealth, education, and health, but are the political values and ideas of citizens in these countries different? This chapter continues with the topic of liberal democracies but relies primarily on individual-level data for citizens. As such, you'll use the CROSS-TABULATION task and learn several new techniques that will be useful throughout the remainder of the workbook. But before we jump into analysis of survey data with the CROSS-TABULATION task, let's start with an example using our familiar GLOBAL file and the MAPPING task.

➤ *Data File:* **GLOBAL**
➤ *Task:* **Mapping**
➤ *Variable 1:* **109) TRUST?**
➤ *View:* **List: Rank**

TRUST?: Percent who say that most people can be trusted

RANK	CASE NAME	VALUE
1	Norway	65
2	Sweden	60
3	Denmark	58
4	Netherlands	55
5	China	52
5	Canada	52
7	Finland	48
8	Ireland	47
9	Iceland	44
10	Japan	42

The TRUST? variable is based on data from surveys that were conducted in 61 countries as part of the World Values Survey. What is shown here is the *average* response given by a sampling of the population in each country to the following survey question: "Generally speaking, would you say that most people can be trusted or that you can't be too careful in dealing with people?" As you can see, 65% of people interviewed in Norway indicate that they trust most people. At the bottom of the list is Brazil, in which only 3% of survey respondents indicate that they trust other people.

This example and most others in the first three chapters of this workbook used the "nation-state" as the *unit of analysis*. The term *unit of analysis* refers to the "things" or "cases" being analyzed. Since we are comparing data across nation-states, we say that nation-states are the unit of analysis. Of course, political scientists use other units of analysis besides nation-states and individuals. For example, a researcher in the United States might analyze the laws of the 50 U.S. states, and therefore the state would be her unit of analysis (each variable would list one value for each state). Or she might use the 254 counties of Texas, or the census tracts of New York City, or the neighborhood areas of Chicago, and so on. Perhaps the most widely used unit of analysis is individuals. When a political scientist conducts a survey or poll, the analyses are usually based on the combined responses that individuals gave during the survey (e.g., "In a national survey of Canadians, 52% indicate that they trust their neighbors."). It's important that you always recognize the unit of analysis that is being used.

In the last example, you used a variable in the GLOBAL file that is based on the World Values Survey. Did you wonder how the "average response" for each nation was obtained? That is, what process was used to come up with the value of 65% for Norway? As it happens, there is a very large data file used by researchers that contains the responses of all 78,574 people interviewed in more than 50 countries that were part of the World Values Survey. This data file is a bit overwhelming for our purposes, but you have a smaller version named WVS97all that includes all 14,097 people interviewed in 8 of the 61 countries. Although only a few of the original survey questions are included in this file, it will give you a good sense of how this source of data (where the *individual* is the unit of analysis) can be used to create data where the nation-state is the unit of analysis. Let's look at the same survey question above (trust in fellow citizens) using individual-level data for eight countries.

➤ *Data File:* **WVS97all**
➤ *Task:* **Cross-tabulation**
➤ *Row Variable:* **3) TRUST PEOP**
➤ *Column Variable:* **1) COUNTRY**
➤ *View:* **Tables**
➤ *Display:* **Column %**

TRUST PEOP by COUNTRY
Cramer's V: 0.239 **

		COUNTRY								
		Germany	USA	Japan	Russia	S Korea	Mexico	Turkey	Nigeria	TOTAL
TRUST PEOP	Can trust	651	543	419	474	378	399	104	488	3456
		33.3%	35.9%	42.3%	23.9%	30.3%	28.1%	5.5%	19.2%	25.5%
	Be careful	1305	968	571	1506	869	1021	1788	2054	10082
		66.7%	64.1%	57.7%	76.1%	69.7%	71.9%	94.5%	80.8%	74.5%
	Missing	70	31	64	60	2	90	16	227	559
	TOTAL	1956	1511	990	1980	1247	1420	1892	2542	13538
		100.0%	100.0%	100.0%	100.0%	100.0%	100.0%	100.0%	100.0%	

Note that this task uses a new data file. To create these results, open the file named WVS97all. Then select the CROSS-TABULATION task and 3) TRUST? as the row variable and 1) COUNTRY as the column variable. When the table is showing, select the [Column %] option. You may need to scroll the table to view all the columns.

The top row of this table shows the percentage of people in each of the eight countries who indicate that you "can trust" people. The bottom row shows the percentage of people who indicate that you should "be careful." The eight countries included in this data set are listed across the top of the columns. As you learned in Chapter 3, the easiest way to read a cross-tabulation result is to pick a row and read it from left to right (just like a book). If you read across the top row, you'll see that 33.3% of citizens in Germany are apt to trust people, compared to 35.9% in the U.S. and 42.3% in Japan. As you work your way across the table, you'll also find the percentages for Russia (23.9%), South Korea (30.3%), Mexico (28.1%), Turkey (5.5%), and Nigeria (19.2%). So this is the answer to our original question: In order to obtain the average response for each nation-state on a survey question, you simply create a table like this to determine the percentaged results of individuals in each category. In fact, if you repeat the opening analysis of this chapter, you'll see that the values you obtained with the GLOBAL file match those shown here.[1]

The eight countries selected for the WVS97all data set were not arbitrary. In fact, they will be the focus of many discussions in the latter half of this workbook. These countries were selected because they represent five of the seven major categories of nation-states:

Liberal Democracies: Germany; USA; Japan.

Communist or Postcommunist: Russia

NICs: S. Korea; Mexico

Islamic: Turkey

LDCs: Nigeria

We are unable to include any marginal or microstates in this analysis. This is the case for marginal states because it is too difficult to conduct reliable surveys in states torn apart by civil war. Microstates were not included in the analysis because the World Values Survey focuses most of its resources on the most populous nations. These countries were also selected because they contain some of the best illustrations of the themes we will explore in the chapters that follow. In fact, let's see if there is a difference in trust between these different categories.

Data File:	**WVS97all**
Task:	**Cross-tabulation**
Row Variable:	**3) TRUST PEOP**
➤ Column Variable:	**2) WORLDS.7**
➤ View:	**Tables**
➤ Display:	**Column %**

TRUST PEOP   by   WORLDS.7
Cramer's V: 0.234 **

		WORLDS.7					
		Lib.Dems	Comm/P-com	NICs	Islamic	LDC	TOTAL
TRUST PEOP	Can trust	1613	474	777	104	488	3456
		36.2%	23.9%	29.1%	5.5%	19.2%	25.5%
	Be careful	2844	1506	1890	1788	2054	10082
		63.8%	76.1%	70.9%	94.5%	80.8%	74.5%
	Missing	165	60	92	15	227	559
	TOTAL	4457	1980	2667	1892	2542	13538
		100.0%	100.0%	100.0%	100.0%	100.0%	

In this table we see that there is a difference in citizens' level of trust in others across the different types of nation-states. Liberal democracies have the highest degree of trust in others (36.2%), the communist/postcommunist state is lower with only 23.9% of the population saying that you can trust others. NICs are slightly higher (29.1%), the Islamic state has the lowest (5.5%), and the LDC falls between the two of them (19.2%).

---

[1] The values in the GLOBAL file have been rounded up to the nearest percent. For example, the actual percentage of the population in Turkey that believes you can trust others is 5.5%, but this has been rounded in the GLOBAL file to 6%.

One of the leading hypotheses on the development of democracy suggests that stable democracies must be ideologically centrist. That is, a majority of the population must identify itself with the political center rather than the left or the right. Let's use this same data file to examine political ideology across these eight nations.

Data File: **WVS97all**
Task: **Cross-tabulation**
➤ Row Variable: **4) LT-RT-3**
➤ Column Variable: **1) COUNTRY**
➤ View: **Tables**
➤ Display: **Column %**

LT-RT-3   by   COUNTRY
Cramer's V: 0.195 **

		Germany	USA	Japan	Russia	S Korea	Mexico	Turkey	Nigeria	TOTAL
	Left	766	232	115	287	424	266	432	824	3346
		40.7%	17.0%	15.3%	26.1%	34.3%	21.0%	24.5%	33.7%	28.3%
	Center	852	725	387	662	470	521	687	709	5013
		45.2%	53.2%	51.5%	60.3%	38.1%	41.1%	39.0%	29.0%	42.5%
	Right	266	406	249	149	341	480	641	913	3445
		14.1%	29.8%	33.2%	13.6%	27.6%	37.9%	36.4%	37.3%	29.2%
	Missing	142	179	303	942	14	243	147	323	2293
	TOTAL	1884	1363	751	1098	1235	1267	1760	2446	11804
		100.0%	100.0%	100.0%	100.0%	100.0%	100.0%	100.0%	100.0%	

To see the entire table, click the right arrow of the bottom scroll bar.

Here we see that Germans are most likely to identify with the left (40.7%) and that Japanese citizens are least likely (15.3%). Examine the next two rows of the cross-tabulation and see if you notice other interesting differences. For example, 60.3% of Russians describe themselves as centrists; those in Russia who identify with either the left or right are in the small minority. On the other hand, citizens in South Korea, Mexico, Turkey, and Nigeria are fairly evenly distributed across each of the three ideology categories. If we use 45% as the threshold for what constitutes a "centrist political culture," then we can see that Germany, Japan, the United States, and Russia fit this criterion. Mexico, South Korea, and Turkey are the next closest to achieving this centrist political culture, while Nigeria is relatively far from this goal. Certainly we would have to do a lot more analysis to test the ideology hypothesis, but based on the analysis we have done here, ideological centrism does seem to be a valid indicator of democratic development.

Now we used an arbitrary threshold for what constitutes the difference between a centrist political culture and a noncentrist political culture. How do we know that the difference between the percentage of people that identify with the center in Mexico and Germany is meaningful? To understand the answer to this question, we have to understand a bit more about polling itself.

Most people are familiar with public opinion polling because it is widely used in the news media. But did you ever wonder how a survey of 1,000 people can be used to represent the opinions among more than 270 million Americans, 125 million Japanese, or more than 1 billion Chinese? The answer is found in the *laws of probability*.

Just as a sophisticated gambler can calculate the odds involved in a particular bet, so too political scientists know how to calculate the odds that findings based on a sample of the population can yield an accurate portrait of the entire population. And just as gamblers assume that they are participating in a random game (that the deck has not been stacked or the dice loaded), so too the odds on a sample being accurate depend on the sample being selected at random from the population.

Thus, the first principle of accurate polling is that people in the sample are selected by *random techniques*. For example, in advanced industrial democracies, interviewers conducting telephone polls often use random dialing software to place their calls. This produces a random sample of all telephones (including those with unlisted numbers) and a random sample of households (except for the percentage of the population without phones). Often, the media will report surveys of public opinion that consist of percentages in favor of or against something—usually something controversial. Unfortunately these surveys are often not based on randomly selected samples, such as when people are invited to register their opinions by dialing a phone number, "hitting" a web page, or faxing in a response. If the sample is selected at random, we can use the laws of probability to calculate the odds that what we find accurately reflects the population from which the sample was drawn. These odds are determined by two factors: the size of the sample and the size of the observed differences within the sample.

First of all, the sample must be sufficiently large. Obviously, we couldn't use a sample of two people as the basis for describing the population of Great Britain (59 million). If we did so, there is a very high probability that they would both be female and then the population would appear to be entirely female. For this reason, survey studies include enough cases (individuals) so that they can accurately reflect the population in terms of variations in such characteristics as age, sex, education, religion, and the like. The accuracy of a sample is a function of its size: the larger the sample, the more accurate it is. Oddly enough, accuracy depends only on the size of the sample, not on the size of the sample relative to the size of the population from which the sample is drawn. Thus, a sample of 1,000 people will yield an equally accurate description of the populations of Luxembourg (425,000) and the United States (270 million).

We can use the UNIVARIATE task to see how many people were included in each of the nine surveys for the WVS97all file.

Data File: **WVS97all**
➤ *Task:* **Univariate**
➤ *Primary Variable:* **1) COUNTRY**
➤ *View:* **Bar - Freq.**

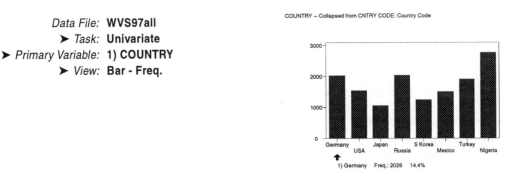

Click on any of the bars to see the number of people surveyed in each country and the percentage of the population in this survey from each country.

Good survey samples include around 1,000 people. For the eight nations included here, we see that the sample from Germany includes 2,026 people while the Nigerian survey includes 2,769. Japan has the fewest number of people surveyed (1,056), but all of the countries in this file have more than 1,000 people surveyed so we have a relatively high degree of confidence in our results. Generally it is good practice to have a higher number of people in your sample where there is a great deal of diversity. Japan, a relatively homogeneous society, has a smaller sample than Nigeria where there is a high degree of religious and ethnic diversity.

While the GLOBAL and WVS97all files are great for quick examinations of attitudes across different countries, they are not especially useful for examining issues within nations. For example, from the analysis of the GLOBAL file we know that the Norwegians are more trusting of fellow citizens than are the Brazilians, but we don't know whether older people in these two countries are more trusting than younger people, or whether women are more trusting than men, or whether those who are wealthier are more trusting than those who are poor. In order to do this type of analysis, it's necessary to examine the survey data for the individual nations. Your book came with 14 data files that allow you to do just that.

Also, we have seen that the political culture in liberal democracies is very different from that of other types of nation-states, so in this chapter, and the three chapters that follow, we will focus our analysis on liberal democracies. Let's start with Germany

➤ *Data File:* **WVS97–GERMANY**
➤ *Task:* **Univariate**
➤ *Primary Variable:* **4) LT-RT-3**
➤ *View:* **Pie**

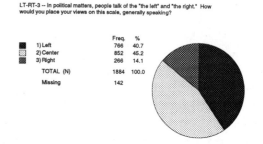

LT-RT-3 -- In political matters, people talk of the "the left" and "the right." How would you place your views on this scale, generally speaking?

	Freq.	%
1) Left	766	40.7
2) Center	852	45.2
3) Right	266	14.1
TOTAL (N)	1884	100.0
Missing	142	

This is the ideology distribution for the people surveyed in Germany. Of course, these numbers should (and do) match those obtained above with the eight-country data set: 40.7% are leftists, 45.2% are centrists, and 14.1% are rightists. Now, let's say that you want to know whether people in Germany who identify themselves as rightists are more likely to be from West or East Germany. Germany was a divided country between 1945 and 1989. It is quite possible that this division may still be reflected in the political attitudes that most Germans hold. To answer this question, switch to the CROSS-TABULATION task.

Data File: **WVS97–GERMANY**
➤ *Task:* **Cross-tabulation**
➤ *Row Variable:* **4) LT-RT-3**
➤ *Column Variable:* **1) PRE-1989**
➤ *View:* **Tables**
➤ *Display:* **Column %**

LT-RT-3   by   PRE-1989
Cramer's V: 0.145 **

		PRE-1989		
		West	East	TOTAL
LT-RT-3	Left	332	434	766
		35.2%	46.1%	40.7%
	Center	437	415	852
		46.3%	44.1%	45.2%
	Right	174	92	266
		18.5%	9.8%	14.1%
	Missing	74	68	142
	TOTAL	943	941	1884
		100.0%	100.0%	

Read across the top row and you'll see that 35.2% of people in West Germany indicate that they are leftists, compared to 46.1% of those in East Germany. While the pattern in the center is quite similar (46.3% of West Germans are centrists compared to 44.1% of East Germans), the pattern on the right is also distinct. While 18.5% of those in West Germany identify with the political right, only 9.8% of those from East Germany identify with the right. There does seem to be a pattern to these results: as the region changes from West to East, the percentage of people who identify with the left increases.

Assuming that a random sample is used to select the respondents for a survey, pollsters want to determine the probability that the data they collect is representative of the entire population. As explained earlier in this chapter, the first factor that impacts the probability level is the number of people included in the survey. The second factor that has an impact on the probability level is the size of the differences observed within a cross-tabulation result. Simply put, if the difference between the percentaged results is high (e.g., 90% of rich people are rightists, compared to 30% of poor people), then the odds that a difference also exists in the full population are very good. But if the percentage differences are very similar (e.g., 65% of rich people are rightists, compared to 62% of poor people), then there is an increased chance that these differences are simply due to randomness, rather than some actual difference in the population. Think about it this way. Suppose you have a bag containing 1,000 marbles. If after drawing out 100 of the marbles, you find that 90 are black and 10 are white, you will feel pretty confident in stating that many more black marbles remain in the bag than white marbles. However, if you draw out 55 black marbles and 45 white marbles, you will be less confident in stating that there are substantially more black marbles than white marbles remaining in the bag.

These two limits of survey data (i.e., the size of the sample; the size of the observed differences within the sample) exist because samples are based on the principle of random selection and therefore are subject to some degree of *random fluctuation*. That is, for purely random reasons there can be small differences between the sample and the population. Thus, whenever we examine cross-tabulations such as the one shown above, political scientists always must ask whether what they are seeing is a real difference—one that would turn up if the entire population were examined—or only a random fluctuation, which does not reflect a true difference in the population.

The differences observed in the region/ideology table from Germany seem to be legitimate. People from former West Germany are more likely to identify with the right. But how do we know that these results are not merely the result of random fluctuations? Fortunately, there is a simple technique for calculating the odds that a given difference is real or random. This calculation is called a **test of statistical significance**. Differences observed in samples are said to be statistically significant when the odds against random results are high enough. There is no mathematical way to determine just how high is high enough. But, through the years, social scientists have settled on the rule of thumb that they will ignore all differences (or correlation coefficients) unless the odds are at least 20 to 1 against their being random. Put another way, social scientists reject all findings when the probability that they are random is greater than .05, or 5 in 100. What this level of significance means is that if 100 random samples were drawn independently from the same population, a difference this large would not turn up more than 5 times, purely by chance. In fact, many social scientists think this is too lenient a standard, and some even require that the probability that a finding is random be less than .01, or 1 in 100. To apply these rules of thumb, social scientists calculate the level of significance of the differences in question and compare them against these standards.

There are two ways to see what the level of significance is for this table. If you want to know the exact probability of whether the results may be due to random error, you need to switch to the statistics summary view.

LT-RT-3   by   PRE-1989

Nominal Statistics
Chi-Square: 39.426	(DF =	2; Prob. = 0.000)			
V:	0.145	C:	0.143		
Lambda: (DV=1)	0.108	Lambda: (DV=4)	0.018	Lambda:	0.061

Ordinal Statistics
Gamma:	-0.236	Tau-b:	-0.131	Tau-c:	-0.145
s.error	0.039	s.error	0.022	s.error	0.024
Dyx:	-0.145	Dxy:	-0.119		
s.error	0.024	s.error	0.020		
Prob. =	0.000				

Ignore everything on this screen except for the first two lines of text. At the end of the first line you'll see "Prob. = 0.000." This value indicates that the odds these results are simply due to randomness are less than 1 in 1,000 (.000). Since social scientists require only that these odds be 1 in 20 (.05) or 1 in 100 (.01), we can be confident that these region/ideology differences would be found if we interviewed the entire population of Germany.

There is another number on this screen that you'll find useful. In the second row, locate the value V = 0.145. The V stands for Cramer's V, which is a correlation coefficient developed for cross-tabulations such as this. Cramer's V is similar to Pearson's r in that the measure varies from 0 to 1. If the relationship between these two variables was perfect (that is, if all people from West Germany were rightists and all people from East Germany were leftists), then this would be a value of 1. However, unlike Pearson's r, V does not indicate whether the relationship is positive or negative. In addition, V is much less sensitive than r. For example, if V is greater than .10, the relationship is somewhat strong. If V is greater than .20, you've found a very strong relationship. The value of V for this table is strong (.145). Overall, we can be fairly confident that, in Germany, people who live in the East are more likely to be leftists. Conversely, we can be confident that people who live in the West are more likely to be rightists.

Whenever you do cross-tabulation analysis, you should always examine three things. First, look at the table to see if the observed differences are worth noting. For example, if the categories you are comparing (e.g., low income/high income) differ by fewer than 5 percentage points, it might not be worth pursing the analysis. Also, if you are testing a hypothesis, you need to be sure that the percentages differ in the predicted direction. For instance, if you predict that West Germans will be more likely to be rightists, then the differences in the table should support this. The second step is to see if the correlation coefficient (V) offers support to the apparent differences. If the percentage differences in your table are worth pursuing, and V offers support for the strength of the relationship, the third step is to determine whether the results are statistically significant. That's when you should apply the probability rules discussed in the previous paragraph.

ExplorIt makes it easy to go through these steps by placing all the information you need on one screen. Return to the column percentaging view for this cross-tabulation. Notice that the value of V appears on this screen. In addition, you'll see that two asterisks appear after this value. One asterisk indicates that the probability value is between .01 and .05. Two asterisks indicate that the probability value is less than .01. So to save time, it's not necessary to go to the statistics screen to obtain these results.

Let's return to the issue of ideology. What makes people have the ideological commitments that they have? We already know from our earlier analysis that the nation someone is from seems to have a bearing on one's political outlook. This makes sense because each nation has a distinct history and culture. For example, in Germany, the political ideas were partly shaped by industrialization. For most of the 19th century, only property-owning males could vote, while factory workers were completely without the capacity to participate in politics. Although the political landscape in Germany has changed a great deal since the 19th century, class-based conflict continues to be a defining feature in ideology in this country. In Japan, industrialization happened later than in Germany. Compared to Western societies, conventional wisdom suggests Japanese political culture emphasizes harmony over conflict, but does this affect ideology?

Let's use the WVS97–JAPAN file to find out. We'll also use a variable that measures the income of the person responding to the survey. When they tell the surveyor what their income is, it is put on a scale of low, medium, or high. A low-income person makes no more than 30% of the highest income person in Japan.

➤ *Data File:* **WVS97–JAPAN**
➤ *Task:* **Cross-tabulation**
➤ *Row Variable:* **2) LT-RT-3**
➤ *Column Variable:* **1) INCOME3**
➤ *View:* **Tables**
➤ *Display:* **Column %**

LT-RT-3   by   INCOME3
Cramer's V: 0.071

		INCOME3				
		Low	Middle	High	Missing	TOTAL
LT-RT-3	Left	30	47	20	18	97
		14.0%	18.1%	12.4%		15.3%
	Center	116	138	78	55	332
		54.2%	53.1%	48.4%		52.3%
	Right	68	75	63	43	206
		31.8%	28.8%	39.1%		32.4%
	Missing	85	96	34	88	303
	TOTAL	214	260	161	204	635
		100.0%	100.0%	100.0%		

Read across the row for those who identify with the political left. Are there clear differences between the income categories? Compare it to the overall population of leftists in Japan by looking at the last column. Overall, 15.3% of the Japanese population identifies with the political left. Low-income people are only 1.3% lower than the overall population, middle-income people are only 2.8% higher, and high-income people are only 2.9% lower than the overall population. To follow our earlier guidelines, no category of income exceeds 5% in difference compared to the overall population. So, based merely on percentages, about the same percentage of low-, middle-, and high-income Japanese consider themselves leftists. Now examine the next row. A clear pattern is still not evident. However, if you compare high-income rightists (39.1%) to the overall Japanese population (32.4%), you do find about a 6.7% percentage-point difference. Only high-income rightists seem all that different from the overall population. But is this difference statistically significant? As you can see, V is not especially strong (V = 0.071), and it is not significant. If you switch to the statistics summary screen, you'll see that the probability value (Prob.) is 0.175. That means the odds are 175 in 1,000 (or 17.5 in 100) that the results could be due to randomness. From this we can conclude that there is no relationship between income and political ideology in Japan.

What else might be the cause of ideological differences in Japan? In many countries, younger people have a greater tendency to identify with the left than the right—the "new generation" is often the source of social change. Let's see if this holds true in Japan.

Data File: **WVS97–JAPAN**
Task: **Cross-tabulation**
Row Variable: **2) LT-RT-3**
➤ Column Variable: **3) AGE GROUP**
➤ View: **Tables**
➤ Display: **Column %**

LT-RT-3   by   AGE GROUP
Cramer's V: 0.174 **

		AGE GROUP						
		18-24	25-34	35-44	45-54	55-64	65+	TOTAL
LT-RT-3	Left	22	20	27	23	17	6	115
		26.5%	22.2%	16.3%	12.4%	13.8%	5.8%	15.3%
	Center	46	52	96	90	51	52	387
		55.4%	57.8%	57.8%	48.6%	41.5%	50.0%	51.5%
	Right	15	18	43	72	55	46	249
		18.1%	20.0%	25.9%	38.9%	44.7%	44.2%	33.2%
	Missing	48	57	73	65	38	22	303
	TOTAL	83	90	166	185	123	104	751
		100.0%	100.0%	100.0%	100.0%	100.0%	100.0%	

Just based on percentages, there does seem to be a relationship between ideology and age. If you read across the top row for leftists, you see that 18 to 24-year-olds have a much higher rate of identification with the political left (26.5%) than do those who are older. This percentage also differs substantially (+11.2%) compared to the overall population (found in the total column). Similarly, if you read across the bottom row for rightists, you see that only 18.1% of 18 to 24-year-olds identify with the right, compared to those over 65 years old (44.2%). The value for Cramer's V (0.174) suggests that there is a relatively strong relationship, and the two asterisks tell us that these results are statistically significant.

Since we have the WVS97–JAPAN data file open, let's also see if men and women differ in their political ideology.

Data File: **WVS97–JAPAN**
Task: **Cross-tabulation**
Row Variable: **2) LT-RT-3**
➤ Column Variable: **4) GENDER**
➤ View: **Tables**
➤ Display: **Column %**

LT-RT-3   by   GENDER
Cramer's V: 0.041

		GENDER		
		Male	Female	TOTAL
LT-RT-3	Left	65	50	115
		15.4%	15.2%	15.3%
	Center	211	176	387
		49.9%	53.7%	51.5%
	Right	147	102	249
		34.8%	31.1%	33.2%
	Missing	97	206	303
	TOTAL	423	328	751
		100.0%	100.0%	

Not much of a difference is evident here. The value for V is weak (0.041), and it is also not significant (Prob. = 0.533). Ideologically speaking, women in Japan seem very similar to men.

Let's switch back to the WVS97–GERMANY file to see if income, age, and gender are related to ideology in Germany.

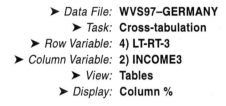

> *Data File:* **WVS97–GERMANY**
> ➤ *Task:* **Cross-tabulation**
> ➤ *Row Variable:* **4) LT-RT-3**
> ➤ *Column Variable:* **2) INCOME3**
> ➤ *View:* **Tables**
> ➤ *Display:* **Column %**

LT-RT-3   by   INCOME3
Cramer's V: 0.065 **

		Low	Middle	High	Missing	TOTAL
LT-RT-3	Left	143	406	127	90	676
		45.1%	41.0%	42.1%		42.0%
	Center	141	462	118	131	721
		44.5%	46.7%	39.1%		44.8%
	Right	33	122	57	54	212
		10.4%	12.3%	18.9%		13.2%
	Missing	32	43	13	54	142
	TOTAL	317	990	302	329	1609
		100.0%	100.0%	100.0%		

If we just review the percentages in this table, there does not seem to be much of a relationship between income and ideology. Low- and middle-income people seem to be very similar to the overall population in terms of ideology. However, high-income people seem to have greater than 5% difference on the center and right. High-income people are 5.7% lower than the population overall in their affiliation with the center, and 5.7% higher in their affiliation with the ideological right. The relationship is relatively weak (V = .065**), but the result is significant.

> *Data File:* **WVS97–GERMANY**
> *Task:* **Cross-tabulation**
> *Row Variable:* **4) LT-RT-3**
> ➤ *Column Variable:* **5) AGE GROUP**
> ➤ *View:* **Tables**
> ➤ *Display:* **Column %**

LT-RT-3   by   AGE GROUP
Cramer's V: 0.096 **

		18-24	25-34	35-44	45-54	55-64	65+	Missing	TOTAL
LT-RT-3	Left	72	236	163	117	111	65	2	764
		39.8%	47.0%	42.9%	37.9%	41.1%	27.7%		40.7%
	Center	87	201	172	142	127	119	4	848
		48.1%	40.0%	45.3%	46.0%	47.0%	50.6%		45.2%
	Right	22	65	45	50	32	51	1	265
		12.2%	12.9%	11.8%	16.2%	11.9%	21.7%		14.1%
	Missing	12	49	25	15	17	24	0	142
	TOTAL	181	502	380	309	270	235	7	1877
		100.0%	100.0%	100.0%	100.0%	100.0%	100.0%		

In Germany, the relationship between age and ideology seems fairly clear. As in Japan, older people are more likely to identify with the right, and younger people are more likely to identify with the left. The correlation coefficient is not as strong in Germany (0.096**) as it was in Japan, but both results are significant. Is there a relationship between gender and ideology in Germany?

> *Data File:* **WVS97–GERMANY**
> *Task:* **Cross-tabulation**
> *Row Variable:* **4) LT-RT-3**
> ➤ *Column Variable:* **3) GENDER**
> ➤ *View:* **Tables**
> ➤ *Display:* **Column %**

LT-RT-3   by   GENDER
Cramer's V: 0.069 *

		Male	Female	TOTAL
LT-RT-3	Left	353	413	766
		39.4%	41.8%	40.7%
	Center	394	458	852
		44.0%	46.4%	45.2%
	Right	149	117	266
		16.6%	11.8%	14.1%
	Missing	32	110	142
	TOTAL	896	988	1884
		100.0%	100.0%	

This table requires careful analysis. If you compare the male and female categories for leftists, there doesn't seem to be much of a difference between men and women. The analysis of center and right also does not reveal much difference between men and women. However, there is a slight difference between men and women in their affiliation with the right (a 4.8% difference between the two). It appears that women are slightly more likely to identify with the center and slightly less likely to identify with the right. Although these results aren't exceptionally strong (V = 0.069), they are statistically significant, as indicated by the one asterisk. So there is a very modest relationship between gender and ideology in Germany.

In the previous analyses, we used demographic factors such as sex, age, and income to see whether they were related to citizens' ideology in Germany and Japan. Comparison of the effects of these relationships helps us to determine whether a characteristic like age transcends national differences. The comparison that follows takes two very different countries, Japan and Germany, and seeks to determine whether these nations have the same relationships between ideology and age. If there are relatively strong relationships, then it suggests that differences, such as national culture, are not as pervasive as we might initially think.

Instead of analyzing the extent to which demographic factors affect differences in ideology, we may want to see whether or not there are important ideological differences between the citizens of nation-states. To answer this type of question, we will use a data set that combines the results of the World Values Survey conducted in eight countries.

➤ Data File: **WVS97all**
➤ Task: **Cross-tabulation**
➤ Row Variable: **4) LT-RT-3**
➤ Column Variable: **1) COUNTRY**
➤ View: **Tables**
➤ Display: **Column %**

LT-RT-3 by COUNTRY
Cramer's V: 0.195 **

		COUNTRY								
		Germany	USA	Japan	Russia	S Korea	Mexico	Turkey	Nigeria	TOTAL
LT-RT-3	Left	766	232	115	287	424	266	432	824	3346
		40.7%	17.0%	15.3%	26.1%	34.3%	21.0%	24.5%	33.7%	28.3%
	Center	852	725	387	662	470	521	687	709	5013
		45.2%	53.2%	51.5%	60.3%	38.1%	41.1%	39.0%	29.0%	42.5%
	Right	266	406	249	149	341	480	641	913	3445
		14.1%	29.8%	33.2%	13.6%	27.6%	37.9%	36.4%	37.3%	29.2%
	Missing	142	179	303	942	14	243	147	323	2293
	TOTAL	1884	1363	751	1098	1235	1267	1760	2446	11804
		100.0%	100.0%	100.0%	100.0%	100.0%	100.0%	100.0%	100.0%	

This table displays the relationship between the country that a citizen is from and the person's position on the ideological scale. We have seen this table before, but it is important to note that ideology does differ according to one's country of citizenship. You will remember that these eight countries were selected because they represented different nation-state types throughout the world (e.g., liberal democracies, NICs), but you should also note that these data do not represent a sampling of the values of citizens throughout the world. Therefore, you should use the WVS97all file only with reference to the eight countries within the file.

You can do this by using the variable COUNTRY as a column variable (shown above), or you can cross-tabulate two other variables with the variable COUNTRY selected as the control variable. Let's say that you wanted to know whether citizens' views on economic equality were related to ideology in each of the eight countries in the WVS97all data set.

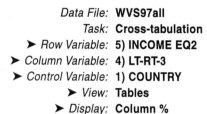

Data File: **WVS97all**

Task: **Cross-tabulation**

➤ Row Variable: **5) INCOME EQ2**

➤ Column Variable: **4) LT-RT-3**

➤ Control Variable: **1) COUNTRY**

➤ View: **Tables**

➤ Display: **Column %**

INCOME EQ2   by   LT-RT-3
Controls: COUNTRY: Germany
Cramer's V: 0.131 **

		Left	Center	Right	Missing	TOTAL
INCOME EQ2	Inc.Equal	385	346	75	63	806
		50.5%	40.9%	28.3%		43.0%
	Center	185	234	59	46	478
		24.3%	27.6%	22.3%		25.5%
	Ind.Effort	192	267	131	29	590
		25.2%	31.5%	49.4%		31.5%
	Missing	4	5	1	4	14
	TOTAL	762	847	265	142	1874
		100.0%	100.0%	100.0%		

The option for selecting a control variable is located on the same screen you use to select other variables. For this example, select 1) COUNTRY as a control variable and then click [OK] to continue as usual. Separate tables for each of the countries will now be shown for the 5) INCOME EQ2 and 4) LT-RT-3 cross-tabulation. Click the appropriate button at the bottom of the task bar to look at the second (or "next") country, and so on.

To analyze the relationship between ideology and opinion on income equality in the eight countries in the data file, you need to examine eight different tables. The first one that you see will be Germany. If you click on the button for the second (or "next") country, you should be able to see the table for the USA, then Japan, and so on. One thing you will notice rather quickly is that it is easy to get overwhelmed by the detail of eight tables. One way to simplify this is to compare the Cramer's V coefficients for the eight different tables. You will notice that the Cramer's V for Germany is 0.131**, for the USA it is 0.161**, Japan 0.197**, Russia 0.098**, South Korea 0.091**, Mexico 0.98**, Turkey 0.123**, Nigeria 0.101**. A comparison of these coefficients indicates that the relationship between views on income equality and ideology is significant in all countries! You are also able to see that the relationship is strongest in Japan, the United States, Germany, Turkey, and Nigeria, weaker in Russia, Mexico, and South Korea. Although it is still important to examine the actual percentages in each table to see where the differences between groups actually lie, the examination of correlation coefficients can help you to narrow the number of countries you need to examine.

We covered a lot of ground in this chapter. Admittedly, a lot of this chapter focused on how to properly use the CROSS-TABULATION task and survey data. Survey data is a staple of political research, so it's important that you learn how to analyze it properly. The worksheet section that follows will give you more experience using the CROSS-TABULATION task. You'll also learn a lot more about political ideology.

WORKSHEET

NAME:

COURSE:

DATE:

CHAPTER

4

Workbook exercises and software are copyrighted. Copying is prohibited by law.

REVIEW QUESTIONS

Based on the first part of this chapter, answer True or False to the following items:

1. People in Brazil are more trusting of fellow citizens than are people in the United States.   T   F

2. A sample of 1,000 people is more accurate in a small country than it is in a large country.   T   F

3. In Germany, people with higher incomes are more likely to be rightists, and those with lower incomes are more likely to be leftists.   T   F

4. In Japan, older people are more likely than younger people to identify with the right.   T   F

5. Young people in Japan are more likely than old people to identify with the left.   T   F

6. Cramer's V is similar to Pearson's r in that both are correlation coefficients.   T   F

7. If Cramer's V is greater than .10, it usually indicates that some relationship exists. If V is greater than .20, it is a strong relationship.   T   F

8. Cramer's V does not indicate whether a relationship is positive or negative.   T   F

9. The units of analysis are the variables being analyzed.   T   F

10. The two factors that determine the odds that survey results are representative of the entire population are (1) the size of the sample and (2) the size of the observed difference within the sample.   T   F

EXPLORIT QUESTIONS

If you have any difficulties using the software to obtain the appropriate information, or if you want to learn more about additional features of ExplorIt's CROSS-TABULATION task, refer to the ExplorIt help topics under the Help menu.

I.   As discussed in the preliminary part of this chapter, the advantage to using individual-level data (opposed to country-level data) is that you can examine differences within specific nations. Your task in this first question is to examine the relationship between political ideology and social change in liberal democracies. In the space below you will compare attitudes on issues and ideology in Australia,

Germany, Japan, Sweden, and the United States. Unlike in the earlier part of the chapter, the variable numbers are not indicated as they may be different for each country's file. We'll use the World Values Survey (WVS) question that asks respondents whether the economic system for their country needs fundamental change. For each country listed below, you will need to open the appropriate data file, conduct the cross-tabulation that is indicated, write down the percentaged results, and indicate if the results are statistically significant for the sample that agrees with the following responses.

Our society must be gradually improved by reforms.

> ➤ *Data Files:* **WVS97–AUSTRALIA**
> **WVS97–GERMANY**
> **WVS97–JAPAN**
> **WVS97–SWEDEN**
> **WVS97–USA**
> ➤ *Task:* **Cross-tabulation**
> ➤ *Row Variable:* **SOCIET CHG**
> ➤ *Column Variable:* **LT-RT-3**
> ➤ *View:* **Tables**
> ➤ *Display:* **Column %**

Fill in the table below with the percentage who favor gradual reform. [Hint: You may want to fill in cells for the whole worksheet country by country.]

% REFORM	LEFT	CENTER	RIGHT	VALUE V	SIGNIFICANT?	
AUSTRALIA	_____%	_____%	_____%	_____	YES	NO
GERMANY	_____%	_____%	_____%	_____	YES	NO
JAPAN	_____%	_____%	_____%	_____	YES	NO
SWEDEN	_____%	_____%	_____%	_____	YES	NO
USA	_____%	_____%	_____%	_____	YES	NO

11. The relationship between political ideology and attitudes toward social change is especially strong in Australia, Germany, and Japan.   T   F

12. In the United States, although the differences are statistically significant, there don't seem to be large ideological differences (greater than 5%) in terms of those who think gradual reforms are preferable.   T   F

13. Regardless of their political ideology, people in Sweden have very similar attitudes toward social change.   T   F

14. A small minority of people within each ideological group in the Germany survey believe that social reform is important.   T   F

II. Repeat the procedures used in the previous question, except use the variable IMPORTS. For each country, fill in the percentaged results for the population of the sample that agrees with the following response:

There should be stricter limits on selling foreign goods here to protect the jobs of people in this country.

Data Files:	**WVS97–AUSTRALIA**
	WVS97–GERMANY
	WVS97–JAPAN
	WVS97–SWEDEN
	WVS97–USA
Task:	**Cross-tabulation**
➤ Row Variable:	**IMPORTS**
➤ Column Variable:	**LT-RT-3**
➤ View:	**Tables**
➤ Display:	**Column %**

Fill in the table below.

% PRO IMPORT	LEFT	CENTER	RIGHT	VALUE V	SIGNIFICANT?
AUSTRALIA	_____%	_____%	_____%	_____	YES NO
GERMANY	_____%	_____%	_____%	_____	YES NO
JAPAN	_____%	_____%	_____%	_____	YES NO
SWEDEN	_____%	_____%	_____%	_____	YES NO
USA	_____%	_____%	_____%	_____	YES NO

15. In each of the five nations examined, there is a statistically significant relationship between political ideology and the individual opinion on free trade.   T   F

16. The people on the political left in Australia, Germany, and the United States are more in favor of free trade than people on the political right.   T   F

17. Ideology does not seem to be an important factor in Japan, in terms of the public's openness to free trade.   T   F

18. Regardless of ideology, the majority of the people in Japan believe imports should not be allowed at the expense of jobs.   T   F

III. We have noted in our discussion of ideology that it can also be an indicator of a citizen's view of social issues. The following two variables examine public opinion toward two social issues that governments can regulate: immigration and assistance to the poor. For each country, fill in the percentaged results for the population of the sample that agrees with the following response:

Place **strict limits** on the number of foreigners who can come here.

Data Files:	**WVS97–AUSTRALIA**
	WVS97–GERMANY
	WVS97–JAPAN
	WVS97–SWEDEN
	WVS97–USA
Task:	**Cross-tabulation**
➤ Row Variable:	**IMMIGRANTS**
➤ Column Variable:	**LT-RT-3**
➤ View:	**Tables**
➤ Display:	**Column %**

Fill in the table below.

% LIMITS	LEFT	CENTER	RIGHT	VALUE V	SIGNIFICANT?
AUSTRALIA	_____%	_____%	_____%	_____	YES NO
GERMANY	_____%	_____%	_____%	_____	YES NO
JAPAN	_____%	_____%	_____%	_____	YES NO
SWEDEN	_____%	_____%	_____%	_____	YES NO
USA	_____%	_____%	_____%	_____	YES NO

19. In all five nations, the majority of people agree with the idea of strict limits on immigration.   T   F

20. Although the relationship between ideology and immigration in Germany is statistically significant, the relationship is very weak.   T   F

21. Political ideology helps us understand why certain people in the United States feel that government should have strict limits on immigration.   T   F

22. Sweden and Japan are similar in that there is no relationship between ideology and citizens' views on immigration.   T   F

IV. Examine the relationship between ideology and citizens' opinions on their governments' policies on poverty. For each country, fill in the percentaged results for the population of the sample that agrees with the following response:

*The government is doing **too little** for people in poverty in this country.*

Data Files:	**WVS97–AUSTRALIA**
	WVS97–GERMANY
	WVS97–JAPAN
	WVS97–SWEDEN
	WVS97–USA
Task:	**Cross-tabulation**
➤ *Row Variable:*	**PV:GOVT**
➤ *Column Variable:*	**LT-RT-3**
➤ *View:*	**Tables**
➤ *Display:*	**Column %**

Fill in the table below.

% TOO LITTLE	LEFT	CENTER	RIGHT	VALUE V	SIGNIFICANT?
AUSTRALIA	_____%	_____%	_____%	_____	YES NO
GERMANY	_____%	_____%	_____%	_____	YES NO
JAPAN	_____%	_____%	_____%	_____	YES NO
SWEDEN	_____%	_____%	_____%	_____	YES NO
USA	_____%	_____%	_____%	_____	YES NO

23. From this analysis we may conclude that the majority of the population in each country believes that the government is doing too little to combat poverty.   T   F

24. In every country, political ideology is strongly associated with one's view on the government's policies on poverty.   T   F

25. In terms of this analysis, political ideology seems to make the strongest difference in Sweden.   T   F

26. The relationship between ideology and the opinion on poverty policy is the weakest in
    a. Australia.
    b. Germany.
    c. Japan.
    d. Sweden.
    e. USA.

27. We can judge the strength of the relationship between two variables by looking at
    a. the percentage differences that exceed 5% in either direction when we read across the rows.
    b. the percentage differences that exceed 5% in either direction when we read down the columns.
    c. the Cramer's V statistic.
    d. the probability statistic.

28. In _____ a majority of the population in every ideological category believes that the government is doing too little about poverty.
    a. Australia
    b. Germany
    c. Japan
    d. Sweden
    e. USA

V. In some nation-states, the issue of abortion has been hotly debated along ideological lines. Let's see if this holds true for all five nation-states, using the survey question "Do you think that abortion can be justified?" For the table below, fill in the percentaged results for those who think abortion is NEVER justified.

Do you think that abortion can be justified?

Data Files:	**WVS97–AUSTRALIA**
	WVS97–GERMANY
	WVS97–JAPAN
	WVS97–SWEDEN
	WVS97–USA
Task:	**Cross-tabulation**
➤ *Row Variable:*	**ABORT-3**
➤ *Column Variable:*	**LT-RT-3**
➤ *View:*	**Tables**
➤ *Display:*	**Column %**

Fill in the table below.

% NEVER	LEFT	CENTER	RIGHT	VALUE V	SIGNIFICANT?	
AUSTRALIA	_____%	_____%	_____%	_____	YES	NO
GERMANY	_____%	_____%	_____%	_____	YES	NO
JAPAN	_____%	_____%	_____%	_____	YES	NO
SWEDEN	_____%	_____%	_____%	_____	YES	NO
USA	_____%	_____%	_____%	_____	YES	NO

Comparative Politics

29. Of these five nations, Sweden is the only one in which less than half of the people in each ideological group think abortion is never justified.   T   F

30. In terms of views on abortion, ideology seems to play the strongest role in Germany and the United States.   T   F

31. In Sweden, although the results for the entire table are statistically significant, there doesn't seem to be a strong relationship between ideology and the belief that abortion is never justified.   T   F

32. The majority of people in each ideological group in Japan agree that abortion is never justified, but the ideological differences among Japanese on this issue are not statistically significant.   T   F

33. These results suggest that abortion is more likely to be a politically volatile issue in Japan than in the United States.   T   F

VI. Does ideology play a role in one's belief of whether prostitution is ever justified? For the table below, fill in the percentaged results for those people who think prostitution is NEVER justified.

Do you think that prostitution can be justified?

Data Files:	**WVS97–AUSTRALIA**
	WVS97–GERMANY
	WVS97–JAPAN
	WVS97–SWEDEN
	WVS97–USA
Task:	**Cross-tabulation**
➤ *Row Variable:*	**PROST-3**
➤ *Column Variable:*	**LT-RT-3**
➤ *View:*	**Tables**
➤ *Display:*	**Column %**

Fill in the table below.

% NEVER	LEFT	CENTER	RIGHT	VALUE V	SIGNIFICANT?	
AUSTRALIA	_____%	_____%	_____%	_____	YES	NO
GERMANY	_____%	_____%	_____%	_____	YES	NO
JAPAN	_____%	_____%	_____%	_____	YES	NO
SWEDEN	_____%	_____%	_____%	_____	YES	NO
USA	_____%	_____%	_____%	_____	YES	NO

34. In this analysis, political ideology seems to play the biggest role in (choose all that apply)
    a. Australia.
    b. Germany.
    c. Japan.
    d. Sweden.
    e. USA.

35. In Japan, an individual's view of prostitution is related to his or her political ideology. T F

36. In all statistically significant results, people on the right are more likely than people on the left to indicate that prostitution is never justified. (Ignore the center categories.) T F

VII. In the table below, place a checkmark (✔) in each column to indicate if the issue is related to political ideology in each country. Then tally the marks and place the total in the column at the right. The first country has already been done for you.

Fill in the table below.

ISSUE/ COUNTRY	SOCIAL CHANGE	IMPORT	IMMIGRANTS	POVERTY	ABORTION	PROSTI- TUTION	TOTAL
AUSTRALIA	✔	✔	✔	✔	✔	✔	6
37. GERMANY	___	___	___	___	___	___	___
38. JAPAN	___	___	___	___	___	___	___
39. SWEDEN	___	___	___	___	___	___	___
40. USA	___	___	___	___	___	___	___

IN YOUR OWN WORDS

In your own words, please answer the following questions.

1. In a paragraph, respond to the following statement: "Ideology is universal. In every nation, people are divided on issues according to their ideology." Support your statement with specific examples from the analyses you conducted in this chapter.

2. "The left-right ideological spectrum fits best with economic issues, and less well with moral issues." Support or refute this statement on the basis of your analysis.

3. "Ideology is essentially a European concept. The left and right do not make much sense to people outside of Europe." Support or refute this statement on the basis of your analysis.

CHAPTER 5

POLITICAL PARTICIPATION: MAKING DEMOCRACY WORK

Politics ought to be the part-time profession of every citizen.

DWIGHT D. EISENHOWER, 1954

Tasks: Mapping, Scatterplot, ANOVA, Cross-tabulation
Data Files: GLOBAL, WVS97–AUSTRALIA, WVS97–GERMANY, WVS97–JAPAN,
WVS97–SWEDEN, WVS97–USA

In the previous chapter we examined some of the cultural values that support democratic political participation. But what makes democracy consistently work over time? In this chapter we will examine the relationship between the public and the government in a number of nation-states to better understand some of the answers to this question.

Political participation refers to the actions taken by ordinary citizens in pursuit of their political goals. Most people assume that in democratic societies participation usually takes a number of very conventional forms. For example, voting, signing petitions, or volunteering for political campaigns are all conventional modes of political participation. But we also know that in some countries free elections and the rights associated with political participation are not available to the public. When these basic rights are not guaranteed, we can also assume that participation in more conventional modes of political participation will be much lower.

But we don't need to assume, we can actually test this hypothesis. Let's look at the percentage of the population that has signed a petition.

> *Data File:* **GLOBAL**
> *Task:* **Mapping**
> *Variable 1:* **106) PETITION?**
> *View:* **List: Rank**

PETITION?: Percentage of the population that has signed a petition

RANK	CASE NAME	VALUE
1	Australia	78
2	Canada	77
3	United States	73
4	Sweden	72
5	Norway	65
6	Switzerland	64
7	Germany	62
8	United Kingdom	58
9	Japan	56
10	France	54

Notice that all of the top ten countries happen to be advanced industrial democracies. In fact, you don't find a country that is not a liberal democracy in the top fifteen! And you do not find a single liberal democracy in the bottom ten. This would indeed support the notion that conventional participation is associated with a high level of democratic development.

What about more unconventional forms of participation, like sit-ins where citizens occupy buildings or factories? If our hypothesis is accurate, then we should expect that these actions would be lower in countries where a full range of participatory options is available (liberal democracies) and higher where these options are not as readily available.

SIT-INS: Percentage of the population sampled that has occupied a building or factory

Data File: **GLOBAL**
Task: **Mapping**
➤ Variable 1: **105) SIT-INS**
➤ View: **List: Rank**

RANK	CASE NAME	VALUE
1	Uruguay	7.6
2	Ghana	5.6
3	Nigeria	5.3
4	Mexico	4.6
4	Dominican Republic	4.6
6	Argentina	3.1
7	Peru	2.9
8	Brazil	2.7
9	Venezuela	2.6
10	Bulgaria	2.4

The first thing that you should notice is that the percentage of the population that has engaged in this kind of participation is low for every country. However, you will also notice that not a single liberal democracy appears in the top ten. From this preliminary examination of conventional and unconventional forms of political participation, it seems that that those countries with established protections of civil liberties tend to have the highest percentage of the population engaging in conventional forms of participation (such as petitioning). Those with a weaker tradition of protecting these freedoms tend to have a higher percentage of the population engaged in unconventional forms of participation (like sit-ins).

To better understand the relationship between participation and the type of state, we could rank each participation variable and then try to identify the number of countries in the top ten and bottom ten in each category, but there is actually a better way to do this.

Let's examine the relationship between political participation and the type of nation-state using the WORLDS.7 variable. Our hypothesis will be that "conventional forms of political participation are higher in developed democracies than in those that are less developed." One of the most conventional forms of participation is voter turnout. What we want to do is look at the relationship between the percentage of the population that turns out to vote at an election and the WORLDS.7 variable. Before we continue, though, the introduction of one last lesson in research methodology is in order. Conduct the following analysis and then I'll explain why the results aren't useful to us.

Data File:	**GLOBAL**
➤ Task:	**Scatterplot**
➤ Dependent Variable:	**57) %TURNOUT**
➤ Independent Variable:	**80) WORLDS.7**
➤ View:	**Reg. Line**

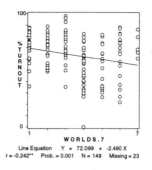

Line Equation   Y = 72.099 + -2.490 X
r = -0.242**   Prob. = 0.001   N = 149   Missing = 23

Carefully examine the regression line and think about how you might summarize the relationship between these two variables. In scatterplot analysis (or any type of correlation analysis), you want to be able to say that as the values for one variable increase, the values for the other variable increase (a positive correlation) or decrease (a negative correlation). However, in order to make such an interpretation, the category values for both variables must have some type of natural or intrinsic meaning. That is, a category of 2 (Communist/Postcommunist) must have more of whatever the variable is measuring than a category coded 1 (Liberal Democracy). A category of 3 (New Industrializing Country) must have more of that something than a category coded 2 (Communist/Postcommunist), and so forth. But as you examine the WORLDS.7 variable, you quickly notice that the categories 1 through 7 do not have an intrinsic order. For example, it wouldn't make any sense to say that as the type of state *increases*, the voter turnout *decreases*. Nor would it make any sense to say that a liberal democratic state is less of a state than a newly industrialized country (NIC). With the WORLDS.7 variable, the values 1 through 7 are used strictly to represent different groupings of countries. The category numbers have no other meaning. Hence, this variable cannot be used in correlation or scatterplot analysis.

You might be thinking, "Why don't we use the CROSS-TABULATION task?" Good question. The WORLDS.7 variable can be used in cross-tabulations. The problem is with the other variable, %TURNOUT. The voter turnout variable is a decimal variable that has over 100 different category values ranging from 4.0% to 98.0%. Cross-tabulations work best when both variables have predetermined or grouped categories (e.g., First World, Second World, Third World; Yes, No). If you try to create a cross-tabulation using WORLDS.7 and %TURNOUT, your table will have 3 columns and about 100 rows! Such a table would be useless. (In fact, ExplorIt won't even let you create a table that has more than 100 categories.)

So, what do you do when one variable has a limited set of categories (e.g., WORLDS.7) and the other variable has a wide range of values that go from low to high? If the independent variable (i.e., the variable causing the effect in the other variable) is the one that has a limited set of categories, you can use ExplorIt's Analysis Of Variance task. Return to the main menu and select ANOVA (the acronym for ANalysis Of VAriance).

Data File: **GLOBAL**
➤ Task: **ANOVA**
➤ Dependent Variable: **57) %TURNOUT**
➤ Independent Variable: **80) WORLDS.7**
➤ View: **Graph**

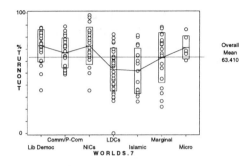

To reproduce this graphic, select the ANOVA task, and select 57) %TURNOUT as the dependent variable and 80) WORLDS.7 as the dependent variable. The first view shown is the Graph view.

What does this graph tell us? To begin with, just like a scatterplot, each nation is represented by one of the dots on the graph. The location of a nation on the graph is based on the percentage of voter turnout in the nation's national election and its category in the Seven Worlds classification. First the dot is placed horizontally according to its category. You will notice that on the bottom of the graph, each category in the Seven Worlds classification is represented. For example, the country of Iceland would be placed in the Liberal Democracy category. Then Iceland is placed vertically according to its voter turnout in the last election (approximately 87.8%), which is scaled on the left side of the graph.

The rectangle shown for each category of the independent variable (WORLDS.7) indicates the high and low range in which most countries in that category are located. While some countries will be located outside of this range, the majority (around 70%) will be found within the range of this rectangle.

When you read an ANOVA graphic, focus on the mean in this graphic (i.e., the average voter turnout) for each category of the independent variable (WORLDS.7). The location of the mean is shown with a flat line in the center of each rectangle. Your task, then, is to compare the mean for one category against the means for the other categories. It's fairly easy to see whether a mean for one category is higher or lower than a mean for another category because there is a line that connects each of these mean points. The flatter the lines between the means, the less difference there is between the categories. For example, there is a very substantial difference in average voter turnout between NICs and Islamic countries, but very little difference between Islamic countries and less developed countries (LDCs).

We can now easily compare different types of nation-states. In this graph you can see that liberal democracies, NICs, and microstates have the highest levels of voter turnout. The average voter turnout in communist/postcommunist systems is slightly lower than the liberal democracies and NICs. LDCs and Islamic countries have the lowest levels of voter turnout, and marginal states are slightly higher. You can also look at the average turnout values themselves in the form of a table.

Task: **ANOVA**

Dependent Variable: **57) %TURNOUT**

Independent Variable: **80) WORLDS.7**

➤ View: **Means**

Means, Standard Deviations and Number of Cases of Dependent Var: %TURNOUT
by Categories of Independent Var: WORLDS.7
Difference of means across groups is statistically significant (Prob. = 0.000)

	N	Mean	Std.Dev.
Lib Democ	24	72.825	13.350
Comm/P-Com	28	66.739	12.471
NICs	21	72.762	15.383
LDCs	34	52.979	17.918
Islamic	17	51.835	18.939
Marginal	19	62.805	20.801
Micro	6	71.300	9.620

If you are continuing from the previous example, select the [Means] button.

This table shows the actual average level of voter turnout within each category of the independent variable (WORLDS.7). As we can see, liberal democratic systems have the highest average level of voter turnout (72.8%). Communist/postcommunist states have lower average turnout (66.7%), and NICs are at almost exactly the same level as liberal democracies (72.8%). LDCs (53.0%) and Islamic states (51.8%) also have very similar voter turnout rates. Interestingly enough, marginal states (states in the midst of civil wars) have much higher voter turnout rates (62.8%). Microstates (71.3%), with very small populations, tend to have turnout rates similar to those in liberal democracies and NICs.

The ANOVA task is pretty easy to use. The initial graphic generally provides a clear picture of whether the pattern supports your initial hypothesis. If it does, then go to the screen with the means to view the actual numbers behind the table. There is one more issue: statistical significance. How do you know if the differences between the means are due to chance or if you can consider the results statistically significant? Simple. As in our earlier analyses with Cramer's V, there is a probability value shown directly above the table containing the means. If the difference is statistically significant, there is a sentence that states that the "difference of means across groups is statistically significant." This can be verified by examining the probability value. If it is between .000 and .05, we can feel confident that the differences between the means are not random findings. If the value is over .05, there is a chance that our findings are due to randomness. In this case, since the probability value is 0.000, we know that these results are statistically significant. If the significance is greater than .05, then we cannot say that there is a relationship between the two variables in our analysis.

In the worksheet section that follows, we'll examine how political participation helps us to better understand the factors that make democracy work.

WORKSHEET

CHAPTER

5

NAME:

COURSE:

DATE:

REVIEW QUESTIONS

Based on the first part of this chapter, answer True or False to the following items:

1. Signing a petition and voting are conventional forms of political participation. T F

2. Liberal democracies tend to have higher levels of voter turnout and petitioning than LDCs. T F

3. Because they guarantee civil liberties, liberal democracies tend to have a higher number of people occupying buildings and having sit-ins. T F

4. Scatterplots are not that useful when you are using a variable that has a few categories without any meaning to their order. T F

5. When your independent variable has a specific set of categories (e.g., Yes, No; Free Free, Not Free) and the dependent variable has a wide range of values that go from 0 to 50, it is more appropriate to use the ANOVA task than the CROSS-TABULATION or SCATTERPLOT tasks T F

6. The ANOVA task is different than the CROSS-TABULATION or SCATTERPLOT tasks in that it does not require you to determine statistical significance. T F

7. The differences in voter turnout across different types of nation-states are statistically significant. T F

EXPLORIT QUESTIONS

If you have any difficulties using the software to obtain the appropriate information, or if you want to learn more about additional features of ExplorIt's ANOVA task, refer to the ExplorIt help topics under the Help menu.

I. In this chapter you compared voter turnout and the type of nation-state around the world. Now let's look at a few other indicators of political participation. Almond and Verba have argued that citizens in liberal democracies will have a higher level of interest in politics. Thus, we might also hypothesize that citizens in liberal democracies will be more likely to discuss politics with others than those in less democratic countries. Let's look at the first part of this hypothesis.

➤ *Data File:* **GLOBAL**
➤ *Task:* **ANOVA**
➤ *Dependent Variable:* **107) P.INTEREST**
➤ *Independent Variable:* **80) WORLDS.7**
➤ *View:* **Means**

> **You may need to use both the Graph view and the Means view to answer the following questions.**

8. The graph indicates that citizens in liberal democracies have a higher interest in politics than do citizens in other types of nation-states.   T   F

9. What is the mean level of political interest for citizens in liberal democracies?   _____

10. What is the mean level of political interest for citizens in communist/post-communist societies?   _____

11. Is the difference in political interest between these countries significant?   Yes   No

12. What is the probability?   _____

13. As predicted, citizens in liberal democracies have higher rates of political interest than do citizens in other types of nation-states.   T   F

Now let's analyze the willingness to discuss politics, which is the second part of Almond and Verba's hypothesis.

               Data File: **GLOBAL**
               Task: **ANOVA**
➤ *Dependent Variable:* **108) TALK POL.**
➤ *Independent Variable:* **80) WORLDS.7**
➤ *View:* **Means**

> **You may need to use both the Graph view and the Means view to answer the following questions.**

In the space provided, write the mean percentage of the population who often discuss politics with friends.

14. Lib Democ.   _____

15. Comm/P-Com   _____

16. NICs   _____

17. LDCs   _____

18. Islamic   _____

19. Marginal   _____

20. Are the differences between these countries significant?   Yes   No

21. What is the probability?   _____

22. As predicted, citizens in liberal democracies discuss politics more than
    citizens in any other type of nation-state.   T   F

23. From these results, we can support a new hypothesis: Citizens in
    communist and postcommunist societies discuss politics more than
    citizens in liberal democracies.   T   F

II. Let's return to the issue with which we started this chapter: political participation in liberal democracies. Is there a certain characteristic to liberal democracies compared to other types of states? In the
analysis below, examine each of the dependent variables provided in relation to the independent
variable WORLDS.7.

> Data File: **GLOBAL**
> Task: **ANOVA**
> ➤ Dependent Variables: **106) PETITION?**
>   **103) BOYCOTT?**
>   **104) DEMONSTRAT**
>   **105) SIT-INS**
> ➤ Independent Variable: **80) WORLDS.7**
> ➤ View: **Means**

In the space provided, write down the mean percentage for the four types of states (ignore the categories for Islamic, marginal, and microstates) and the significance for each variable.

STATE TYPE	PETITION	BOYCOTT	DEMON-STRATION	SIT-IN
LIBERAL DEMOC.	_____	_____	_____	_____
COMM/P-COM	_____	_____	_____	_____
NICs	_____	_____	_____	_____
LDCs	_____	_____	_____	_____
SIGNIFICANT?	Y N	Y N	Y N	Y N

24. Citizens in liberal democracies are more accustomed to signing petitions
    and boycotting products than citizens in other types of states.   T   F

25. The percentage of citizens who participate in demonstrations is likely to be higher in countries with underdeveloped democratic systems.   T   F

26. We cannot draw conclusions about the relationship between the level of participation in demonstrations and the type of state because the relationship is not significant.   T   F

27. Citizens are more likely to have occupied buildings or factories (SIT-INS) in liberal democracies than in NICs.   T   F

III. So far we have examined participation at the nation-state level, but in reality, political participation has more to do with individual decisions to relate to the political process. To better understand individual political participation, we need to use individual-level data.

What factors make people more likely to sign petitions? What factors influence people to participate in demonstrations? Let's explore this using the CROSS-TABULATION task. As in the worksheet section for Chapter 4, the variable numbers are not indicated as they may be different for each country's file. We'll use the World Values Survey (WVS) question that asks respondents whether they have ever signed a petition. For each country listed below, you will need to open the appropriate data file, conduct the cross-tabulation that is indicated, write down the percentaged results for the first row of the table (i.e., Have done), write down the value for V, and then indicate whether the results are statistically significant.

> **If you have not used the CROSS-TABULATION task with survey data, you may wish to review Chapter 4.**

>   *Data Files:*   **WVS97-AUSTRALIA**
>   **WVS97-GERMANY**
>   **WVS97-JAPAN**
>   **WVS97-SWEDEN**
>   **WVS97-USA**
>   *Task:*   **Cross-tabulation**
>   *Row Variables:*   **SIGN PETN**
>   **DEMONSTR**
>   *Column Variables:*   **CLASS3**
>   **GENDER**
>   **WATCH TV**
>   *View:*   **Tables**
>   *Display:*   **Column %**

Fill in the table below with the percentage that have signed petitions and then answer the "In Your Own Words" questions at the end of this chapter. [Hint: Complete all analyses for one country and then continue to the next.]

SIGN PETN by CLASS-3

% HAVE DONE	UPPER	MIDDLE	WORKING	VALUE V	SIGNIFICANT?	
AUSTRALIA	_____%	_____%	_____%	_____	YES	NO
GERMANY	_____%	_____%	_____%	_____	YES	NO
JAPAN	_____%	_____%	_____%	_____	YES	NO
SWEDEN	_____%	_____%	_____%	_____	YES	NO
USA	_____%	_____%	_____%	_____	YES	NO

SIGN PETN by GENDER

% HAVE DONE	MALE	FEMALE	VALUE V	SIGNIFICANT?	
AUSTRALIA	_____%	_____%	_____	YES	NO
GERMANY	_____%	_____%	_____	YES	NO
JAPAN	_____%	_____%	_____	YES	NO
SWEDEN	_____%	_____%	_____	YES	NO
USA	_____%	_____%	_____	YES	NO

SIGN PETN by WATCH TV

% HAVE DONE	NO TV	1–2 HOURS	2–3 HOURS	3+ HOURS	VALUE V	SIGNIFI-CANT?
AUSTRALIA	_____%	_____%	_____%	_____%	_____	Y N
GERMANY	_____%	_____%	_____%	_____%	_____	Y N
JAPAN	_____%	_____%	_____%	_____%	_____	Y N
SWEDEN	_____%	_____%	_____%	_____%	_____	Y N
USA	_____%	_____%	_____%	_____%	_____	Y N

Fill in the table below with the percentage that have participated in demonstrations and then answer the "In Your Own Words" questions.

DEMONSTR by CLASS-3

% HAVE DONE	UPPER	MIDDLE	WORKING	VALUE V	SIGNIFICANT?	
AUSTRALIA	_____%	_____%	_____%	_____	YES	NO
GERMANY	_____%	_____%	_____%	_____	YES	NO
JAPAN	_____%	_____%	_____%	_____	YES	NO
SWEDEN	_____%	_____%	_____%	_____	YES	NO
USA	_____%	_____%	_____%	_____	YES	NO

DEMONSTR by GENDER

% HAVE DONE	MALE	FEMALE	VALUE V	SIGNIFICANT?	
AUSTRALIA	_____%	_____%	_____	YES	NO
GERMANY	_____%	_____%	_____	YES	NO
JAPAN	_____%	_____%	_____	YES	NO
SWEDEN	_____%	_____%	_____	YES	NO
USA	_____%	_____%	_____	YES	NO

DEMONSTR by WATCH TV

% HAVE DONE	NO TV	1–2 HOURS	2–3 HOURS	3+ HOURS	VALUE V	SIGNIFI-CANT?
AUSTRALIA	_____%	_____%	_____%	_____%	_____	Y N
GERMANY	_____%	_____%	_____%	_____%	_____	Y N
JAPAN	_____%	_____%	_____%	_____%	_____	Y N
SWEDEN	_____%	_____%	_____%	_____%	_____	Y N
USA	_____%	_____%	_____%	_____%	_____	Y N

IN YOUR OWN WORDS

In your own words, please answer the following questions.

1. What is the nature of the relationship between political participation (measured by signing petitions and participating in demonstrations) and social class? In which countries is class strongly related to political participation? Where is it weakest? Be sure to support your generalizations with evidence from your analysis.

2. Do women have higher or lower rates of political participation? What is the nature of the relationship between political participation and gender? In which countries is gender strongly related to political participation? Where is it weakest? Be sure to support your generalizations with evidence from your analysis.

3. Is TV watching associated with higher or lower rates of political participation? What is the nature of the relationship between TV watching and political participation? In which countries is TV watching strongly related to political participation? Where is it weakest? Be sure to support your generalizations with evidence from your analysis.

CHAPTER **6**

ELECTORAL SYSTEMS IN LIBERAL DEMOCRACIES

Democracy is still upon its trial. The civic genius of our people is its only bulwark.

WILLIAM JAMES, 1897

Tasks: Mapping, Univariate, ANOVA, Cross-tabulation
Data Files: GLOBAL, EUROPE

With so many new democratic governments across the world, it seems necessary to examine the different types of electoral systems that are currently in place. Elections are one of the ways that citizens attempt to influence the politics in their country. In a sense, elections translate the sentiments of citizens into a formal government. Most democracies hold elections every three to five years so citizens can express their political, economic, and even social preferences. These expressions often change the composition of the leadership that governs each democratic nation-state.

Most people who are unfamiliar with comparative politics are surprised when they learn of the many different types of electoral systems. The Institute for Democracy and Electoral Assistance (IDEA) has classified the world's electoral system into nine different types.

➤ *Data File:* **GLOBAL**
➤ *Task:* **Univariate**
➤ *Primary Variable:* **63) ELECTSYSTM**
➤ *View:* **Bar - Freq**

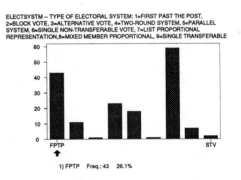

ELECTSYSTM -- TYPE OF ELECTORAL SYSTEM: 1=FIRST PAST THE POST, 2=BLOCK VOTE, 3=ALTERNATIVE VOTE, 4=TWO-ROUND SYSTEM, 5=PARALLEL SYSTEM, 6=SINGLE NON-TRANSFERABLE VOTE, 7=LIST PROPORTIONAL REPRESENTATION, 8=MIXED MEMBER PROPORTIONAL, 9=SINGLE TRANSFERABLE

1) FPTP   Freq.: 43   26.1%

Make sure you select the [Bar - Freq.] option. Move the right or left arrows on your keyboard to see the frequency percentage of each electoral system type.

We don't have time to go into the differences between these electoral systems, but this graph does give you a sense of the variation that exists. As shown below, each of these systems can be reduced to three categories: plurality-majority electoral systems, proportional electoral systems, and semi-proportional electoral systems.

Plurality-majoritarian	Semi-proportional	Proportional representation
First Past the Post	List Proportional Representation	Parallel System
Block Voting	Mixed Member Proportional	Single-Nontransferable Vote
Alternative Vote	Single Transferable Vote	
Two Round System		

Plurality-majoritarian electoral systems (or simply, majoritarian electoral systems) favor majorities or large parties and limit the number of parties in the system. For the most part, legislators in these systems are elected by a majority (50% + 1) of votes in a district or by the plurality of the votes cast (i.e., he/she who has the most votes wins). **Proportional** electoral systems seek to translate the percentage of votes for a given party directly to the number of seats that will be in a legislature. **Semi-proportional** electoral systems fall in between these two extremes. As such, these electoral systems can be placed along a spectrum, with majoritarian systems on one end and proportional systems on the other end.

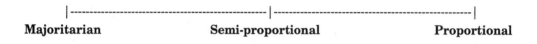

| Majoritarian | Semi-proportional | Proportional |

Let's look at the percentage of the world's electoral systems that fall into these three categories.

Data File: **GLOBAL**
Task: **Univariate**
➤ Primary Variable: **64) ELECSYSTM2**
➤ View: **Pie**

ELECSYSTM2 -- GENERAL ELECTORAL SYSTEM: 1=PLURALITY-MAJORITY, 2=SEMI-PROPORTIONAL, 3=PROPORTIONAL REPRESENTATION (IDEA, 1997)

	Freq.	%
1) Plur-Major	79	47.9
2) Semi-PR	19	11.5
3) PR	67	40.6
TOTAL (N)	165	100.0
Missing	7	

Nearly half of the world's countries use some kind of majority system, about 40% use proportional representation, and around 11% use a semi-proportional system. Because of the prevalence of majoritarian and proportional systems, our analysis below will concentrate primarily on them.

Majoritarian systems tend to eliminate small parties and strengthen large parties. This is the type of system that exists in the United States and the United Kingdom. Most majoritarian (or modified majoritarian) systems divide the nation into relatively similar-sized districts. When elections occur, several parties run against each other for each seat that is available. The majoritarian system favors the winning party by overrepresenting it in the legislature. The advantage of this type of electoral system is that it creates a strong majority and often a strong minority to govern the country. To illustrate a majoritarian system, examine Table 6.1 for the United Kingdom election of 2001. The first column of numbers shows the percentage of vote that each party obtained, the second column shows the percentage of seats the party actually won, and the last column indicates the percentage of over- or underrepresentation of each party in the United Kingdom's Parliament.

Table 6.1. UK Election and Party Representation, 2001 Results

Party	% Vote	% Seats	Over/Under Represented
Labour	40.7	62.7	+22.0
Liberal Democrats	18.3	7.9	−10.4
Conservatives	31.7	25.2	−6.5
Other	9.3	4.2	−5.1

The Labour Party won only 40.7% of the vote, but it wields a virtual super-majority (62.7%) in Parliament thanks to the majoritarian electoral system. At the expense of the liberal democrats, the conservatives, and the other small parties, the Labour Party is overrepresented in Parliament by 22%! The liberal democrats, which obtained 18.3% of the votes and received only 7.9% of the seats, are underrepresented by 10.4%. Other parties without a plurality of votes also suffer the same fate.

Proportional electoral systems are at the other end of the spectrum. Instead of trying to ensure a majority in parliament, these systems seek to ensure fair representation of voter preference. Sweden is a good example of a country that uses a proportional electoral system. As shown in Table 6.2, the Social Democratic Party received the greatest percentage of votes in the 1998 election (37.5%), and it ended up obtaining 37.5% of the seats in the Swedish Riksdag (Parliament). The Swedish voting rules specify that seats in the legislature must be allocated in proportion to the percentage of the vote that each party received in the election. As you look down the list, you'll see that all parties are within 0.8 percentage point of this desired goal. Parties that receive less than 4% of the popular vote are not represented in Parliament.

Table 6.2. Swedish Election and Party Representation, 1998 Results

Party	% Vote	% Seats	Over/Under Represented
Left Party	12.0	12.3	+0.3
Greens	4.5	4.6	+0.1
Social Democrats	37.5	37.5	+0.0
Liberals	4.7	4.9	+0.2
Center	5.1	5.2	+0.1
Moderates	22.7	23.5	+0.8
Christian Democrats	11.8	12.0	+0.2
Other Parties	1.7	0.0	−1.7

As indicated above, the great advantage of a proportional electoral system is that it fairly represents the voters' preferences. The disadvantage is that no single party has a majority of the seats in the legislature. In order to govern in this type of system, parties must cooperate with one another and form coalitions. This makes the task of governing more challenging.

From this example it is clear that electoral systems can influence the composition of power among the leadership. But do electoral systems shape other features of politics, government, and policy? Let's examine the effect of the electoral system on the representation of women in parliament to better understand this issue. The following variable measures the percentage of parliamentary members who are elected to that nation's parliament (or legislature).

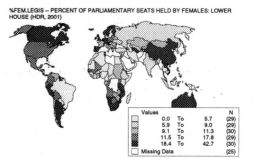

> Data File: **GLOBAL**
> ➤ Task: **Mapping**
> ➤ Variable 1: **95) %FEM.LEGIS**
> ➤ View: **Map**
> ➤ Display: **Legend**

Click on the nation of Sweden to see where it ranks. The percentage of women in parliament and Sweden's rank will appear at the bottom of the graphic. Now click on the United States.

As you can see, the representation of women varies widely. It also seems as though there are some regional patterns in the map. Clearly, most of the countries with high representation of women in parliament are located in Europe. But there are also some exceptions to this pattern. Women seem well represented in Argentina, Peru, South Africa, Namibia, Mozambique, and Tanzania. What causes women to be better represented in some countries and not so well represented in others?

Let's examine this relationship to see if the electoral system that a nation-state uses is associated with the representation of women. What we want to do is look at the relationship between the representation of women in the legislature and the ELECSYSTM2 variable. (If you have not used the ANOVA task before now, you may want to review this task as it is introduced in Chapter 5).

> Data File: **GLOBAL**
> ➤ Task: **ANOVA**
> ➤ Dependent Variable: **95) %FEM.LEGIS**
> ➤ Independent Variable: **64) ELECSYSTM2**
> ➤ View: **Graph**

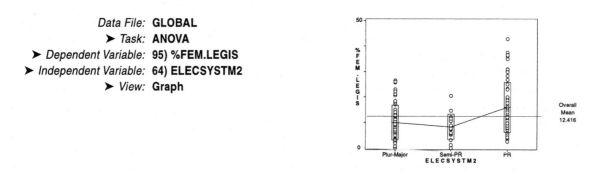

What does this graph tell us? We can now easily compare different types of electoral systems. In this graph you can see that the first category, plurality-majority systems, has the second lowest level of female representation in the legislature. The average score of semi-proportional systems is just lower than that of plurality-majority systems. And now for the purpose of this analysis. The third category (PR systems) has substantially higher levels of female representation than the other two electoral systems. You can also look at these mean values themselves in the form of a table.

	Data File:	**GLOBAL**
	Task:	**ANOVA**
	Dependent Variable:	**95) %FEM.LEGIS**
	Independent Variable:	**64) ELECSYSTM2**
	➤ View:	**Means**

Means, Standard Deviations and Number of Cases of Dependent Var: %FEM.LEGIS
by Categories of Independent Var: ELECSYSTM2
Difference of means across groups is statistically significant (Prob. = 0.000)

	N	Mean	Std.Dev.
Plur-Major	64	9.948	6.805
Semi-PR	17	8.265	4.972
PR	64	15.986	9.849

If you are continuing from the previous example, select the [Means] button.

As we learned in Chapter 5, this table shows the actual average level of women's representation within each category of the independent variable (ELECSYSTM2). As we can see, PR systems have the highest average level of women's representation in the legislature (16.0%). The semi-PR systems have the lowest average level of women's representation (8.2%). The plurality-majority systems are far below the PR systems, with a mean level of representation at 9.9%, but they are higher than the semi-PR systems.

It is one thing to note that women's representation is higher in PR systems and quite another to understand why this is the case. In plurality-majority systems, voters generally elect a single representative. Often each candidate represents a single party and voters face choosing one or another candidate. Imagine that you prefer to elect women to office because they are underrepresented in the United States. You are faced with electing a female candidate from the Democratic Party or a male from the Republican Party. This puts the voter on the horns of a dilemma. Generally speaking, for most people ideology is more important than the gender of a candidate. If you are like those who care more about ideology than gender, you would probably vote for the Republican male candidate.

There are a wide variety of PR systems, but in most PR-list systems, voters do not have to choose between the gender of a candidate and the party of their choice. If you live in Sweden and prefer women in leadership, you can actualize both of these preferences at the polls. In its simplest form, List PR involves each party presenting a list of candidates to the electorate, voters voting for a party, and parties receiving seats in proportion to their overall share of the national vote. Winning candidates are taken from the lists in order of their position on the lists. So when a voter enters the voting booth in Sweden, she selects one party's list of candidates. In many countries she can also vote for candidates who are lower on the list so that they are moved up the list. For example, she may want to promote more women candidates in her chosen party, so she would give a vote to a candidate on her list. In PR-list systems, voters can choose a party and influence the representation of the types of candidates that they prefer at the same time.

In the worksheet section that follows, you'll examine how election models have an impact on factors such as election turnouts and the number of parties that participate in the election process.

WORKSHEET

NAME: _____

COURSE: _____

DATE: _____

CHAPTER

6

Workbook exercises and software are copyrighted. Copying is prohibited by law.

REVIEW QUESTIONS

Based on the first part of this chapter, answer True or False to the following items:

1. Majoritarian electoral systems encourage coalition building in the legislature to achieve majorities.   T   F

2. Proportional electoral systems seek to ensure fair representation in the legislature by allocating seats according to the percentage of votes each party obtained.   T   F

3. Majoritarian systems of representation tend to overrepresent larger parties.   T   F

4. Most countries use a semiproportional electoral system for electing their leaders, rather than one that is majoritarian or proportional.   T   F

5. The differences in the representation of women across the various types of electoral systems are statistically significant.   T   F

EXPLORIT QUESTIONS

I. In this chapter you compared electoral systems and outcomes in political systems around the world. Now let's look at democracy in Europe. The variable GOVERNMEN2 divides the European countries into those with new political systems since 1989 and those with democratic political systems in existence prior to 1989. Let's see if the nations of Europe have election systems that are majoritarian, semi-proportional, or proportional.

> *Data Files:* **EUROPE**
> *Task:* **Cross-tabulation**
> *Row Variable:* **28) ELECTSYST2**
> *Column Variable:* **15) GOVERNMEN2**
> *View:* **Tables**
> *Display:* **Column % (Frequency)**

You may need to use both column percentaging and the frequency options to answer the following questions.

6. Over three-quarters of older democracies in Europe have proportional electoral systems.   T   F

7. Transitional countries in Europe are spread across all three types of electoral systems.   T   F

8. Over half of the 17 transitional countries in Europe have majoritarian or semi-proportional types of electoral systems. This is a stark contrast to the proportional systems found in older European democracies.   T   F

II. Do new democracies in Europe have higher levels of voter turnout than old democracies? We might hypothesize that there will be higher rates of voter turnout in transitional European governments because democratic elections give these citizens rights they didn't previously have.

> Data Files: **EUROPE**
> ➤ Task: **ANOVA**
> ➤ Dependent Variable: **29) %TURNOUT**
> ➤ Independent Variable: **15) GOVERNMEN2**
> ➤ View: **Means**

You may need to use both the Graph view and the Means view to answer the following questions.

9. The graph indicates that old democracies have higher voter turnout than transitional countries   T   F

10. What is the mean voter turnout for old democracies?   _____

11. What is the mean voter turnout for transitional governments?   _____

12. Is the difference in turnout between old democracies and transitional governments significant?   Yes   No

13. What is the probability?   _____

14. As predicted, transitional nations in Europe have higher rates of voter turnout than do older democratic nations.   T   F

Let's look at this same hypothesis (whether transitional nations will have higher voter turnout rates) using the entire GLOBAL data file. The GOVERNMENT variable in the GLOBAL data file is the same as the GOVERNMEN2 variable in the EUROPE file. However, because we are talking about nation-states around the world there is greater variety for this variable in the GLOBAL file. Write the entire variable description for 65) GOVERNMENT in the space provided below.

_____

_____

_____

_____

> *Data Files:* **GLOBAL**
> *Task:* **ANOVA**
> *Dependent Variable:* **57) %TURNOUT**
> *Independent Variable:* **65) GOVERNMENT**
> *View:* **Means**

You may need to use both the Graph view and the Means view to answer the following questions.

In the space provided, write down the mean voter turnout for each government system.

15. Old Democracy _____

16. Transitional _____

17. One Party _____

18. Autocratic _____

19. Civil War _____

20. Is the difference in turnout between old democracies and transitional
    governments significant?   Yes   No

21. What is the probability?   _____

22. As predicted, transitional nation-states are more likely than older
    democracies to have higher voter turnouts.   T   F

Given this variable description, you may wonder why we would study voter turnout in countries where one-party rule, autocracy, or civil war makes elections less relevant. The fact is that many of these kinds of nation-states still convene elections or elect members of parliament. While these states still hold elections, we might hypothesize that citizens in these countries know that elections don't mean much, so they are less inclined to turn out to vote. Let's check this out.

23. One-party governments have the highest voter-turnout rates.   T   F

24. Nation-states experiencing civil war have the lowest voter-turnout rates because
    the government is not stable.   T   F

25. In terms of voter turnout, the analysis containing all transitional nation-states
    differs substantially from the analysis that includes only European countries.   T   F

III. Now let's look at the effect that the electoral system has on voter turnout. Is turnout higher among PR systems or majoritarian systems? How does the analysis of global turnout compare to the analysis of European turnout?

Data Files:	**GLOBAL**
Task:	**ANOVA**
➤ *Dependent Variable:*	**57) %TURNOUT**
➤ *Independent Variable:*	**64) ELECSYSTM2**
➤ *View:*	**Means**

In the space provided, write down the mean voter turnout for each election system.

26. Plurality-Majority _____

27. Semi-PR _____

28. PR _____

29. Is the difference in turnout between the three electoral systems significant?   Yes   No

30. What is the probability? _____

31. Proportional systems tend to have higher voter turnout than the plurality-majority systems or semi-PR systems.   T   F

Now analyze voter turnout for the European systems using the EUROPE data file. Be sure to write down the mean voter turnout for each electoral system using 28) ELECTSYST2.

32. Plurality-Majority _____

33. Semi-PR _____

34. PR _____

35. Is the difference in turnout between the three electoral systems significant?   Yes   No

36. What is the probability? _____

37. In Europe, proportional systems tend to have higher voter turnout than the plurality-majority systems or semi-PR systems.   T   F

IV. Now we will use the EUROPE data file to examine the relationship between the type of electoral system a country has and the number of political parties in the country. Since majoritarian electoral systems favor larger parties, we would expect to find fewer political parties in those nation-states and more political parties in those countries with proportional and semi-proportional electoral systems.

➤ *Data Files:*	**EUROPE**
➤ *Task:*	**ANOVA**
➤ *Dependent Variable:*	**26) #PARTIES2**
➤ *Independent Variable:*	**28) ELECTSYST2**
➤ *View:*	**Graph (Statistics: Means)**

In the space provided, write the mean number of parties for each election system.

38. Plurality-Majority _____

39. Semi-PR _____

40. PR _____

41. Is the difference in the number of parties between the three electoral systems significant?   Yes   No

42. What is the probability?   _____

43. European countries with majoritarian electoral systems have fewer political parties than countries with PR systems.   T   F

IN YOUR OWN WORDS

Open the GLOBAL file, select the ANOVA task and use 64) ELECSYSTM2 as the independent variable and 61) POL RIGHTS, 59) CIV LIBS, 72) NO CORRUPT; and 15) MULTI-CULT as dependent variables. Then answer the following questions.

1. Based on the analysis of the relationship between ELECSYSTM2 and 61) POL RIGHTS, 59) CIV LIBS, and 72) NO CORRUPT, indicate whether or not there seems to be a relationship between the type of election system that a nation chooses and its level of political freedom. Support your conclusions with evidence.

2. Based on the analysis of the relationship between ELECSYSTM2 and MULTI-CULT, indicate whether or not you agree with the following statement. "It is not good for highly diverse societies to have too many political parties to choose from. Proportional representation makes sense only in relatively homogeneous societies." Support your conclusion with evidence.

3. Based on all of the analysis that you have conducted in this chapter, indicate whether or not you agree with the following assertion: "Electoral systems don't really matter all that much to democracy." Support your conclusion with evidence.

Europe

ICELAND

North Atlantic
Ocean

SWEDEN   FINLAND

NORWAY

ESTONIA

LATVIA   RUSSIA

DENMARK

LITHUANIA

NETHERLANDS

IRELAND

U. K.   POLAND   BELARUS

GERMANY

BELGIUM   UKRAINE

LUXEMBURG

CZECH
REPUBLIC   SLOVAKIA

MOLDOVA

FRANCE   AUSTRIA   HUNGARY

SWITZERLAND   ROMANIA

SLOVENIA

Black Sea

CROATIA   BOSNIA

YUGOSLAVIA

ANDORRA   ITALY   BULGARIA

PORTUGAL   CORSICA   MACEDONIA

SPAIN   ALBANIA   TURKEY

SARDINIA   GREECE

SICILY   CYPRUS

MALTA   LEBANON

Mediterranean Sea

POLITICAL PARTIES IN THE UNITED KINGDOM AND GERMANY

> *Party-spirit . . . at best is but the madness of many for the gain of a few.*
>
> ALEXANDER POPE, 1714

Tasks: Mapping, Historical Trends, Univariate, Cross-tabulation
Data Files: EUROPE, HISTORY, CSES-GERMANY, CSES-UK, WVS97–GERMANY
WVS97–SWEDEN

One way to think comparatively about European political parties is to divide them into "families" of parties that are ideologically similar. Since the end of World War II there have been about 12 main party families in Europe. Not every family is in every country. In fact, a country like the United Kingdom will have only four of the twelve party families represented here. But organizing political parties does help us to simplify the study of political parties so that we can compare one nation to another (see Table 7.1).

Table 7.1. Party Families in Europe

Extreme Left	Left	Center	Right	Extreme Right	Other
Communist	Social Dem.	Liberal	Christian Dem.	Nationalist	Regionalist
Socialist	Labour	Agrarian	Conservative		
Former Communist	Greens				

The extreme left consists of those parties that are more radical in their orientation to democratic politics. In a few countries they are still called communist parties, but many of them have changed their names to something that sounds a bit more up to date. In most European countries these parties support the democratic process but are also willing to use strikes, demonstrations, and the nationalization of industry to achieve their goals. Communists usually have strong ties to labor unions in their respective countries. Open the EUROPE data file and rank the percentage of the vote obtained by extreme left parties in recent elections.

%EXT.LEFT: Percentage of vote for extreme left parties (including communist and former communist)

➤ *Data File:* **EUROPE**
➤ *Task:* **Mapping**
➤ *Variable 1:* **31) %EXT.LEFT**
➤ *View:*` **List: Rank**

RANK	CASE NAME	VALUE
1	Moldova	51.6
2	Ukraine	38.3
3	Slovak Republic	28.3
4	Russia	24.3
5	Serbia	13.9
6	Czech Republic	11.0
7	Greece	5.5
8	Italy	5.0
9	Portugal	2.4
10	Norway	1.2

As you can see from the ranking, the extreme left is popular only in a few countries in Eastern and Southern Europe. An analysis of the support for communism over time in Germany, Sweden, and France also reveals some interesting patterns.

➤ *Data File:* **HISTORY**
➤ *Task:* **Historical Trends**
➤ *Variables:* **4) %COMMGM**
5) %COMMFR
6) %COMMSW

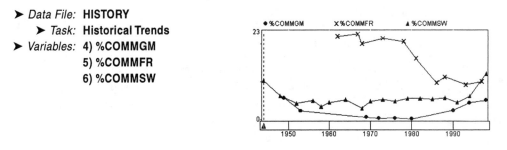

Electoral support for communists in Germany, France, and Sweden

In Sweden (red) and Germany (blue), electoral support for communist parties has been relatively low compared to France (green). In France, support for communist parties was highest during the 1960s and 70s when around 20% of the vote went to the Communist Party. Since 1980, the French Communist Party has fallen on hard times.

Data File: **HISTORY**
Task: **Historical Trends**
➤ *Variables:* **7) %SOCIALFR**
5) %COMMFR

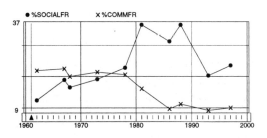

Electoral support for the socialist and communist parties in France

This graph again shows the communist vote in France over the last three decades, but this time it's contrasted with the trend line for the French Socialist Party (shown in blue). Scroll through the events until you get to the 1981 election of socialist François Mitterrand as president of the French Republic.

Comparative Politics

You will also notice that since this time, the socialists have dominated the political left of French politics consistently outpacing the communists at every election.

Let's take a look at the Socialist Party across all of Europe.

➤ Data File: **EUROPE**
➤ Task: **Mapping**
➤ Variable 1: **33) %SOCIALIST**
➤ View: **Map**
➤ Display: **Legend**

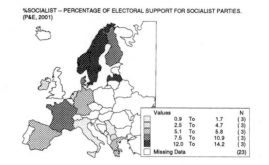

%SOCIALIST -- PERCENTAGE OF ELECTORAL SUPPORT FOR SOCIALIST PARTIES. (P&E, 2001)

Although socialist parties are categorized on the extreme left, they are slightly more moderate than their communist counterparts. A key factor that sets socialists apart from social democrats (categorized as "left") is that the former are more prone to advocate state ownership of industry. More recently, former communists and other extreme leftists have become the leading opponents of globalization on the left.

As this map shows, socialist parties have been fairly popular in Scandinavia and Southern Europe and continue to be quite popular in Eastern Europe as well. If you look at the ranked list for this variable, you see that Latvia (14.2%), Norway (12.4%), and Sweden (12.0%) are strongholds for the socialist parties.

Let's look at the map for social democrats.

Data File: **EUROPE**
Task: **Mapping**
➤ Variable 1: **35) %SOC.DEM**
➤ View: **Map**
➤ Display: **Legend**

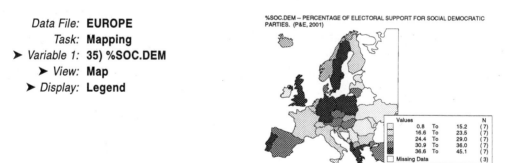

%SOC.DEM -- PERCENTAGE OF ELECTORAL SUPPORT FOR SOCIAL DEMOCRATIC PARTIES. (P&E, 2001)

Historically, social democrats have been avid defenders of democracy, but they have also actively promoted the construction of an extensive welfare state in the European nations where they reside. Innovations such as old-age pensions, universal health care, and child care have been the issues championed by the social democrats.

Social democrats have been among the largest parties on the left in Europe. If you look at the ranked list for social democrats, you see that in recent elections between 40% and 50% of the vote in Albania, Portugal, Greece, the United Kingdom, and Poland went to social democrats. Over 20% of the vote was obtained in 25 European nations. Historically speaking, social democrats have been significant actors in the party politics of Europe. Their influence in countries like Germany, Sweden, and the United Kingdom has profoundly shaped these nations.

➤ *Data File:* **HISTORY**
   ➤ *Task:* **Historical Trends**
➤ *Variables:* 8) **%LABOURUK**
        9) **%SOCDEMSW**
       10) **%SOCDEMGM**

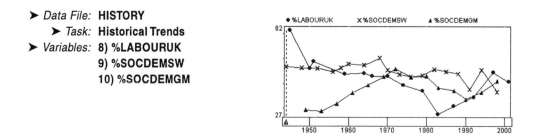

Electoral support for social democratic parties in UK, Sweden, and Germany

This graphic shows the electoral fortunes of social democratic parties in the United Kingdom (called the Labour Party), Sweden, and Germany. Notice that with the exception of the Labour Party's strong showing in the 1945 election, social democratic strength in the three countries was at its highest in the late 1960s and early 70s. All three of the parties declined with the economic crises of the 1970s and early 80s. Interestingly enough, following the end of the Cold War, most of these parties started to bounce back.

The Green Party is a recent upstart that is also categorized as a party on the left. It emphasizes local control of the government and environmental concerns. It's not exactly clear where a party like this should be placed on the political spectrum, but because of its emphasis on political equality and, sometimes, radical change, the Green Party is placed on the left side of the political spectrum. Let's see how it has fared over the last couple of decades in France, Sweden, and Germany.

Data File: **HISTORY**
   Task: **Historical Trends**
➤ *Variables:* 11) **%GREENFR**
       12) **%GREENSW**
       13) **%GREENGM**

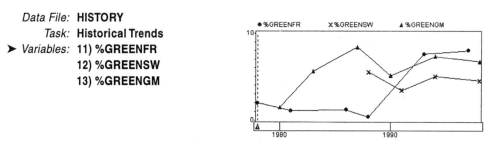

Electoral support for green parties in France, Sweden, and Germany

The Green Party in France received around 1% of the vote in the 1980s, but by the mid-1990s this grew to 8% of the vote. Across all three countries, though, the Green Party has never obtained as much as 10% of the vote.

Here are two ranked lists for all European countries that have a green party. The top list shows the percentage of vote for green parties in the most recent election. The bottom list shows the actual percentage of parliamentary seats that were allocated to the green parties as a result of these elections.

                                                                                 Comparative Politics

> Data File: **EUROPE**
> Task: **Mapping**
> Variable 1: **37) %GREEN**
> Variable 2: **38) STS.GREEN**
> View: **List: Rank**

%GREEN: Percent of vote for green parties

RANK	CASE NAME	VALUE
1	Belgium	14.3
2	Iceland	9.1
3	Portugal	9.0
4	Luxembourg	8.5
5	Finland	7.5

STS.GREEN: Percentage of parliamentary seats allocated to green parties

RANK	CASE NAME	VALUE
1	Belgium	13.3
2	Iceland	9.5
3	Luxembourg	8.3
4	Austria	7.7
5	Portugal	7.41

You can see from the rank list for the map that only 17 of the 38 nations in Europe even have green parties that have made a political showing in a recent election. They retain parliamentary seats in almost all of the countries where they have won a measurable percentage of the vote. With the exception of the Ukraine, where the Chernobyl nuclear meltdown mobilized the environmental movement, green parties are strongest in Western Europe.

Liberal parties tend to be at the center of the political spectrum. These parties were the first "reforming" parties in Europe. Originally, they sought to make the political processes more democratic, advocated voting rights for women and workers, and have also been strong advocates of free-market economics. They occupy the center of the political spectrum in most countries where they exist.

Data File: **EUROPE**
Task: **Mapping**
> Variable 1: **39) %LIBERAL**
> View: **Map**
> Display: **Legend**

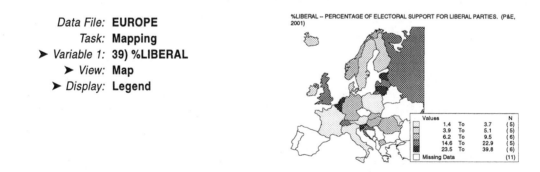

%LIBERAL -- PERCENTAGE OF ELECTORAL SUPPORT FOR LIBERAL PARTIES. (P&E, 2001)

Values			N
1.4	To	3.7	(5)
3.9	To	5.1	(5)
6.2	To	9.5	(6)
14.6	To	22.9	(5)
23.5	To	39.8	(6)
Missing Data			(11)

The pattern of this map isn't especially clear. If you look at the ranked list, you'll see that many of the Eastern European nations have high percentages of votes going to liberal parties, such as Lithuania (39.8%), Slovenia (37.1%), Estonia (23.5%), and others. Perhaps the democratic and free-market ideas espoused by the liberal parties have more salience in countries where democracy and market economies are only now emerging.

Once again, let's see how the liberal democratic parties have fared over the last several decades. We'll pick Sweden, the United Kingdom, and the free democrats of Germany as illustrations.

> *Data File:* **HISTORY**
> > *Task:* **Historical Trends**
> *Variables:* **14) %FREEDEMGM**
> **15) %LIBRLSW**
> **16) %LIBDEMUK**

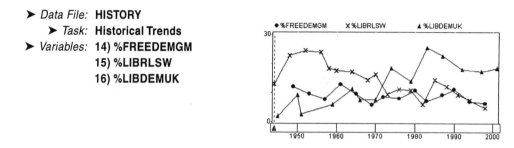

Electoral support for liberal parties in UK, Sweden, and Germany

Since World War II, liberal democratic parties have generally been too small to govern on their own or to lead coalitions in any parliament, but they have often served as effective partners to parties of both the left and the right. As a result of this pattern of partnership, these parties have remained relatively vital, albeit small. In Germany, the free democrats have fluctuated around the same rate of support (around 10%) for 50 years. In Sweden, the liberals were once fairly strong, but their influence has waned in recent years. In the UK, the liberals have suffered several divisions but have recently reconstituted themselves to become a force for the other parties to reckon with.

> *Data File:* **HISTORY**
> *Task:* **Historical Trends**
> *Variables:* **16) %LIBDEMUK**
> **17) STS.LIB.UK**

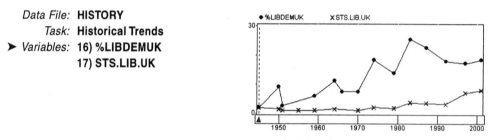

Liberal electoral support vs. seats in Parliament in the UK

Due to the United Kingdom's majoritarian electoral system, the representation of liberal democrats in the British Parliament has always been well below the proportion of votes they receive during the election, as is evident in this graph.

Like the liberals, parties of the political center have not done well in recent years. In Scandinavia, center parties are usually the representatives of agricultural interests. In France the Center Party has been a coalition of moderate conservatives. As you can see in the following graph, both parties have seen large declines since their peak in the early 1970s.

> *Data File:* **HISTORY**
> *Task:* **Historical Trends**
> *Variables:* **18) %CENTERFR**
> **19) %CENTERSW**

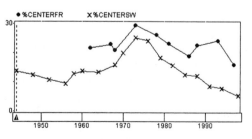

Liberal electoral support vs. seats in Parliament in the UK

Comparative Politics

Now let's examine the percentage of the vote that center parties received across all of Europe.

> Data File: **EUROPE**
> Task: **Mapping**
> Variable 1: **41) %CENTER**
> View: **Map**
> Display: **Legend**

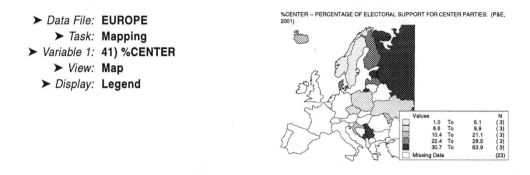

Center parties with agrarian ties are primarily a phenomenon common to Northern and Central Europe. Most of these countries have long traditions of agrarian parties in politics.

Let's shift to the right side of the political spectrum and look at Christian democratic parties and conservative parties.

Data File: **EUROPE**
Task: **Mapping**
> Variable 1: **43) %CH.DEM**
> View: **Map**
> Display: **Legend**

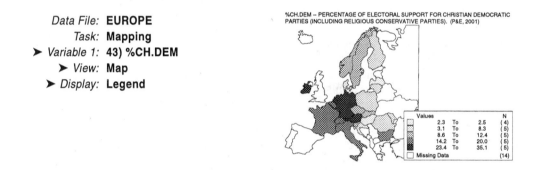

If the social democrats have been the dominant party on the left in postwar Europe, then either Christian democratic parties or secular conservative parties have been the dominant parties on the political right. Some scholars describe Christian democracy as having three distinct strands.[1] The predominately Catholic version of the party was founded in many Catholic countries (Austria, Belgium, Italy, Luxembourg, and Switzerland) to advance the interests of the Catholic Church as governments became more secular during the 19th century. In Germany, Christian democrats draw support from Catholics and Protestants. And in Northern Europe (Denmark, Norway, Sweden, Netherlands), there are very small Protestant evangelical Christian democratic parties. These parties have usually been advocates for a more "socially conservative" agenda, meaning that the defense of traditional morality has been important. Unlike American religious conservatives, the Christian democrats have also usually been moderate advocates for social benefits such as pensions and worker rights, and, they exhibit a reluctance to pursue policies that result in class conflict.

---

[1] This characterization of Christian democratic parties is drawn from Michael Gallagher, Michael Laver, and Peter Mair, *Representative Government in Modern Europe* (New York: McGraw-Hill, 1995), pp. 192–194.

➤ *Data File:* **HISTORY**
  ➤ *Task:* **Historical Trends**
➤ *Variables:* **20) %CHDEMSW**
        21) %CHDEMGM

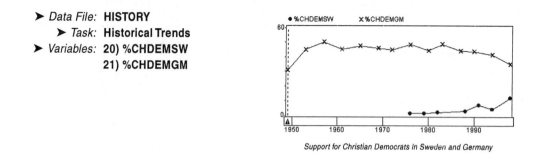

Support for Christian Democrats in Sweden and Germany

One can see from the analysis of historical trends that the inclusion of Protestants and Catholics has served the German party well (shown in green). The German party has consistently dominated the center-right of German politics since the end of War World II. The Swedish party only began to be represented in the 1970s, but has actually performed better in recent times. In 1991 the Christian democrats in Sweden even served as a partner in the government with a coalition of center-right political parties.

The conservative party, operating from a secular platform, is also on the right side of the political spectrum. Let's start by looking at trend lines for the conservative parties in France, Sweden, and the United Kingdom.

Data File: **HISTORY**
  Task: **Historical Trends**
➤ *Variables:* **22) %CONSERVFR**
        23) %CONSERVSW
        24) %CONSERVUK

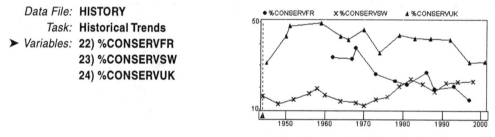

Support for conservatives in France, Sweden, and the UK

Historically speaking, secular conservatives peaked in Britain and France during the 1950s and 60s respectively. In both countries the party experienced a resurgence in the 1980s, but its support has dropped off since then. In Sweden, secular conservatives have been the largest party on the right, but they have only recently approached the level of support for secular conservatives found in other European countries.

➤ *Data File:* **EUROPE**
  ➤ *Task:* **Mapping**
➤ *Variable 1:* **45) %CONSERVAT**
    ➤ *View:* **Map**
  ➤ *Display:* **Legend**

%CONSERVAT -- PERCENTAGE OF ELECTORAL SUPPORT FOR CONSERVATIVE
PARTIES. (P&E, 2001)

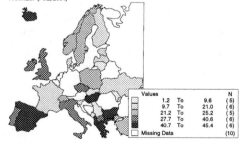

As is evident from the map legend, 18 European nations have over 20% of their votes going to secular conservative parties. If you look at the list of nations, you see that Hungary tops the list with 45.4%, followed by Spain (44.5%) and Bulgaria (42.7%). In general, secular conservative parties are most popular in the southern part of Europe. Secular conservatives are usually placed farther on the right because of their more strident opposition to socialism and social democracy, their free-market libertarianism, and a strong emphasis on patriotism and the promotion of "national interests."

The extreme right is a very difficult group to categorize. Generally these types of parties have strong nationalist tendencies and very high levels of antipathy toward foreigners, whether they are immigrants or citizens of neighboring countries.

    Data File: **EUROPE**

       Task: **Mapping**

➤ *Variable 1:* **47) %EXT.RIGHT**

   ➤ *View:* **Map**

   ➤ *Display:* **Legend**

Recently the extreme right has had some success in elections in the southern European countries of Italy (15.9%), France (14.9%), and Austria (26.9%). But these types of parties have also been fairly popular in Eastern European countries like Yugoslavia (13.9%), Romania (20.9%), and most notably, Croatia (29.1%).

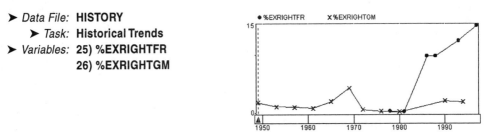

   ➤ *Data File:* **HISTORY**

    ➤ *Task:* **Historical Trends**

➤ *Variables:* **25) %EXRIGHTFR**

           26) %EXRIGHTGM

Electoral support for extreme right parties in France and Germany

Of recent concern to a number of political observers has been the popularity of extreme right movements in southern Europe. France, in particular, is growing increasingly wary of the success of the far-right National Front, which won almost 15% of the vote in the last parliamentary election.

The final group of parties is also hard to classify because it is neither right nor left. The parties in this group are usually organized around a specific ethnic identity that exists under the sovereignty of a larger, dominant nation. For example, Scottish people have organized the Scottish National Party to press for the interests of Scots in the English-dominated nation of Great Britain.

➤ *Data File:* **EUROPE**
➤ *Task:* **Mapping**
➤ *Variable 1:* **49) %REGIONAL**
➤ *View:* **Map**
➤ *Display:* **Legend**

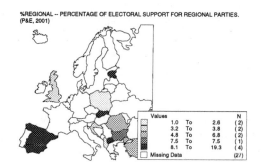

%REGIONAL -- PERCENTAGE OF ELECTORAL SUPPORT FOR REGIONAL PARTIES.
(P&E, 2001)

Values			N
1.0	To	2.6	(2)
3.2	To	3.8	(2)
4.8	To	6.8	(2)
7.5	To	7.5	(1)
8.1	To	19.3	(4)
Missing Data			(27)

Twelve European countries have regionalist parties that obtained at least some percentage of the vote in the most recent elections. Here, Macedonia (19.3%) leads the pack, followed by the Slovak Republic (9.1%), Estonia (8.1%), and Spain (8.1%).

PARTY AFFILIATION IN GERMANY AND UK

In the Comparative Study of Electoral Systems survey, citizens from a number of countries around the world were asked to name the party that they voted for at the last election. These surveys were conducted immediately following that nation's most recent election. In Germany, citizen responses from the 1998 national election are shown in the next graph.

➤ *Data File:* **CSES-GERMANY**
➤ *Task:* **Univariate**
➤ *Primary Variable:* **1) PARTY VOTE**
➤ *View:* **Pie**

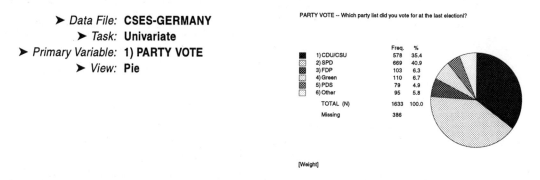

PARTY VOTE -- Which party list did you vote for at the last election!?

		Freq.	%
■	1) CDU/CSU	578	35.4
	2) SPD	669	40.9
	3) FDP	103	6.3
	4) Green	110	6.7
	5) PDS	79	4.9
□	6) Other	95	5.8
	TOTAL (N)	1633	100.0
	Missing	386	

[Weight]

If we examine the political parties of Germany, we find that citizens identify with two major political parties, the Christian Democrats and the Social Democrats, and three minor political parties, the Free Democrats, the Greens, and the Party of Democratic Socialism. We can better understand where these parties stand when we compare citizens' party preferences to their own placement on the left-right ideological scale.

Data File: **CSES-GERMANY**
➤ Task: **Cross-tabulation**
➤ Row Variable: **2) LT-RT-3**
➤ Column Variable: **1) PARTY VOTE**
➤ View: **Tables**
➤ Display: **Column %**

LT-RT-3 by PARTY VOTE
Weight Variable: GERMWT3
Cramer's V: 0.368 **

		CDU/CSU	SPD	FDP	Green	PDS	Other	Missing	TOTAL
LT-RT-3	Left	145	368	35	86	51	14	145	700
		26.3%	62.0%	34.5%	84.9%	88.8%	16.3%		46.9%
	Center	251	172	50	12	6	13	99	504
		45.5%	29.0%	49.7%	11.7%	10.4%	15.2%		33.8%
	Right	156	53	16	3	0	58	39	287
		28.2%	9.0%	15.8%	3.3%	0.8%	68.4%		19.3%
	Missing	26	75	2	8	22	10	102	244
	TOTAL	552	594	101	102	57	85	386	1491
		100.0%	100.0%	100.0%	100.0%	100.0%	100.0%		

This analysis relies on some of the lessons learned in Chapter 4. If your instructor has assigned this chapter out of order, you may need to review Chapter 4 to understand how we use Cramer's V and significance.

There is a very strong correlation between ideology and party preference in Germany (V = 0.368**). Of the people who express a preference for the Social Democratic Party (SPD), 62.0% place themselves on the left of the political spectrum. But also note that 29.0% of those with a preference for the SPD place themselves in the political center of the ideological spectrum. Most of the citizens in Germany who prefer the other large party, the Christian Democrats, place themselves in the political center (45.5%). But another significant portion of those who prefer the Christian Democrats (28.2%) would place themselves on the right of the political spectrum. Because smaller parties are able to be more ideologically focused, it should not be surprising that the smaller parties seem more uniform in their ideological makeup. Supporters of the Free Democrats are strongly concentrated in the ideological center (49.7%), and most Green Party identifiers place themselves on the ideological left (84.9%). The Party of Democratic Socialism is the most leftist of the parties in Germany with 88.8% of their voters identifying with the political left. The PDS is a very interesting phenomenon in Germany. Let's explore this a bit more.

Data File: **CSES-GERMANY**
Task: **Cross-tabulation**
➤ Row Variable: **15) EAST/WEST**
➤ Column Variable: **1) PARTY VOTE**
➤ View: **Tables**
➤ Display: **Column %**

EAST/WEST by PARTY VOTE
Weight Variable: GERMWT3
Cramer's V: 0.376 **

		CDU/CSU	SPD	FDP	Green	PDS	Other	Missing	TOTAL
EAST/WEST	East	81	104	10	12	64	25	83	295
		14.0%	15.5%	9.4%	11.2%	80.5%	26.7%		18.1%
	West	497	565	93	98	15	70	302	1338
		86.0%	84.5%	90.6%	88.8%	19.5%	73.3%		81.9%
	TOTAL	578	669	103	110	79	95	386	1633
		100.0%	100.0%	100.0%	100.0%	100.0%	100.0%		

The variable 15) EAST/WEST indicates where the voter surveyed is from. Prior to the fall of the Berlin wall in 1989, citizens of East Germany lived under a very oppressive communist regime. Since the first full German election, the PDS has gradually emerged as a far left socialist party with its base in the former East Germany. As you can see, a full 80.5% of PDS supporters live in the East. No other party has this level of regional support.

Now let's compare Germany's party system to the party system in the UK. This survey was taken just prior to the 1997 national election that returned the Labour Party to power for the first time in 18 years.

➤ *Data File:* **CSES-UK**
➤ *Task:* **Univariate**
➤ *Primary Variable:* **1) PARTY VOTE**
➤ *View:* **Pie**

PARTY VOTE -- Which party did you vote for in the last election?

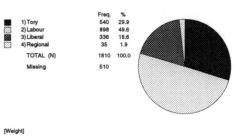

		Freq.	%
■	1) Tory	540	29.9
▨	2) Labour	898	49.6
▩	3) Liberal	336	18.6
░	4) Regional	35	1.9
	TOTAL (N)	1810	100.0
	Missing	510	

[Weight]

As in Germany, the UK has two major parties, the Tories (a nickname for the Conservatives) and the Labour Party. In addition to these two parties, the UK has a small party called the Liberal Democratic Party, a host of even smaller regional parties, and a very small Green Party.

Data File: **CSES-UK**
➤ *Task:* **Cross-tabulation**
➤ *Row Variable:* **2) LT-RT-3**
➤ *Column Variable:* **1) PARTY VOTE**
➤ *View:* **Tables**
➤ *Display:* **Column %**

LT-RT-3   by   PARTY VOTE
Weight Variable: BRITWT
Cramer's V: 0.390 **

		PARTY VOTE					
		Tory	Labour	Liberal	Regional	Missing	TOTAL
LT-RT-3	Left	22	353	87	10	107	471
		4.4%	50.0%	30.8%	39.4%		31.1%
	Center	201	278	156	12	204	647
		40.1%	39.4%	55.4%	48.7%		42.8%
	Right	278	75	39	3	71	395
		55.5%	10.6%	13.8%	11.8%		26.1%
	Missing	39	192	54	11	127	424
	TOTAL	501	706	282	24	510	1513
		100.0%	100.0%	100.0%	100.0%		

Like Germany, there is a very strong correlation between party preference and ideological placement (V = 0.390**). In the United Kingdom, Conservatives lean to the right of the political spectrum (55.5%), but a fairly large percentage still claim the center (40.1%). While 50.0% of Labour supporters are on the political left, 39.4% are in the ideological center. Most supporters of the Liberal Democratic Party (55.4%) are in the center of the political spectrum, while the regional parties are at the center leaning left.

From this analysis we can see that the party systems in the UK and Germany share at least one attribute in common. They are both characterized by large parties that are close to the political center in terms of their ideological composition and character. What we don't know is what other factors influence citizens' party preference. So it's your turn to figure this out.

Comparative Politics

NAME: _____

COURSE: _____

DATE: _____

REVIEW QUESTIONS

Based on the first part of this chapter, answer True or False to the following items:

1. Over the last couple of decades, the Communist Party in France has lost ground to less radical parties, such as the Socialist Party.   T   F

2. When a Socialist Party receives a high percentage of the vote in a country, the Social Democratic Party also tends to do well.   T   F

3. Liberal parties in Europe are similar to liberal parties in the United States in that they are all located on the left side of the ideological spectrum.   T   F

4. The Christian Democratic Party is considered to be a radical party because of its religious ideology.   T   F

5. Green parties tend to be stronger in Western Europe than in Eastern Europe. The extreme right has been showing substantial growth in some southern European countries, such as France.   T   F

6. Ideology and party preference are strongly associated with one another both in Germany and in the UK.   T   F

7. The majority of Liberal Democrats in the United Kingdom are more to the left than they are in the center.   T   F

EXPLORIT QUESTIONS

In the preliminary part of this chapter, we examined the ideological differences between citizens with different party preferences in Germany and the United Kingdom. In this first section, you'll look at how supporters of these parties differ in terms of sex, education, religion, and socioeconomic status.

I. Use the CSES–GERMANY data file and then the CSES–UK file to perform the series of cross-tabulations indicated. For each result, you need to fill in the percentaged results for the row that is specified in the table below. Also indicate whether the results are statistically significant (circle Y for Yes, N for No).

GERMANY SURVEY

> ➤ *Data File:* **CSES–GERMANY**
> ➤ *Task:* **Cross-tabulation**
> ➤ *Row Variables:* **3) SEX**
> **4) EDUCATION**
> **5) RELIGION**
> **7) UNION?**
> ➤ *Column Variable:* **1) PARTY VOTE**
> ➤ *View:* **Tables**
> ➤ *Display:* **Column %**

Fill in the table below.

	CHR.DEM	SPD	FREE DEM.	GREEN	PDS	V =	SIGNIFI-CANT?
3) SEX % Female	_____%	_____%	_____%	_____%	_____%	_____	Y N
4) EDUCATION % University	_____%	_____%	_____%	_____%	_____%	_____	Y N
5) RELIGION % Catholic	_____%	_____%	_____%	_____%	_____%	_____	Y N
7) UNION? % Yes	_____%	_____%	_____%	_____%	_____%	_____	Y N

UK SURVEY

> ➤ *Data File:* **CSES–UK**
> ➤ *Task:* **Cross-tabulation**
> ➤ *Row Variables:* **3) SEX**
> **4) EDUCATION**
> **5) RELIGION2**
> **7) UNION?**
> ➤ *Column Variable:* **1) PARTY VOTE**
> ➤ *View:* **Tables**
> ➤ *Display:* **Column %**

Fill in the table below.

	TORY	LABOUR	LIBERAL	REGIONAL	V =	SIGNIFICANT?
3) SEX % Female	_____%	_____%	_____%	_____%	_____	Y N
4) EDUCATION % University	_____%	_____%	_____%	_____%	_____	Y N
5) RELIGION2 % Anglican	_____%	_____%	_____%	_____%	_____	Y N
7) UNION? % Yes	_____%	_____%	_____%	_____%	_____	Y N

8. In the UK, each party has a relatively similar percentage of female support. This suggests that the differences between male and female vote choices in the analysis are not statistically significant.   T   F

9. In both Germany and the UK, people who support the two parties farthest to the left tend to have more schooling than people who support other political parties.   T   F

10. In both Germany and the UK, people who support ideologically centrist political groups are more likely to be union members.   T   F

11. Of all political groups in Germany, the PDS has the lowest proportions of female supporters.   T   F

12. Christian Democrats and the Tories are much more likely to have high levels of affiliation with the Catholic Church and the Anglican Church respectively.   T   F

II. Do people who prefer different parties have different levels of *political efficacy* and knowledge? Efficacious individuals believe that their opinions and actions are meaningful in the political process. For example, do people who voted for certain parties believe that their votes matter, or that elections matter, while other people do not? Do they vary in their contact with politicians and political knowledge? Again use the GERMANY and UK data files to complete the indicated cross-tabulations. For each result, fill in the percentaged results for the row that is specified in the table below. Also indicate whether the results are statistically significant.

GERMANY SURVEY

➤ *Data File:* **CSES–GERMANY**
➤ *Task:* **Cross-tabulation**
➤ *Row Variables:* **9) OPINION**
10) VOTE MATER
11) WHO POWER
12) CONTACT
13) POL KNOW
➤ *Column Variable:* **1) PARTY VOTE**
➤ *View:* **Tables**
➤ *Display:* **Column %**

Fill in the table below.

	CHR.DEM	SPD	FREE DEM.	GREEN	PDS	V =	SIGNIFI-CANT?
9) OPINION % Hide	_____%	_____%	_____%	_____%	_____%	____	Y N
10) VOTE MATER % Makes diff.	_____%	_____%	_____%	_____%	_____%	____	Y N
11) WHO POWER % Makes diff.	_____%	_____%	_____%	_____%	_____%	____	Y N
12) CONTACT % Yes	_____%	_____%	_____%	_____%	_____%	____	Y N
13) POL KNOW % Don't know	_____%	_____%	_____%	_____%	_____%	____	Y N

UK SURVEY

➤ *Data File:* **CSES–UK**
➤ *Task:* **Cross-tabulation**
➤ *Row Variables:* **9) OPINION**
10) VOTE MATER
11) WHO POWER
12) CONTACT
13) POL KNOW
➤ *Column Variable:* **1) PARTY VOTE**
➤ *View:* **Tables**
➤ *Display:* **Column %**

Fill in the table below.

	TORY	LABOUR	LIBERAL	REGIONAL	V =	SIGNIFICANT?
9) OPINION % Hide	_____%	_____%	_____%	_____%	_____	Y N
10) VOTE MATER % Makes diff.	_____%	_____%	_____%	_____%	_____	Y N
11) WHO POWER % Makes diff.	_____%	_____%	_____%	_____%	_____	Y N
12) CONTACT % Yes	_____%	_____%	_____%	_____%	_____	Y N
13) POL KNOW % Don't know	_____%	_____%	_____%	_____%	_____	Y N

13. In Germany, the PDS and the SPD are more likely to believe that people have to hide their opinions. T F

14. Although it appears that Greens in Germany are less likely to believe that they should hide their opinions, the UNIVARIATE task would allow us to test this idea most accurately. T F

15. In Germany, the party with the highest percentage of persons who believe that their vote matters is _____. _____

16. In Germany, the party with the lowest percentage of persons who believe that their vote matters is _____. _____

17. In the UK, the party with the highest percentage of persons who believe that their vote matters is _____. _____

18. In the UK, the party with the lowest percentage of persons who believe that their vote matters is _____. _____

III. Now let's look at some actual issues to see if there is a difference in the way that political parties approach issues from country to country. The World Values Survey asked respondents which party they would vote for if an election were held tomorrow, and a number of issue questions. The five issues that we are interested in relate to (1) paying taxes to improve the environment, (2) whether or not abortion can ever be justified, (3) confidence in the European Union, (4) confidence in the women's movement, and (5) whether or not people believe that the poor have a chance to move out of poverty. This time we will use the GERMANY and SWEDEN World Values Survey files to complete the indicated cross-tabulations. For each result, fill in the percentaged results for the row that is specified in the table below. Also indicate whether the results are statistically significant.

GERMANY SURVEY

> *Data File:* **WVS97–GERMANY**
> *Task:* **Cross-tabulation**
> *Row Variables:* **18) ENV:TAX**
> **19) CONF:EURO**
> **11) ABORT-3**
> **20) CONF:WOMEN**
> **21) PV: ESCAPE**
> *Column Variable:* **17) PARTY #1**
> *View:* **Tables**
> *Display:* **Column %**

Fill in the table below.

	CHR.DEM	SPD	FREE DEM.	GREEN	PDS	V =	SIGNIFI-CANT?
18) ENV:TAX % S.Agree	_____%	_____%	_____%	_____%	_____%	_____	Y N
19) CONF:EURO % None	_____%	_____%	_____%	_____%	_____%	_____	Y N
11) ABORT-3 % Never	_____%	_____%	_____%	_____%	_____%	_____	Y N
20) CONF:WOMEN % None	_____%	_____%	_____%	_____%	_____%	_____	Y N
21) PV: ESCAPE % Chance	_____%	_____%	_____%	_____%	_____%	_____	Y N

SWEDEN SURVEY

The parties in Sweden are little different from those in Germany, but they still fit the party families model that you learned in this chapter. In fact, Sweden has a pretty fair representation of most of the major party families in Europe from right to left.

Swedish Party	Party Family
Moderate	Conservative
Christian Dem.	Christian Democrat
Liberal Party	Liberal
Center Party	Agrarian
Environment Party	Greens
Social Democrats	Social Democrats
Left Party	Socialist

Now conduct the same issue analysis that you conducted in the previous analysis of Germany. However, you will not need to write down the percentage for every party. Actually, in the analysis that follows, we are interested in issues that divide specific parties.

> ➤ *Data File:* **WVS97–SWEDEN**
> ➤ *Task:* **Cross-tabulation**
> ➤ *Row Variables:* **16) ENV:TAX**
> **14) CONF:EURO**
> **7) ABORT-3**
> **15) CONF:WOMEN**
> **17) PV:ESCAPE**
> ➤ *Column Variable:* **13) PARTY #1**
> ➤ *View:* **Tables**
> ➤ *Display:* **Column %**

Fill in the table below.

	MODERATE	CHR.DEM	GREENS	SDP	V =	SIGNIFICANT?
16) ENV:TAX % S.Agree	____%	____%	____%	____%	____	Y N
14) CONF:EURO % No	____%	____%	____%	____%	____	Y N
7) ABORT-3 % Never	____%	____%	____%	____%	____	Y N
15) CONF:WOMEN % None	____%	____%	____%	____%	____	Y N
17) PV:ESCAPE %Chance	____%	____%	____%	____%	____	Y N

19. In Sweden, all five issues show significant differences between political party supporters.   T   F

20. In Germany, all five issues show significant differences between political party supporters.   T   F

21. In Germany the CDU/CSU and the FDP are the least likely to have no confidence in the European Union.   T   F

22. With the exception of the Green Party, most party supporters in Germany are fairly similar in their views on abortion.   T   F

23. Based on these results, which of these five issues is the most controversial in Sweden? (That is, where is the greatest percentage difference?)

    a. Taxes for the environment

    b. Confidence in the EU

    c. Abortion

    d. Confidence in the women's movement

    e. Chance to escape from poverty

24. Which political party supporters have the lowest level of approval of the women's movement in Sweden?

    a. Moderates

    b. Christian Democrats

    c. Greens

    d. SPD

IN YOUR OWN WORDS

In your own words, please answer the following questions.

1. Based on the analyses in Part I of this worksheet section, write a paragraph that summarizes the similarities and differences of those who are most likely to prefer parties of the left in the UK (Labour and Regional) or in Germany (Social Democrats and Greens).

2. Based on your analysis of OPINION, VOTE MATER, WHO POWER, CONTACT, and POL KNOW in Part II, respond to the following statement: "In both Germany and the UK, supporters of parties on the right have more political efficacy." Be sure to support your answer with evidence.

3. Which issues in Part III seem specific to only one country, and which seem relevant to both countries? In your own nation, which of these issues do you think are the most divisive in terms of political parties? Do any of these results surprise you? Why or why not? Where appropriate, your brief essay should include support from the evidence found in the previous question.

Part III

COMMUNIST AND POSTCOMMUNIST SOCIETIES

CHAPTER 8

AFTER COMMUNISM

Under capitalism, man exploits man. Under communism, it's just the opposite.

JOHN KENNETH GALBRAITH

Communism doesn't work 'cause people like to own stuff.

FRANK ZAPPA

> *Tasks:* Mapping, Historical Trends, Univariate, Cross-tabulation, ANOVA
> *Data Files:* GLOBAL, EUROPE, ASIA, HISTORY, WVS97all, WVS97–RUSSIA

The Cold War ended with the fall of the Berlin Wall in 1989, but politics across the Eurasian continent is still mostly characterized by the differences that resulted from divisions between East and West for more than 40 years.

➤ *Data File:* **GLOBAL**
➤ *Task:* **Mapping**
➤ *Variable 1:* **66) COMMUNIST**
➤ *View:* **Map**
➤ *Display:* **Legend**

COMMUNIST -- Communist and former communist states. (Le Roy, 2001). 0=Non-communist states; 1=Communist states or former communist states in

Category	N
NON-COMM.	(138)
FMR.COMM	(34)
Missing Data	

You can see from this map that Europe was roughly divided between East and West.

➤ *Data File:* **EUROPE**
➤ *Task:* **Mapping**
➤ *Variable 1:* **20) COLD WAR**
➤ *View:* **Map**
➤ *Display:* **Legend**

COLD WAR -- 1947-1989: SECURITY ALIGNMENTS DURING THE COLD WAR (LE ROY, 1998)

Category	N
NATO	(14)
Neutral	(11)
Warsaw Pct	(13)
Missing Data	

As the legend indicates, the countries highlighted in yellow belonged to the Western bloc of countries associated with a military alliance called the North Atlantic Treaty Organization (NATO), which also included the United States and Canada (not shown on this map). With a few exceptions (i.e., Turkey, Greece, Portugal, and Spain), these nations were democratic and capitalist. The Eastern block of countries, shown in the darkest color, were associated with the Soviet Union and were members of an alliance called the Warsaw Pact. These nations were organized along the lines of a centrally planned economy and a communist political system. There were also a few neutral countries between the two blocs. Switzerland, Austria, Ireland, Finland, and Sweden were neutral, but democratic and capitalist. Albania and Yugoslavia were communist but did not affiliate with the Warsaw Pact.

In the first chapter of this workbook, you examined the independence dates of nation-states. Let's revisit the graph that shows the number of countries that became independent during each decade between the late 1700s and late 1900s.

> *Data File:* **HISTORY**
> > *Task:* **Historical Trends**
> *Variables:* **3) IND/DECADE**

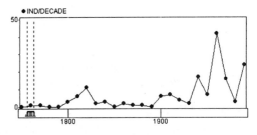

The number of independent countries per decade

From the graph you can see that the 1990s saw the proliferation of independent countries. In 1989, communism collapsed due to revolutions in much of Eastern Europe. Since 1991 the Soviet Union, Czechoslovakia, and Yugoslavia have broken into smaller, independent nation-states (see Table 8.1).

Table 8.1. Breakup of European Nation-States in the 1990s

Soviet Union	Yugoslavia	Czechoslovakia
Armenia	Bosnia-Herzegovina	Czech Republic
Azerbaijan	Croatia	Slovakia
Belarus	Macedonia	
Estonia	Slovenia	
Georgia	Yugoslavia	
Kazakhstan		
Kyrgyzstan		
Latvia		
Lithuania		
Moldova		
Russia		
Tajikistan		
Turkmenistan		
Ukraine		
Uzbekistan		

The collapse of communism has had a profound effect on Europe. European nation-states are now oriented more toward cooperation than conflict with one another. The North Atlantic Treaty

Organization is also in the midst of radical transformation. In the mid-1990s, NATO formally established partnership agreements with its former Warsaw Pact neighbors. Only those countries with profound internal problems have been left out of increasingly cooperative intergovernmental organizations like NATO. In 1997, the Czech Republic, Hungary, and Poland began the process of joining the Alliance, and a host of other European nations signed partnership agreements with the Alliance. This is what the map of NATO looks like today:

➤ *Data File:* **EUROPE**
➤ *Task:* **Mapping**
➤ *Variable 1:* **21) NATO**
➤ *View:* **Map**
➤ *Display:* **Legend**

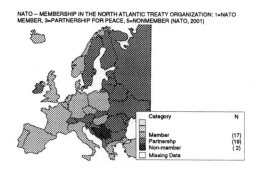

In addition to Europe, the rise and fall of communism has also had a profound effect on the geopolitical situation in South and Central Asia.

➤ *Data File:* **ASIA**
➤ *Task:* **Mapping**
➤ *Variable 1:* **34) COMMUNIST**
➤ *View:* **Map**
➤ *Display:* **Legend**

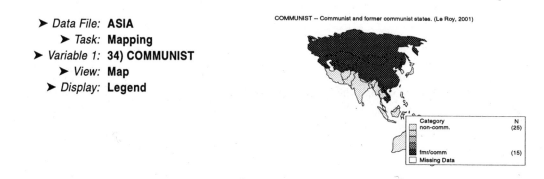

In the wake of the collapse of communism, new independent and former communist states have taken a wide variety of forms. Prior to the collapse of communism, comparative politics researchers classified communist states as totalitarian. Totalitarian states control every element of politics, society, and economy. The following variable indicates the degree of political freedom and civil liberties. Free states now have strong protection of political rights and civil liberties. Authoritarian states may have more restrictive political environments, and states that are not free have not liberalized their political systems to any significant degree since the collapse of the Soviet Union.

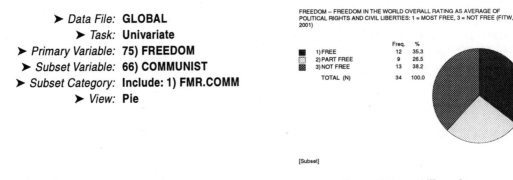

> *Data File:* **GLOBAL**
> *Task:* **Univariate**
> *Primary Variable:* **75) FREEDOM**
> *Subset Variable:* **66) COMMUNIST**
> *Subset Category:* **Include: 1) FMR.COMM**
> *View:* **Pie**

FREEDOM -- FREEDOM IN THE WORLD OVERALL RATING AS AVERAGE OF POLITICAL RIGHTS AND CIVIL LIBERTIES: 1 = MOST FREE, 3 = NOT FREE (FITW, 2001)

		Freq.	%
■	1) FREE	12	35.3
▨	2) PART FREE	9	26.5
▨	3) NOT FREE	13	38.2
	TOTAL (N)	34	100.0

[Subset]

Since we just want to look at states that were communist prior to 1989, we will need to use a subset variable 66) COMMUNIST and select category 1) FMR.COMM for inclusion in the analysis.

Clearly, from a political point of view, former communist nations are not all the same. 35.3% of former communist states are now considered free, and for our purposes we will call them democratic. 26.5% of former communist states have liberalized to a degree but continue to limit political and civil liberties, so they are now classified as partially free. For our purposes we will refer to these as authoritarian. Interestingly enough, 38.2% of former communist states are still not considered free. For our purposes we continue to classify these states as totalitarian.

The same kind of analysis can be conducted about the degree of economic reform.

> *Data File:* **GLOBAL**
> *Task:* **Univariate**
> *Primary Variable:* **46) REGULATION**
> *Subset Variable:* **66) COMMUNIST**
> *Subset Category:* **Include: 1) FMR.COMM**
> *View:* **Pie**

REGULATION -- Index of economic freedom 2001 ranking (HF, 2001)

		Freq.	%
■	1) Capitalist	6	18.8
▨	2) Regulated	19	59.4
▨	3) Statist	7	21.9
	TOTAL (N)	32	100.0
	Missing	2	

[Subset]

Some states (18.8%) have made relatively rapid progress in the transformation of their economies from state-dominated-command economies to free-market-capitalist economies. 59.4% of former communist states have made some reform to their economies. For our purposes we will refer to these economies as "regulated." Finally, you can see that there are a number of states (21.9%) that still have state-dominant economies. Clearly, the majority of former communist states still seem to practice economic policy as though the state has a very significant role to play in economic policy.

Some have emphasized rapid transformation of their political systems, and a few others have rapidly tried to adapt their economies to the global capitalist system. Still others have made very few reforms. We can better understand these new states if we organize them according to their degree of economic and political reform.[1]

---

[1] There are some instances in this chapter (and in the worksheet section that follows) where the cross-tabulation results using the GLOBAL file produce the statement "Warning: Potential significance problem." This is to alert you that the statistical significance value may not be reliable due to the small number of nations used in the analysis. This is not a problem for the type of analysis that we are currently conducting. For our purposes in this chapter, we will often ignore this warning.

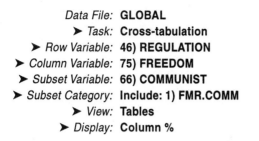

Data File: **GLOBAL**
➤ Task: **Cross-tabulation**
➤ Row Variable: **46) REGULATION**
➤ Column Variable: **75) FREEDOM**
➤ Subset Variable: **66) COMMUNIST**
➤ Subset Category: **Include: 1) FMR.COMM**
➤ View: **Tables**
➤ Display: **Column %**

REGULATION   by   FREEDOM

Cramer's V: 0.596 **
Warning: Potential significance problem. Check row and column totals.

		FREE	PART FREE	NOT FREE	TOTAL
Capitalist		6	0	0	6
		50.0%	0.0%	0.0%	18.8%
Regulated		6	7	6	19
		50.0%	100.0%	46.2%	59.4%
Statist		0	0	7	7
		0.0%	0.0%	53.8%	21.9%
Missing		0	2	0	2
TOTAL		12	7	13	32
		100.0%	100.0%	100.0%	

From this table you can see that 50% of the free states are capitalist and 50% are still highly regulated. You should also note that all partially free states have highly regulated economies. Of the states that are not free, 6 of the 13 states in this category are highly regulated and the rest continue to be state-dominant.

Table 8.2. **Communist/Postcommunist Reform States**

	Democratic	Authoritarian	Totalitarian
Capitalist	Democratic-Capitalist *Poland*	n/a	n/a
Regulated	Democratic-Regulatory *Romania*	Authoritarian-Regulatory *Russia*	Totalitarian-Regulatory *China*
Statist	n/a	n/a	Totalitarian *North Korea*

From this table you can see that there are five basic types of communist and post-communist regimes: democratic capitalist, typified by Poland, democratic-regulatory regimes as in Romania, authoritarian-regulatory regimes as in Russia, totalitarian-regulatory regimes as in China, and totalitarian regimes as in North Korea.

You can see each of these regime types in the following map.

Data File: **GLOBAL**
➤ Task: **Mapping**
➤ Variable 1: **67) COMM TYPE**
➤ View: **Map**
➤ Display: **Legend**

COMM TYPE -- Type of post-communist Regime (Le Roy, 2001)

Category	N
DEM-CAP	(6)
DEM-REG	(6)
AUTH-REG	(7)
TOT-REG	(6)
TOTAL	(7)
Missing Data	(140)

Now we have already described these states as having widely varying approaches to politics and economics. Let's test this typology to see if they vary according to economic political and economic factors.

Chapter 8: After Communism   143

Democratic capitalist societies tend to have much higher rates of access to information. Does the number of daily newspapers in a country depend on the type of communist transition state?[1]

Data File: **GLOBAL**
➤ Task: **ANOVA**
➤ Dependent Variable: **50) NEWS/CP**
➤ Independent Variable: **67) COMM TYPE**
➤ View: **Summary**

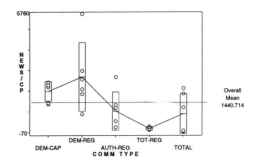

Newspapers are more widely read and distributed in those nations with free politics and markets. Where one party controls the creation and publication of news, the distribution of this information is clearly much lower. Is national wealth related to the type of regime in a country?

Data File: **GLOBAL**
Task: **ANOVA**
➤ Dependent Variable: **38) GDPCAP PPP**
➤ Independent Variable: **67) COMM TYPE**
➤ View: **Summary**

Democratic-capitalist societies also are wealthier than their less free and more regulated counterparts. But is this all dependent on culture or on some other factors that may be associated with type of government? After all, Europe is generally a much wealthier region than East or Central Asia.

Data File: **GLOBAL**
➤ Task: **Cross-tabulation**
➤ Row Variable: **67) COMM TYPE**
➤ Column Variable: **10) REGION**
➤ View: **Tables**
➤ Display: **Column %**

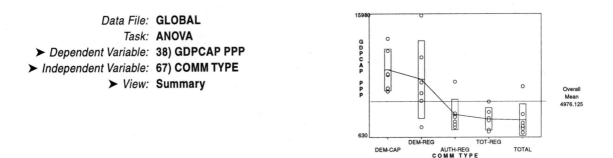

COMM TYPE by REGION
Cramer's V: 0.413
Warning: Potential significance problem. Check row and column totals.

		REGION					
		SUB-SAHARA	ARAB	ASIA/PACIF	WEST.HEMI.	EUROPE	TOTAL
COMM TYPE	DEM-CAP	0	0	0	0	6	6
		0.0%	0.0%	0.0%	0.0%	24.0%	18.8%
	DEM-REG	0	0	1	0	5	6
		0.0%	0.0%	16.7%	0.0%	20.0%	18.8%
	AUTH-REG	0	0	0	0	7	7
		0.0%	0.0%	0.0%	0.0%	28.0%	21.9%
	TOT-REG	0	0	2	0	4	6
		0.0%	0.0%	33.3%	0.0%	16.0%	18.8%
	TOTAL	0	0	3	1	3	7
		0.0%	0.0%	50.0%	100.0%	12.0%	21.9%
	Missing	43	22	26	28	23	142
	TOTAL	0	0	6	1	25	32
		100.0%	100.0%	100.0%	100.0%	100.0%	

---

[1] If you have not learned to use the ANOVA task, please review Chapter 5 where this task is introduced.

From this table we see that there are actually very few communist or former communist countries located anywhere but in Asia or Europe. In Asia all but one of them still has strong totalitarian tendencies, while in Europe these transition states clearly seem to vary much more widely. Let's look at Europe a bit more closely. There may actually be some incentives for developing democratic and capitalist systems.

Following World War II, the nations of Western Europe began to cooperate with one another on a host of economic, social, and political issues. In 1992, the nations of Western Europe established the European Union to promote their common economic agenda. Recently, 11 of the 15 members committed themselves to a common currency. Under the common currency arrangement, the national currencies of countries such as Germany and France will be replaced with a single European currency. We can see by a comparison of maps below that there is a strong overlap between those nations that were in the democratic-capitalist West during the Cold War and those nations that are now members of the European Union.

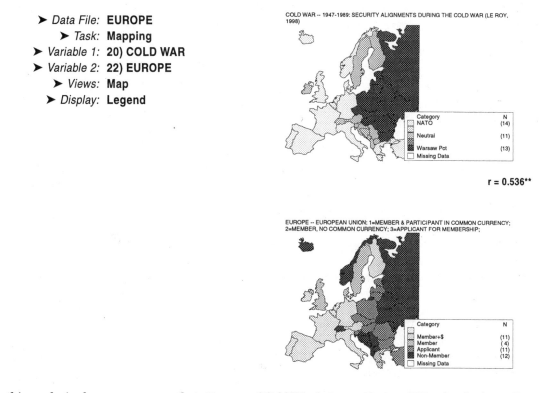

➤ *Data File:* **EUROPE**
➤ *Task:* **Mapping**
➤ *Variable 1:* **20) COLD WAR**
➤ *Variable 2:* **22) EUROPE**
➤ *Views:* **Map**
➤ *Display:* **Legend**

COLD WAR -- 1947-1989: SECURITY ALIGNMENTS DURING THE COLD WAR (LE ROY, 1998)

Category	N
NATO	(14)
Neutral	(11)
Warsaw Pct	(13)
Missing Data	

r = 0.536**

EUROPE -- EUROPEAN UNION: 1=MEMBER & PARTICIPANT IN COMMON CURRENCY; 2=MEMBER, NO COMMON CURRENCY; 3=APPLICANT FOR MEMBERSHIP;

Category	N
Member+$	(11)
Member	(4)
Applicant	(11)
Non-Member	(12)
Missing Data	

As this analysis shows, we can see that 47 years of Cold War between East and West has had an effect on the contemporary shape of membership in the European Union. But the differences between East and West go beyond just organizational membership issues. The divisions between the two blocs are also associated with strong cross-national differences in wealth.

Data File: **EUROPE**
Task: **Mapping**
Variable 1: **20) COLD WAR**
➤ Variable 2: **11) GDPCAP PPP**
 ➤ Views: **Map**
 ➤ Display: **Legend**

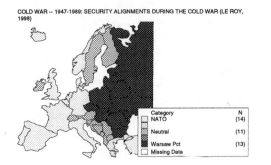

COLD WAR -- 1947-1989: SECURITY ALIGNMENTS DURING THE COLD WAR (LE ROY, 1998)

Category	N
NATO	(14)
Neutral	(11)
Warsaw Pct	(13)
Missing Data	

r = −0.661**

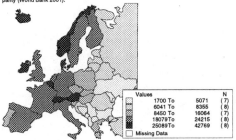

GDPCAP PPP -- Gross Domestic Product per capita based on purchasing power parity (World Bank 2001).

Values		N
1700 To	5071	(7)
6041 To	8355	(8)
8450 To	16064	(7)
18079 To	24215	(8)
25089 To	42769	(8)
Missing Data		

From this comparison of maps we see that there is strong correlation between GDPCAP PPP and COLD WAR.

The changes throughout Eastern Europe extend beyond economic and military factors. As discussed earlier, the 1990s led to creation of many new nation-states in Eastern Europe. Let's use the CROSS-TABULATION task to compare European nation-states in terms of those having relatively new democracies and those having older, more established democracies.

Data File: **EUROPE**
➤ Task: **Cross-tabulation**
➤ Row Variable: **15) GOVERNMEN2**
➤ Column Variable: **20) COLD WAR**
 ➤ View: **Tables**

GOVERNMEN2   by   COLD WAR
Cramer's V: 0.860 **

		COLD WAR			
		NATO	Neutral	Warsaw Pct	TOTAL
GOVERNMEN2	Old Demos	14	6	0	20
		100.0%	60.0%	0.0%	54.1%
	Transition	0	4	13	17
		0.0%	40.0%	100.0%	45.9%
	Missing	0	1	0	1
	TOTAL	14	10	13	37
		100.0%	100.0%	100.0%	

The pattern is very clear. All 13 of the Warsaw Pact nation-states are in a current state of transition. All 14 of the NATO nation-states have older, established democracies. Due to Eastern Europe's recent arrival on the democratic scene, laws and practices in these countries reflect a great deal of uncertainty about the norms associated with Western democratic behavior. For example, the variable CENSORSHIP refers to a state's infringement on freedoms of belief, expression, communication, and movement.

Comparative Politics

Data File: **EUROPE**
Task: **Cross-tabulation**
➤ Row Variable: **23) CENSORSHIP**
➤ Column Variable: **15) GOVERNMEN2**
➤ View: **Tables**
➤ Display: **Column %**

CENSORSHIP by GOVERNMEN2
Cramer's V: 0.681 **
Warning: Potential significance problem. Check row and column totals.

		GOVERNMEN2			
		Old Demos	Transition	Missing	TOTAL
C E N S O R S H I P	Mild	18	4	0	22
		90.0%	23.5%		59.5%
	Severe	1	10	0	11
		5.0%	58.8%		29.7%
	Draconian	1	3	1	4
		5.0%	17.6%		10.8%
	TOTAL	20	17	1	37
		100.0%	100.0%		

The results of this table are very clear. Thirteen of the 17 nation-states that are transition states practice severe or draconian levels of censorship, whereas only 2 of the 20 established democracies have severe or draconian levels of censorship.

Do transition states differ in terms of capital punishment?

Data File: **EUROPE**
Task: **Cross-tabulation**
➤ Row Variable: **24) CAP PUNISH**
➤ Column Variable: **15) GOVERNMEN2**
➤ View: **Tables**
➤ Display: **Column %**

CAP PUNISH by GOVERNMEN2
Cramer's V: 0.706 **
Warning: Potential significance problem. Check row and column totals.

		GOVERNMEN2			
		Old Demos	Transition	Missing	TOTAL
C A P P U N I S H	Abolished	14	5	0	19
		70.0%	29.4%		51.4%
	Condition	3	0	0	3
		15.0%	0.0%		8.1%
	No use	2	0	0	2
		10.0%	0.0%		5.4%
	Retained	1	12	1	13
		5.0%	70.6%		35.1%
	TOTAL	20	17	1	37
		100.0%	100.0%		

Most people in the United States are surprised to find that, in general, established democracies in Europe have abolished capital punishment. As this table shows, only 1 of the 20 established democracies in Europe still uses capital punishment. However, 12 of the 17 newly established democracies use capital punishment for ordinary crimes (e.g., murder). Throughout Europe and the rest of the world, the longer a nation has been a democracy, the less likely it is to use capital punishment.

What was once a single world living behind an iron curtain is now a tremendously diverse set of nations. Some have changed very little, whereas others have made a very distinct break from the past. In the worksheet section that follows, it will be your turn to explore these new nations.

WORKSHEET

NAME: _____

COURSE: _____

DATE: _____

CHAPTER

8

REVIEW QUESTIONS

Based on the first part of this chapter, answer True or False to the following items:

1. During the Cold War, all European nations were divided between NATO and the Warsaw Pact.   T   F

2. The decade of the 1990s saw a large increase in the number of nation-states that became independent because of the breakup of the Soviet Union, Yugoslavia, and Czechoslovakia.   T   F

3. Transition states in Europe tend to have more liberal democratic regimes than transition states in Asia.   T   F

4. The Cold War division of Europe did not appear to have any effect on communist countries' capacity to accumulate wealth.   T   F

5. Established democracies are more likely to retain capital punishment laws than new democracies.   T   F

EXPLORIT QUESTIONS

I. Corruption and the lack of respect for the rule of law is said to be one of the leading challenges to democratic transition and economic development in former communist countries. Prior to the fall of communism, bureaucratic authorities and political elites dominated individual and collective decision-making. Now, in an environment of declining state capacity to enforce the laws, corruption is said to be rampant. Please write out the variable description for 72) NO CORRUPT in the space below:

_____

_____

_____

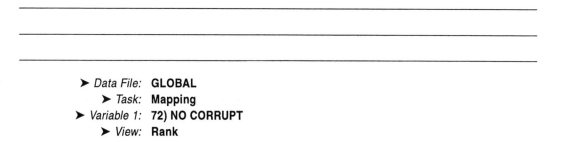

> ➤ *Data File:* **GLOBAL**
> ➤ *Task:* **Mapping**
> ➤ *Variable 1:* **72) NO CORRUPT**
> ➤ *View:* **Rank**

6. List the top and bottom five countries rank-ordered in terms of their level of corruption.

    LEAST CORRUPT   **MOST CORRUPT**

    _____   _____

    _____   _____

    _____   _____

    _____   _____

    _____   _____

7. Most of the countries with low corruption are in

    a. Africa.

    b. Europe.

    c. East Asia.

    d. the Americas.

    e. South Asia.

8. Most of the countries with high corruption are in

    a. Africa.

    b. Europe.

    c. East Asia.

    d. the Americas.

    e. South Asia.

II. Now let's analyze corruption using the WORLDS.7 variable.

> Data File: **GLOBAL**
> ➤ Task: **ANOVA**
> ➤ Dependent Variable: **72) NO CORRUPT**
> ➤ Independent Variable: **80) WORLDS.7**
> ➤ View: **Means**

> You may need to use both the Graph view and the Means view to answer the following questions.

9. Levels of corruption in communist and postcommunist societies are most
    similar to levels of corruption in Islamic nation-states.   T   F

10. Based on the graph alone, list the type of country that has the lowest
    level of corruption.   _____

11. Now list the three types of countries that have the highest levels of corruption and their mean
    corruption scores.

    COUNTRY TYPE   **MEAN CORRUPTION SCORE**

    _____   _____

    _____   _____

    _____   _____

12. Are the differences between types of nations and the levels corruption
    statistically significant?   Yes   No

Now let's see if the type of transition state makes a difference in the level of corruption.

> | | |
> |---|---|
> | Data File: | **GLOBAL** |
> | Task: | **ANOVA** |
> | Dependent Variable: | **72) NO CORRUPT** |
> | ➤ Independent Variable: | **67) COMM TYPE** |
> | ➤ View: | **Means** |

> **You may need to use both the Graph view and the Means view to answer the following questions.**

13. Based on the ANOVA graph alone, the types of countries in the transition
    states typology do not differ in their levels of corruption.   T   F

14. Based on the graph alone, list the type of country that has the lowest
    level of corruption.   _____

15. Now list the three types of regimes that have the highest levels of corruption and their mean
    corruption scores.

    REGIME TYPE   **MEAN CORRUPTION SCORE**

    _____   _____

    _____   _____

    _____   _____

Assume that the regime-type variable is based on the level of government regulation of the economy and the level of democratization, and then answer the following questions.

16. The level of democratization and economic liberalization in a country is related to the level of corruption; specifically, the lower the level of democratization and economic liberalization, the higher the rate of corruption. This suggests that democratization and economic liberalization play an important role in the level of corruption in society   T   F

17. Based on these results, one might conclude that (circle one of the following)

    a. economic liberalization appears to be more important than democratization in determining the level of corruption in a country.

    b. democratization appears to be more important than economic liberalization in determining the level of corruption in a country.

    c. both democratization and economic liberalization seem to have an impact on the level of corruption in society.

III. Now that you have analyzed what businesspeople and investors think about corruption in communist societies, what do the actual people in these countries think about corruption?

> *Data File:*   **WVS97all**
> *Task:*   **Cross-tabulation**
> *Row Variable:*   **7) CORRUPTION**
> *Column Variable:* **1) COUNTRY**
> *View:*   **Tables**
> *Display:*   **Column %**

18. What percentage of U.S. citizens believes that all public officials are corrupt?   _____%

19. What percentage of Russian citizens believes that all public officials are corrupt?   _____%

20. With respect to citizens' perceptions of public corruption, Russian citizens are more like

    a. Americans.

    b. Mexicans.

    c. South Koreans.

    d. Germans.

IN YOUR OWN WORDS

In your own words, please answer the following questions.

1. Are the perceptions of businesspeople and analysts that characterize Russia as corrupt similar to the perceptions of the citizens of Russia? Answer this question and explain your answer on the basis of evidence.

2. Is there a difference in the attitudes that citizens have toward the democratization process depending on whether they were part of the Soviet Union or a satellite? Open the WVS97–RUSSIA data file and look at the variables 2) PRE REGIME and 3) NOW REGIME using the UNIVARIATE task. Do the results surprise you? If so, why? If not, why not? As always, base your written response on evidence.

3. Do older people remember communism with greater nostalgia or wrath? Using the WVS97–RUSSIA data file, look at 2) PRE REGIME and 3) NOW REGIME to see if there is a relationship between age and one's view of the regime. Put the two regime variables in the row and 5) AGE GROUP in the column. Use column percentages. Is there a relationship between these variables? Explain your answer on the basis of evidence.

CHAPTER **9**

RUSSIA, POLAND, AND DEMOCRATIC TRANSITION

*I cannot forecast to you the action of Russia. It is a
riddle, wrapped in a mystery, inside an enigma . . .*
SIR WINSTON CHURCHILL, 1939

Tasks: Mapping, Scatterplot, Historical Trends, Univariate, Cross-tabulation
Data Files: GLOBAL, EUROPE, HISTORY, WVS97–RUSSIA, WVS97–POLAND, WVS97–USA,
WVS97–GERMANY

What Winston Churchill perceived in 1939 is still true in the new millennium. Most of the
problems that interest researchers in comparative politics today—democratic transition,
political economy, nationalism, and ethnic conflict—are all present in the study of the
politics of Russia. These issues are also present in the study of the former Soviet satellites, but you will
see that they exist to a much lesser degree. In this chapter we will examine the political culture,
behavior, and attitudes of citizens in Russia and Poland. You will recall that in Chapter 8 we determined that there is a wide variety of regimes in states that were formerly communist.

➤ *Data File:* **GLOBAL**
➤ *Task:* **Mapping**
➤ *Variable 1:* **67) COMM TYPE**
➤ *View:* **Map**
➤ *Display:* **Legend**

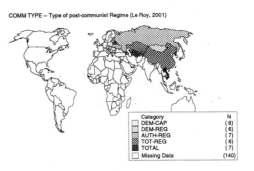

You remember that we classified Russia as an authoritarian-regulatory regime and Poland as a democratic-capitalist regime. But as you have read about Russia, you probably wonder why we have classified it as "authoritarian." After all, Russia still convenes regular elections and has a competitive party
system. Let's take a closer look at these two countries using the EUROPE file.

155

➤ *Data File:* **EUROPE**
➤ *Task:* **Mapping**
➤ *Variable 1:* **60) POL RIGHT2**
➤ *View:* **Map**
➤ *Display:* **Legend**

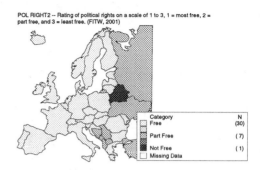

POL RIGHT2 -- Rating of political rights on a scale of 1 to 3, 1 = most free, 2 = part free, and 3 = least free. (FITW, 2001)

Category	N
Free	(30)
Part Free	(7)
Not Free	(1)
Missing Data	

According to Freedom House, which is the source of the data, political rights in Russia are still somewhat limited. By comparison, Poland emerges with a relatively strong rating. According to Freedom House, the political rights measure is based on a number of factors:

> free and fair elections, competitive parties or other political groupings, and the opposition plays an important role and has actual power. Citizens enjoy self-determination or an extremely high degree of autonomy (in the case of territories), and minority groups have reasonable self-government or can participate in the government through informal consensus.

According to Freedom House, Russia's political rights ratings are relatively low due to significant allegations of corruption at the last election, President Vladimir Putin's tendency toward the concentration of power in the hands of the executive, and the activities of the military in the civil war in Chechnya.[1]

By comparison, Poland's new democratic system is relatively strong, elections are fair, and the leadership is adhering to constitutional norms.

Civil liberties are another measure of a nation's commitment to democratic norms and values. How well does a nation protect free expression, a free press, freedom of association, minority opinions, and the right to worship?

Data File: **EUROPE**
Task: **Mapping**
➤ *Variable 1:* **61) CIV LIBS2**
➤ *View:* **Map**
➤ *Display:* **Legend**

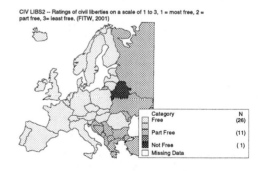

CIV LIBS2 -- Ratings of civil liberties on a scale of 1 to 3, 1 = most free, 2 = part free, 3= least free. (FITW, 2001)

Category	N
Free	(26)
Part Free	(11)
Not Free	(1)
Missing Data	

According to this map, Poland is more free than Russia in the area of civil liberties. In Freedom House's report on Poland, the only problem cited is the considerable backlog of criminal cases in the Polish legal system. These cases may actually serve to deny due process of law to Polish defendants, so Poland is cited for improvement in this area.

---

[1] *Freedom in the World*, 2000–2001.

Russia, on the other hand, has considerable problems in the area of civil liberties. A Freedom House survey of the press in Russia reports that Russian police have engaged in persistent harassment of media outlets that report on corruption or criticize the government for its war in Chechnya. Reporters and editors have been harassed, beaten, and detained without charge for their press activities. Freedom House also reports that "uneven respect for religious freedom characterizes the local authorities' relationship to religious organizations." Under a 1997 law, churches must be registered with the government and prove that they have been in existence for more than 15 years. The reports also site problems in union representation and organization and the independence of the judiciary.

In spite of these problems, concern, for the economy in Poland and Russia overwhelms most other issues. Open the HISTORY file so that you can see the annual growth in GDP since 1990.

> *Data File:* **HISTORY**
>> *Task:* **Historical Trends**
> *Variables:* **48) GR:RUSSIA**
>> **49) GR:POLAND**

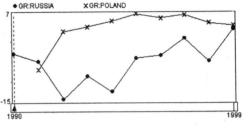

Annual GDP growth in Russia and Poland, 1990–1999

As you can see, the collapse of communism and the Soviet Union has actually been beneficial for economic growth in Poland. In Russia this is another story. Until recently, Russia's economy shrunk in almost every year since 1990.

Was this divergent pattern of growth the norm everywhere else? Were all the economies within the former Soviet Union hurt by the transition that occurred between 1989 and 1991? The following variable measures the average annual rate of economic growth from 1990–1999.

> *Data File:* **EUROPE**
>> *Task:* **Mapping**
> *Variable 1:* **12) GROW 90–99**
>> *View:* **Map**
>> *Display:* **Legend**

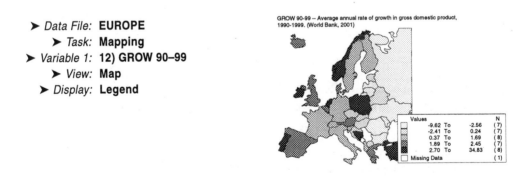

From this map it appears that almost all of the former communist nations of Europe grew at an average annual rate that is either negative or near zero during the period 1990–99. Poland is one of a few exceptions to this rule. Poland grew at a remarkable rate of 3.7% per year, whereas Russia's economy shrunk at a rate of 5.22% per year. This means that Poland's economy increased by more than 30% during this period while Russia's economy shrunk by 50%!

Why is this the case? Some would argue that it has to do with the level of government intervention in the economy. The Wall Street Journal and Heritage Foundation have co-published a rating system that assesses economic freedom in a country.

> *Data File:* **EUROPE**
> *Task:* **Mapping**
> ➤ *Variable 1:* **55) FREE2001**
> ➤ *View:* **Map**
> ➤ *Display:* **Legend**

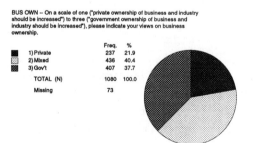

FREE2001 -- Index of economic freedom 2001 ranking (Heritage Foundation, 2001)

Values			N
1.65	To	1.90	(5)
2.05	To	2.25	(9)
2.30	To	2.55	(7)
2.65	To	3.30	(7)
3.45	To	4.25	(8)
Missing Data			(2)

A low number in this ranking indicates a low level of government intervention in the economy, whereas a high number indicates a high level of government intervention in the economy. As you can see, Russia has the fourth highest level of government intervention in the economy. If you look at the rankings for this variable [List:Rank], the only nations with more government intervention are Ukraine, Bosnia, and Belarus. In the worksheet section that follows, you will begin to explore the relationship between government intervention in the economy and economic growth, but first let's turn to the people of Russia and Poland. How do these citizens view the changes to their society?

> ➤ *Data File:* **WVS97–RUSSIA**
> ➤ *Task:* **Univariate**
> ➤ *Primary Variable:* **6) BUS OWN**
> ➤ *View:* **Pie**

BUS OWN -- On a scale of one ("private ownership of business and industry should be increased") to three ("government ownership of business and industry should be increased"), please indicate your views on business ownership.

		Freq.	%
■	1) Private	199	10.2
▨	2) Mixed	774	39.5
▨	3) Gov't	987	50.4
	TOTAL (N)	1960	100.0
	Missing	80	

Only 10.2% of the population in Russia seems to favor more private ownership of business and industry, while 50.4% of the population favors more government ownership of business.

> ➤ *Data File:* **WVS97–POLAND**
> ➤ *Task:* **Univariate**
> ➤ *Primary Variable:* **5) BUS OWN**
> ➤ *View:* **Pie**

BUS OWN -- On a scale of one ("private ownership of business and industry should be increased") to three ("government ownership of business and industry should be increased"), please indicate your views on business ownership.

		Freq.	%
■	1) Private	237	21.9
▨	2) Mixed	436	40.4
▨	3) Gov't	407	37.7
	TOTAL (N)	1080	100.0
	Missing	73	

Polish citizens don't have as much hesitation about private ownership. While 21.9% of the population favors more privatization, 37.7% favors more government intervention. The plurality of the Polish population favors a more mixed perspective. Poland does seem more receptive to private ownership of industry and a little more hesitant to want to return to the days of government ownership. Compare these results in Russia and Poland to the same question asked of the U.S. population.

➤ *Data File:* **WVS97–USA**
➤ *Task:* **Univariate**
➤ *Primary Variable:* **15) BUS OWN**
➤ *View:* **Pie**

BUS OWN -- On a scale of one ("private ownership of business and industry should be increased") to three ("government ownership of business and industry should be increased"), please indicate your views on business ownership.

		Freq.	%
■	1) Private	186574	62.7
▨	2) Mixed	95570	32.1
▦	3) Gov't	15376	5.2
	TOTAL (N)	297520	100.0
	Missing	10749	

[Weight]

The overwhelming majority of the U.S. population surveyed favors more private ownership in the United States. While a belief in private or public ownership does not make an economy run, a population in favor of private enterprise will make the transition to capitalism much easier.

Some scholars have suggested that the simultaneous introduction of democratic and market ideals to countries like Russia and Poland is unfortunate. Analysts fear that as the Russian economy deteriorates, the population will be inclined to blame democracy for their economic woes. The World Values Survey asks a question to try to understand this sentiment. They asked respondents to agree or disagree with the statement "In democracy, the economic system runs badly."

➤ *Data File:* **WVS97–RUSSIA**
➤ *Task:* **Univariate**
➤ *Primary Variable:* **8) DEM:ECONOM**
➤ *View:* **Pie**

DEM:ECONOM -- In democracy, the economic system runs badly.

		Freq.	%
■	1) Agree	1005	60.1
▨	2) Disagree	666	39.9
	TOTAL (N)	1671	100.0
	Missing	369	

In Russia, the majority of the population (60.1%) agrees or strongly agrees with this idea, and they may have a point. If you recall our earlier examination of economic growth over time, you will remember that Russia has suffered badly since it introduced democratic political reforms. But what about Poland? We would guess that its better economic performance might actually lead its citizens to have a more positive attitude about democracy.

➤ *Data File:* **WVS97–POLAND**
➤ *Task:* **Univariate**
➤ *Primary Variable:* **7) DEM:ECONOM**
➤ *View:* **Pie**

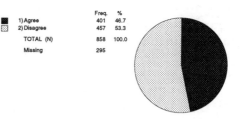

		Freq.	%
■	1) Agree	401	46.7
▨	2) Disagree	457	53.3
	TOTAL (N)	858	100.0
	Missing	295	

In Poland, the majority of the population (53.3%) tends to disagree with the assertion that "in democracy, the economic system runs badly." However, this response is also consistent with the Polish experiences during the 1990s. Let's compare this to the population in Germany, but this time we should see if there is a difference of opinion on this matter between citizens from the former Communist East Germany and those living in the West.

➤ *Data File:* **WVS97–GERMANY**
➤ *Task:* **Cross-tabulation**
➤ *Row Variable:* **29) DEM:ECONOM**
➤ *Column Variable:* **1) PRE-1989**
➤ *View:* **Tables**
➤ *Display:* **Column %**

DEM:ECONOM   by   PRE-1989
Cramer's V: 0.139 **

		PRE-1989		
		West	East	TOTAL
DEM:ECONOM	Agree	121	220	341
		12.3%	22.9%	17.5%
	Disagree	863	741	1604
		87.7%	77.1%	82.5%
	Missing	33	48	81
	TOTAL	984	961	1945
		100.0%	100.0%	

Both the East and West Germans disagree with the assertion that "in democracy, the economic system runs badly" to a far greater extent than citizens in Poland or Russia, but there are more East Germans who agree with this statement than West Germans. So far, this analysis does suggest that citizens of a nation-state with a longer tradition of communism have a far deeper suspicion of democracy and capitalism than citizens in societies with democratic-capitalist traditions.

There are likely to be other factors that are responsible for this low opinion of democracy. In the previous chapter, you explored the relationship between age and one's attitude toward the current regime in Russia. Now it's your turn to do more comparative politics.

NAME: _____

COURSE: _____

DATE: _____

REVIEW QUESTIONS

Based on the first part of this chapter, answer True or False to the following items:

1. Russia is characterized as an authoritarian-regulatory regime because of its weak protection of political rights and civil liberties.　　T　F

2. The Russian government protects civil liberties better than the Polish government.　　T　F

3. Free and fair elections, competitive party systems, and minority participation are all examples of civil liberties.　　T　F

4. The GDP of Russia grew at a negative rate in the 1990s.　　T　F

5. During the 1990s Poland's economy also suffered significant negative growth.　　T　F

6. Compared to other European nation-states, the Russian government is not very involved in the regulation of the economy.　　T　F

7. Russians are generally more inclined than Poles to believe that in democracy the economy runs badly.　　T　F

8. In surveys of Germans, Poles, and Russians, Germans are the most inclined to believe that in democracy the economic system runs badly.　　T　F

EXPLORIT QUESTIONS

I. Do economies that are more highly regulated have higher rates of economic growth than those that are less regulated? Analyze the relationship between FREE2001 and GROW 90–99 in the GLOBAL file and then the EUROPE file and answer the questions that follow.

> ➤ *Data File:* **GLOBAL**
> ➤ *Task:* **Scatterplot**
> ➤ *Dependent Variable:* **40) GROW 90–99**
> ➤ *Independent Variable:* **45) FREE2001**
> ➤ *View:* **Reg. Line**

9. What is the value of r?　　r = _____

10. Is the result statistically significant?   Yes   No

Now remove three outliers from the analysis by clicking on the [Outlier] button and then clicking on [Remove] for each case that appears. You should remove Iraq, Bosnia and Herzegovina, and Equatorial Guinea. The scatterplot will rescale.

11. After you have removed the outlier, what is the value of r?   r = _____

12. Is the relationship significant?   Yes   No

Now conduct the same analysis with the nations of Europe.

> ➤ *Data File:* **EUROPE**
> ➤ *Task:* **Scatterplot**
> ➤ *Dependent Variable:* **12) GROW 90–99**
> ➤ *Independent Variable:* **55) FREE2001**
> ➤ *View:* **Reg. Line**

13. What is the value of r?   r = _____

14. Is the result statistically significant?   Yes   No

Now remove one outlier from the analysis by clicking on the [Outlier] button and then clicking on [Remove]. The scatterplot will rescale.

15. Which case did you remove?   _____

16. After you have removed the outlier, what is the value of r?   r = _____

17. Is the relationship significant?   Yes   No

On the basis of this analysis, answer Question 1 in the "In Your Own Words" section at the end of this chapter.

II. Has a democratic culture taken root in Poland and Russia? In spite of increased freedoms, many Poles and Russians do not see the contemporary political and social situations in their countries in a positive light. In fact, in our analysis of attitudes toward the pre-1989 communist regimes in Chapter 8 we saw that there are still many people who see that era in a positive light. Have these individuals come to value democracy? Is there a significant difference in democratic values between those who liked the previous political regime and those who did not? Complete the table below for Russia and Poland and then answer the questions that follow. For each country listed below, you will need to open the appropriate data file, conduct the cross-tabulation that is indicated, write down the percentaged results for the first row of the table (e.g., Good, Bad), write down the value for V, and then indicate whether the results are statistically significant.

> *Data Files:* **WVS97–RUSSIA**
> **WVS97–POLAND**
> *Task:* **Cross-tabulation**
> *Row Variables:* **CONF:EURO**
> **DEMOCRACY (Russia only)**
> **AUTOCRAT (Russia only)**
> **DEM:BETTER**
> **ORDER-FREE**
> *Column Variable:* **PRE-REGIM2**
> *View:* **Tables**
> *Display:* **Column %**

Fill in the table below.

RUSSIA

	BAD	SAME	GOOD	VALUE V	SIGNIFICANT?
10) CONF:EURO % High Confidence	_____%	_____%	_____%	_____	Y N
11) DEMOCRACY % Good	_____%	_____%	_____%	_____	Y N
12) AUTOCRAT % Bad	_____%	_____%	_____%	_____	Y N
13) DEM:BETTER % Agree	_____%	_____%	_____%	_____	Y N
14) ORDER-FREE % Freedom	_____%	_____%	_____%	_____	Y N

18. In general, do Russians who think that the communist regime in Russia was good generally value democracy as much as those who thought communism was bad?   Yes   No

19. Which group of Russians tend to be more inclined to support autocratic or authoritarian government?

   a. Those who believe that the former communist regime was bad.

   b. Those who believe that the former communist regime was about the same.

   c. Those who believe that the former communist regime was good.

   d. None of the above. All groups felt generally the same way about autocracy.

20. Which group of Russians is more likely to believe that "democracy may have its problems, but it is better than all other forms of government"?

   a. Those who believe that the former communist regime was bad.

   b. Those who believe that the former communist regime was about the same.

   c. Those who believe that the former communist regime was good.

   d. None of the above. All groups felt generally the same way about autocracy.

Fill in the table below.

POLAND

	BAD	SAME	GOOD	VALUE V	SIGNIFICANT?
10) CONF:EURO % Low Confidence	_____%	_____%	_____%	_____	Y N
11) DEM:BETTER % Disagree	_____%	_____%	_____%	_____	Y N
12) ORDER-FREE % Order	_____%	_____%	_____%	_____	Y N

21. Are Poles who think that the communist regime was bad less confident in the European Union than those who think it was good?   Yes   No

22. Which group of Poles is more likely to believe that "democracy may have its problems, but it is better than all other forms of government"?

   a. Those who believe that the former communist regime was bad.

   b. Those who believe that the former communist regime was about the same.

   c. Those who believe that the former communist regime was good.

   d. None of the above. All groups felt generally the same way about autocracy.

III. One of the historical features of Russian and Polish political culture is a very large, conservative peasant-farmer class. Historically, this group is associated with political submissiveness and resistance to change. One way that we can measure this is to see whether or not people who live in small towns have different attitudes toward democracy and their relationship to the European Union than those who live in larger cities. City sizes have been divided into towns or villages of fewer than 20,000 people, cities from 20,000 to 100,000, and "big cities" with more than 100,000 people. Complete the table below for Russia and Poland and then answer the questions that follow.

> Data Files: **WVS97–RUSSIA**
>   **WVS97–POLAND**
> Task: **Cross-tabulation**
> Row Variables: **CONF:EURO**
>   **DEMOCRACY (Russia only)**
>   **AUTOCRAT (Russia only)**
>   **DEM:BETTER**
>   **ORDER-FREE**
> Column Variable: **TOWN SIZE**
> View: **Tables**
> Display: **Column %**

Fill in the table below.

RUSSIA

	TOWN	CITY	BIG CITY	VALUE V	SIGNIFICANT?
10) CONF:EURO % Low Confidence	_____%	_____%	_____%	_____	Y N
11) DEMOCRACY % Bad	_____%	_____%	_____%	_____	Y N
12) AUTOCRAT % Good	_____%	_____%	_____%	_____	Y N
13) DEM:BETTER % Disagree	_____%	_____%	_____%	_____	Y N
14) ORDER-FREE % Order	_____%	_____%	_____%	_____	Y N

23. In terms of Russians' confidence in the European Union, do people from towns feel less confident in the EU than those from the big cities?   Yes   No

24. In terms of democracy, are people from small towns more disposed to see democracy as a negative development than those from big cities?   Yes   No

25. Are people from small towns more likely to favor an autocrat who dispenses with parliament and elections?   Yes   No

26. In which town size are people less likely to disagree with the statement that "democracy may have its problems, but it is better than all other forms of government"?   _____

Fill in the table below.

POLAND

	TOWN	CITY	BIG CITY	VALUE V	SIGNIFICANT?
10) CONF:EURO % Low Confidence	_____%	_____%	_____%	_____	Y N
11) DEM:BETTER % Disagree	_____%	_____%	_____%	_____	Y N
12) ORDER-FREE % Order	_____%	_____%	_____%	_____	Y N

27. In terms of Poles' confidence in the European Union, do people from towns feel less confident in the EU than those from the big cities?   Yes   No

28. In which town size are people more likely to disagree with the statement that "democracy may have its problems, but it is better than all other forms of government"?   _____

IN YOUR OWN WORDS

In your own words, please answer the following questions.

1. In the analysis of the relationship between economic growth and economic regulation in the GLOBAL file, the relationship was extremely weak. But in the EUROPE file, once the outlier was removed the relationship was very strong. Why would this relationship be weak in the analysis of countries around the world, but strong among European countries? Also, how can we justify the removal of an outlier like Bosnia?

2. In the analysis of town size and support for democracy, how are Poland and Russia similar? How are they different? Be sure to support your answer with evidence.

3. Based on all of your analysis in this chapter, which country is more likely to have a backlash against democratic reform? Which is the least likely? Why?

Part IV

NEWLY INDUSTRIALIZED COUNTRIES

DEVELOPING NATIONS: WHAT DETERMINES WEALTH AND POVERTY?

No society can be flourishing and happy of which the far greater part of the members are poor and miserable.
ADAM SMITH

Tasks: Mapping, Scatterplot
Data File: GLOBAL

W e've covered a lot of ground so far in this workbook. From a topical standpoint, we have learned about the basics of comparative politics, examined the politics of liberal democracies, and explored the democratic transition of postcommunist states. The last section of this book will explore a group of states that are distinct from the other two types because of their relatively late political and economic development. However, you may remember that these countries that were formerly called Third World states are a very diverse bunch of countries. Some are wealthier than others, some are more democratic than others. Some are divided by war and others are blessed with oil.

This chapter will survey the determinants of wealth and poverty—a topic we've encroached on many times in the past nine chapters. Indeed, it's impossible to talk about social and political issues apart from economics because they are all so interrelated. This chapter will not introduce you to any new methodological techniques; rather, it will be an expansion of topics already touched on.

Economic factors are important to political scientists because they can significantly influence the behavior of politicians, the position of a nation-state in international politics, and the overall welfare of the state. Earlier in this workbook we determined that the year in which a country became independent is related to its current national wealth. Clearly, though, we are not asserting that all variations in wealth and poverty are determined by nation-states' dates of independence. We cannot even suggest that historical, political, and social factors are the only determinants of wealth and poverty. For instance, a nation-state's natural resources, size, and location can also have an impact on its economic situation. A nation-state located on a small island 2,000 miles from the nearest city or continent has a distinctly different economic situation than, say, Canada or France. The same is true of a country whose land consists largely of deserts or mountainous regions, or one that has no coastline.

Let's make a statement that is not especially daring: "The size of a nation-state is related to its national wealth." When social scientists make a theoretical generalization such as this, they usually break the statement down into testable assertions called *hypotheses*. We've already done hypothesis testing in earlier chapters, but we skimmed over the details of the process because there were so many other things to learn. A good hypothesis requires terminology that is clearly defined and theoretical statements that can be tested. To test the above statement, we first need to define what is meant by *national wealth* and the *size* of the nation. Measurement of national wealth is complex, but to simplify the process let's use gross domestic product as an indicator of national wealth. Since size of a country can be defined as both "population" and "land area," we need to develop two hypotheses if we want to test both concepts. Finally, our hypotheses must describe how the two variables will be related. For example, we might state that as values for one variable increase, we expect the values of another variable to increase (a positive relationship). Or we might expect the values of the second variable to decrease as the values of the first variable increase (a negative relationship). If we implement all the above items, our two hypotheses might look like this:

Hypothesis 1: As the population of nation-states increases, so will their gross domestic product.

Hypothesis 2: As the land area of nation-states increases, so will their gross domestic product.

If both hypotheses are supported, we will see that the wealthiest nation-states tend to be highly populous and have large land masses. Conversely, the poorest nation-states will tend to be the least populous and have small land mass. In both situations, we are predicting that we will find a positive correlation between these two variables and GDP.

➤ *Data File:* **GLOBAL**
➤ *Task:* **Mapping**
➤ *Variable 1:* **37) GDP PPP**
➤ *Variable 2:* **12) POPULATION**
➤ *View:* **Map**

GDP PPP -- Gross domestic product in billions of dollars purchasing power parity, (World Bank 2001).

r = 0.595**

POPULATION -- POPULATION IN 1000S (IDB, 1998)

These results are probably not surprising to you. The two maps are very similar, and the correlation coefficient shown on the right side of the screen is fairly strong (r = 0.595**). It does appear that nation-states with large populations tend to have large GDPs. This makes sense because more people should be able to produce more wealth than fewer people could produce.

Comparative Politics

GDP: Gross domestic product in billions of U.S. dollars

RANK	CASE NAME	VALUE
1	United States	8868
2	China	4535
3	Japan	3151
4	India	2242
5	Germany	1949

Data File: **GLOBAL**
Task: **Mapping**
Variable 1: **37) GDP PPP**
Variable 2: **12) POPULATION**
➤ View: **List: Rank**

POPULATION: 1996 population in 1000s

RANK	CASE NAME	VALUE
1	China	1236915
2	India	984004
3	United States	270312
4	Indonesia	212942
5	Brazil	169807

Look at the ranked distributions for each map and make a mental note of which nations are in the top ten positions on each list.

Is the geographic size of a nation-state similar to population in terms of its relationship to GDP? Since people, not land, generate GDP, we might not be surprised if we find different results. On the other hand, if a nation-state has a lot of land, it may be better able to sustain larger populations, and it is more likely to have greater amounts of natural resources.

Data File: **GLOBAL**
Task: **Mapping**
Variable 1: **37) GDP PPP**
➤ Variable 2: **2) AREA**
➤ View: **Map**

GDP PPP -- Gross domestic product in billions of dollars purchasing power parity, (World Bank 2001).

r = 0.533**

AREA -- AREA IN SQUARE MILES (SAUS 1992)

The map for 2) AREA is difficult to interpret because the smallest nation-states (those having the lightest color) are too small to view on this type of map. But the correlation coefficient indicates that there is a strong correlation between the physical size of nation-states and their GDP. Examine the ranked distributions for both maps.

Data File: **GLOBAL**
Task: **Mapping**
Variable 1: **37) GDP PPP**
Variable 2: **2) AREA**
➤ View: **List: Rank**

GDP: Gross domestic product in billions of U.S. dollars

RANK	CASE NAME	VALUE
1	United States	8868
2	China	4535
3	Japan	3151
4	India	2242
5	Germany	1949

AREA: Area in square miles

RANK	CASE NAME	VALUE
1	Russia	6592817
2	China	3600930
3	Canada	3560219
4	United States	3539227
5	Brazil	3265061

Once again we see many of the same nation-states at the top of the list, including China, the United States, Brazil, India, and so on.

If we wanted to take this a step further, we could look at the GDP and control for the physical size of the country. The variable GDP/AREA does just that—it divides GDP by a country's number of square miles of land.

Data File: **GLOBAL**
Task: **Mapping**
➤ Variable 1: **41) GDP/AREA**
➤ View: **Map**

GDP/AREA -- (GDP PPP) per 1000 (AREA) units. (Calculated)

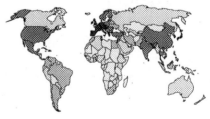

The West European nation-states and a few Asian countries seem to be the most efficient in terms of generating wealth with their available amount of land.

GDP/AREA: GDP per square mile

Data File: **GLOBAL**
Task: **Mapping**
Variable 1: **41) GDP/AREA**
➤ View: **List: Rank**

RANK	CASE NAME	VALUE
1	Singapore	340.25
2	Malta	48.39
3	Bahrain	41.84
4	Taiwan	30.99
5	Netherlands	29.23
6	Barbados	24.10
7	Belgium	22.28
8	Japan	20.67
9	Korea, South	19.41
10	Luxembourg	18.04

The ranked distribution for GDP per square mile is interesting. Singapore is a major outlier, outpacing the second highest nation-state by almost tenfold. With the exception of Japan, none of the top ten nation-states on this list also appeared on the top ten list for GDP or POPULATION. This suggests that the relationship between population and GDP may be stronger than the relationship between land area and GDP.

Let's try one more angle. Instead of controlling the gross domestic product for area, let's use the GDP per capita variable in a correlation analysis with 2) AREA. Recall from Chapter 1 that the reason we often use the *GDP per capita* measure instead of GDP is because it adjusts for highly populous nation-states that are poor (e.g., China, India) and less populous nations that are wealthy (e.g., Luxembourg).

We'll use the SCATTERPLOT task this time.

Data File: **GLOBAL**
➤ Task: **Scatterplot**
➤ Dependent Variable: **38) GDPCAP PPP**
➤ Independent Variable: **2) AREA**
➤ View: **Reg. Line**

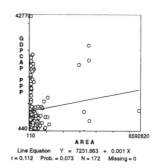

Line Equation Y = 7231.663 + 0.001 X
r = 0.112   Prob. = 0.073   N = 172   Missing = 0

Now that we have controlled for the population, we see that there is no relationship between national wealth and land area (r = 0.112). This tells us that population and land area are related. It also suggests that population has a greater impact on GDP than does land area.

What about natural resources? Do nation-states with vast amounts of natural resources have an economic edge? Unfortunately, there are no variables in this data set that allow us to analyze the percentage of the GDP that is based on specific natural resources. Nor do we have variables that allow us to investigate important underground natural resources (e.g., oil, coal, precious metals). But we do have a few basic measures that assess the general terrain of a nation-state, such as the percentage of the land that is arable (usable for farming), the percentage of the land that is forest and woodland, and the length of coastline (an important factor for both the seafood industry and international trade). In each of these analyses, we'll continue to control for population differences by using GDP per capita.

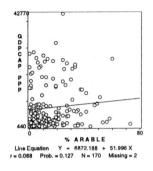

There seems to be no relationship between the percentage of land that can support crops and GDP per capita (r = 0.088). What about forests?

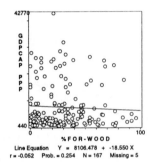

Nor do nation-states with high percentages of forests and woodlands seem to have especially high GDP per capita (r = –0.052). What about length of coastline?

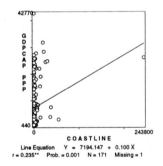

There does seem to be a modest correlation (r = 0.235**) between length of coastline and GDP per capita. Perhaps the natural resources of the ocean and the ability to easily trade with other countries do have some positive economic impact. Even with the removal of the outlier (Canada), there seems to be a modest relationship (r = 0.215**).

It's too bad we don't have a variable that allows us to examine oil reserves or oil exports, because this is one natural resource that we know has a major impact on GDP per capita. But, in general, the limited analyses we conducted above don't suggest that natural resources are a major determinant of economic wealth.

Perhaps national wealth is really a function of how *efficiently* natural resources are transformed by workers into goods and services. We might postulate that efficiency is influenced by the level of education in a country. Is the investment in human capital related to the level of national wealth achieved? We can explore this question using two different measures of education.

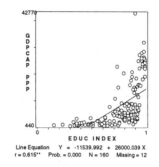

Data File: **GLOBAL**
Task: **Scatterplot**
Dependent Variable: **38) GDPCAP PPP**
➤ Independent Variable: **16) EDUC INDEX**
➤ View: **Reg. Line**

Line Equation   Y = -11539.992 + 26000.039 X
r = 0.615**   Prob. = 0.000   N = 160   Missing = 12

The results of this analysis reveal that there is a very strong relationship between national wealth and education levels in nation-states (r = 0.615**). If we carefully examine the location of specific cases in this scatterplot, some interesting patterns are revealed. For example, click on the dots located high above the midpoint of the regression line. These countries have a high GDP per capita but have relatively low levels of education compared to countries at a similar level of GDP per capita. So, if our hypothesis states that nation-states with low education will tend to have low levels of GDP per capita, these cases do not offer support for it. Is there something in common about these cases? By clicking on the dots we can see that we have located the wealthy oil-producing nations alluded to above (Kuwait, Brunei, Qatar, United Arab Emirates). The fact that these Middle Eastern countries contradict our hypothesis makes sense because their wealth is related not to education but to the good fortune of possessing vast oil reserves. Also notice that Singapore is in this group of cases. Singapore is often an outlier in analyses because it is a small, rapidly developing nation-state that is benefiting from large amounts of foreign investment. It has become an investment haven for Western corporations seeking a foothold in Asia.

Now look at some of the cases located below the regression line and to the far right of the scatterplot. These nation-states have a low GDP per capita despite high levels of education, and nearly all are former communist states (Hungary, Poland, Russia, Latvia). This group of cases is interesting because it suggests that high levels of education may not always produce a wealthy economy. In these former communist countries, education was strongly emphasized but it did not produce the same kind of results that we see in the cluster of countries in the upper right corner. Perhaps other factors, such as an inefficient economic system, suppressed the development of these nation-states.

The third group of countries, clustered at the lower left corner of the scatterplot, are too numerous and indistinct to generalize. But if you click on these plots, you will see that there are some important regional clusters. Can you find the clusters for Central and South America? How about sub-Saharan Africa? Central Asia?

The final group of nations is located in the upper right corner. These countries have high levels of GDP per capita and high levels of education. All of them also happen to be categorized as "advanced industrial democracies." This cluster of cases clearly supports our hypothesis. Remember, though, that *correlation does not mean causation*. It is possible that national wealth was accumulated in these countries for reasons unrelated to education levels. In fact, it may be that nation-states use their resources to raise education levels only *after* they have become wealthy. Other statistical techniques that are beyond the scope of this workbook must be used to discern causation with any degree of confidence.

Perhaps a more pertinent question for political scientists is whether government spending on education is related to national wealth. A major task of government leaders is to determine the best way to allocate resources. Since education is, in fact, one of the most expensive forms of government spending (although many of these costs are borne at the local level), this becomes an important question. To ascertain the level of each nation-state's commitment to education, we'll use 17) PUB EDUCAT, which is the amount spent on education as a percentage of GDP.

Data File: **GLOBAL**
Task: **Scatterplot**
Dependent Variable: **38) GDPCAP PPP**
➤ *Independent Variable:* **17) PUB EDUCAT**
➤ *View:* **Reg. Line**

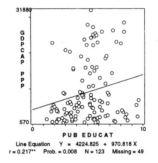

Line Equation Y = 4224.825 + 970.818 X
r = 0.217**   Prob. = 0.008   N = 123   Missing = 49

As you can see, there is a statistically significant correlation between spending on public education and GDP per capita (r = 0.217**). But the relationship is not as strong as what we found above for GDP per capita and the average education level attained by citizens. From this analysis it seems that spending on education is associated with economic development, but we cannot conclude that spending causes development to occur.

Now it's your turn to further examine the determinants of wealth and poverty.

WORKSHEET

NAME:

COURSE:

DATE:

CHAPTER

10

REVIEW QUESTIONS

Based on the first part of this chapter, answer True or False to the following items:

1. A hypothesis is an untestable opinion about the nature of political reality.   T   F

2. An important aspect of hypothesis testing is defining key concepts and terminology.   T   F

3. It's not essential for a hypothesis to predict the "direction" of the relationship (i.e., whether the relationship will be positive or negative).   T   F

4. If the results of the analysis are consistent with the hypothesis, we know we have found a cause-and-effect relationship.   T   F

5. There is a strong positive correlation between GDP and population.   T   F

6. In terms of GDP per square mile, Singapore greatly outpaces all other nation-states.   T   F

7. Nation-states with large proportions of arable or forested land tend to have higher GDPs per capita.   T   F

8. Nation-states with longer coastlines tend to have higher GDPs per capita.   T   F

9. There is a statistically significant relationship between education and GDP.   T   F

10. Our analysis confirmed that, over time, nation-states that spend more money on education will see greater growth in their GDP.   T   F

EXPLORIT QUESTIONS

I. So far we've barely scratched the surface on factors that might influence national wealth. Many other factors, such as political stability, legal structure, values, and social organization, can contribute to the wealth or poverty of nation-states. One theory that dominated the study of international relations and comparative politics, particularly in the 1960s and 70s, held that wealth and poverty were merely a function of whether or not a nation-state had been subjected to colonial domination. The "dependency theory" hypothesized that the wealth of colonies and former colonies was extracted by colonial powers and other developed nations, and that this legacy left recently independent countries in a position of poverty. In Chapter 1, we used the MAPPING task to look at the relationship between year of independence and GDP per capita. We saw a general pattern to the maps, but we can use the SCATTERPLOT task to be more precise in our analysis.

WORKSHEET

> *Data File:* **GLOBAL**
> *Task:* **Scatterplot**
> *Dependent Variable:* **38) GDPCAP PPP**
> *Independent Variable:* **70) IND DATE**
> *View:* **Reg. Line**

11. The countries that appear closest to the top of the scatterplot represent those that have the (circle one of the following)

    1. highest gross domestic product per capita.

    2. lowest gross domestic product per capita.

    3. earliest independence dates.

    4. most recent independence dates.

    5. The location of the dots tells us nothing about the values of the cases on these variables.

12. What is the correlation coefficient for these results?   r = _____

13. Is this relationship positive or negative?   _____

14. Are these results statistically significant?   Yes   No

II. Using the same scatterplot, identify the nation-state that has the highest gross domestic product per capita.

15. What is the name of this case?   _____

16. What is its independence date?   _____

17. What is its value for GDP/capita?   _____

18. Does this nation-state offer support to the dependency-theory hypothesis?   Yes   No

Now use the [Find case] option to locate Belize and then Japan.

19. What is Belize's independence date?   _____

20. What is its value for GDP/capita?   _____

21. What is Japan's independence date?   _____

22. What is its value for GDP/capita?   _____

23. Do these two cases offer support for the dependency-theory hypothesis?   Yes   No

III. Another claim of dependency theorists is that the wealth in poor nation-states is concentrated in the hands of a few. This wealthy minority is said to negotiate deals with developed nations or companies that are beneficial to themselves (i.e., the wealthy minority), but detrimental to the rest of their nation-state. The variable 42) $ RICH 10% represents the percentage of national income that is received by the richest 10% of the population. Our hypothesis is: *As the percentage of the national income controlled by the richest 10% of the population increases, the GDP per capita will decrease.*

> Data File: **GLOBAL**
> Task: **Scatterplot**
> Dependent Variable: **38) GDPCAP PPP**
> ➤ Independent Variable: **42) $ RICH 10%**
> ➤ View: **Reg. Line**

24. What is the correlation coefficient for these results?   r = _____

25. Is this relationship positive or negative?   _____

26. Are these results statistically significant?   Yes   No

IV. An alternative to dependency theory might be a cultural model of political development. This model suggests that cultural diversity creates political, social, and economic conflict. This conflict is said to hurt growth, development, and the accumulation of wealth in nation-states. The variable 15) MULTI-CULT is a measure of the likelihood that any two people in a nation-state would have different cultural identities. A low value, such as Japan's value of 1, indicates a very low likelihood of any two people being from different racial, religious, or ethnic groups. A high value, such as Zaire's value of 91, indicates a very high likelihood that any two people are from different racial, religious, or ethnic groups. Here's the hypothesis: *As cultural diversity within nation-states increases, the GDP per capita will decrease.*

> Data File: **GLOBAL**
> Task: **Scatterplot**
> Dependent Variable: **38) GDPCAP PPP**
> ➤ Independent Variable: **15) MULTI-CULT**
> ➤ View: **Reg. Line**

27. What is the correlation coefficient for these results?   r = _____

28. Is this relationship positive or negative?   _____

29. Are these results statistically significant?   Yes   No

30. Identify the two nation-states that have very high GDPs and very high levels of cultural diversity.   _____

                                                      _____

V. The hypothesis is: *Nation-states with high proportions of women (relative to men) in professional or technical positions are more likely to have greater national wealth.*

> Data File: **GLOBAL**
> Task: **Scatterplot**
> Dependent Variable: **38) GDPCAP PPP**
> ➤ Independent Variable: **92) FEM. PROF**
> ➤ View: **Reg. Line**

31. What is the correlation coefficient for these results?   r = _____

32. Are these results statistically significant?   Yes   No

33. Do these results support the hypothesis?   Yes   No

What about nation-states that have high proportions of women in managerial jobs? The hypothesis is: *Nation-states with high proportions of women (relative to men) in managerial positions are more likely to have greater national wealth.*

> Data File: **GLOBAL**
> Task: **Scatterplot**
> Dependent Variable: **38) GDPCAP PPP**
> ➤ Independent Variable: **93) FEM.MANAGE**
> ➤ View: **Reg. Line**

34. What is the correlation coefficient for these results?   r = _____

35. Are these results statistically significant?   Yes   No

36. Do these results support the hypothesis?   Yes   No

VI. The United Nations has created a measure of women's power in society called the Gender Empowerment Measure (GEM). The variable 102) GEM measures "gender inequality in three basic dimensions of empowerment—economic participation and decision making, political participation and decision making, and power over economic resources. Let's test the following hypothesis: *Nation-states that have higher levels of wealth will also have higher levels of gender empowerment.*

> For this analysis, be sure to create a scatterplot, select 38) GDPCAP PPP as the dependent variable, and select 102) GEM as the independent variable.

37. What is the correlation coefficient for these results?   r = _____

38. Are these results statistically significant?   Yes   No

39. Do these results support the hypothesis?   Yes   No

<u>**IN YOUR OWN WORDS**</u>

In your own words, please answer the following questions.

1. Discuss the validity of the dependency theory and the cultural theory outlined in the chapter. Describe the nature of the relationships between the study of wealth, the concentration of wealth, and the year of independence. Do the results of the analysis support or refute these hypotheses. Which theory do you find more persuasive? Why? Be sure to support your answer with the use of evidence from your analysis.

2. Discuss the relationship between national wealth and the station of women in society. Is there a relationship between these two concepts? Are there wealthy societies that deny women social and political power? Be sure to support your assertions with evidence drawn from your analyses.

Asia

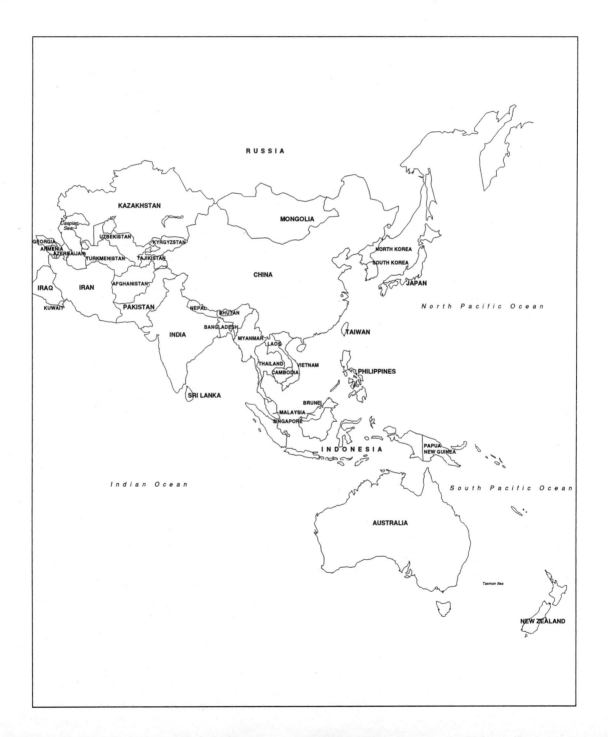

CHAPTER **11**

NEWLY INDUSTRIALIZED
COUNTRIES IN ASIA

*Before, we fought the war for independence, for
freedom, for the unification of the country. Now our
battle is for the development of our country . . .*

NGUYEN XUAN PHONG,
FOREIGN MINISTER, VIETNAM, 1993

Tasks: Mapping, Univariate, Scatterplot, Historical Trends, ANOVA, Cross-tabulation
Data Files: GLOBAL, ASIA, HISTORY

The newly industrialized countries of Asia are among the few former colonies around the world
to begin to develop rapidly. But the region itself is very difficult to define geographically,
because it is so economically and politically diverse. To begin, let's open the GLOBAL data set
and look at the second version of the REGION variable.

➤ *Data File:* **GLOBAL**
➤ *Task:* **Mapping**
➤ *Variable 1:* **11) REGION2**
➤ *View:* **Map**
➤ *Display:* **Legend**

REGION2 -- REGIONS: 1=AFRICA, 2=MIDDLE EAST, 3=ASIA/PACIFIC, 4=WESTERN
HEMISPHERE, 5=EUROPE (LE ROY, 1998)

Category	N
Africa	(51)
Mid. East	(14)
Asia/Pacif	(40)
West.Hemi	(29)
Europe	(38)
Missing Data	

As you can see, the Asia-Pacific region includes the continent of Australia, a country like Russia, which
is usually classified as being part of Europe, and the eastern portion of the Eurasian land mass. Let's
also refresh our memory on where Asian countries stand in terms of gross domestic product.

In Chapter 8 we learned that several different types of states share common borders in Asia. In fact,
Asia possesses the fewest liberal democracies, a lot of newly industrialized countries, and a host of
other types of states.

➤ *Data File:* **ASIA**
➤ *Task:* **Univariate**
➤ *Primary Variable:* **31) WORLDS.7**
➤ *View:* **Bar - Freq**

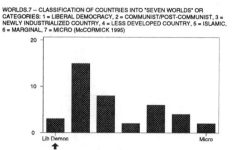

WORLDS.7 -- CLASSIFICATION OF COUNTRIES INTO "SEVEN WORLDS" OR
CATEGORIES: 1 = LIBERAL DEMOCRACY, 2 = COMMUNIST/POST-COMMUNIST, 3 =
NEWLY INDUSTRIALIZED COUNTRY, 4 = LESS DEVELOPED COUNTRY, 5 = ISLAMIC,
6 = MARGINAL, 7 = MICRO (McCORMICK 1995)

1) Lib Democ   Freq.: 3   7.5%

The region is largely characterized by a large presence of communist regimes and nation-states in transition from communism. The second most frequently occurring type of state is New Industrializing Countries followed closely by Islamic states. In fact, there are a few states that fit into both the NIC and Islamic category (Indonesia and Malaysia). While this diversity is interesting, it is also the cause for great concern when we consider that the region is also heavily populated by states with nuclear weapons.

NUKES: Ownership of nuclear weapons: 1 = own nuclear weapons materials, 2 = voluntarily abandoned nuclear weapons program, 3 = own nuclear weapons, 4 = compelled to abandon nuclear weapons program

➤ *Data File:* **GLOBAL**
➤ *Task:* **Mapping**
➤ *Variable 1:* **77) NUKES**
➤ *View:* **List: Rank**

RANK	CASE NAME	VALUE
1	Iraq	Sanctioned
2	Israel	Weapons
2	United Kingdom	Weapons
2	Ukraine	Weapons
2	Belarus	Weapons
2	United States	Weapons
2	France	Weapons
2	India	Weapons
2	Pakistan	Weapons
2	China	Weapons

You will notice that Asia has the highest concentration of nuclear-weapons owners of any region. Of the 11 countries that currently have weapons, 5 are from Asia, including Russia, Kazakhstan, China, India, and Pakistan.

➤ *Data File:* **ASIA**
➤ *Task:* **Mapping**
➤ *Variable 1:* **22) NUKES**
➤ *View:* **Map**
➤ *Display:* **Legend**

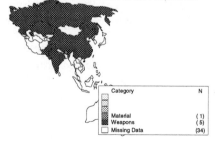

NUKES -- OWNERSHIP OF NUCLEAR WEAPONS: 1=OWN NUCLEAR MATERIAL,
2=VOLUNTARILY ABANDONED WEAPONS, 3=OWN WEAPONS, 4=COMPELLED TO

Category	N
Material	(1)
Weapons	(5)
Missing Data	(34)

Comparative Politics

Another Asian country, North Korea, has materials for making nuclear weapons, but it recently agreed to abandon its program. What is more disturbing is that these nations also have developed capabilities to deliver these weapons quickly through advances in missile technology.

Data File: **ASIA**
Task: **Mapping**
➤ Variable 1: **23) MISSILES**
➤ View: **Map**
➤ Display: **Legend**

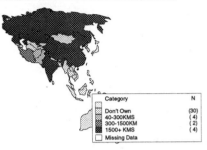

MISSILES -- OWNERSHIP AND RANGE OF BALLISTIC MISSILES (SWPA, 1997)

Category	N
Don't Own	(30)
40-300KMS	(4)
300-1500KM	(2)
1500+ KMS	(4)
Missing Data	

In addition to nuclear weapons, many countries in the region are also suspected of possessing chemical weapons of mass destruction.

Data File: **ASIA**
Task: **Mapping**
➤ Variable 1: **32) CHEM ARMS**
➤ View: **List: Rank**

CHEM ARMS: Chemical weapons possession and research program development

RANK	CASE NAME	VALUE
1	India	Known
1	Russia	Known
3	China	Probable
3	Korea, South	Probable
3	Korea, North	Probable
3	Iran	Probable
3	Pakistan	Probable
3	Myanmar	Probable
3	Vietnam	Probable
3	Taiwan	Probable

A full 10 of the 29 countries in the Asia-Pacific region are known or probable possessors of chemical weapons. The threat of biological weapons in this region is also significant.

Data File: **ASIA**
Task: **Mapping**
➤ Variable 1: **33) BIOL ARMS**
➤ View: **List: Rank**

BIOL WEAPONS: Biological weapons possession and research program development

RANK	CASE NAME	VALUE
1	Pakistan	Prob/Known
1	China	Prob/Known
1	Iran	Prob/Known
1	Korea, North	Prob/Known
1	Russia	Prob/Known
6	Taiwan	Possible
7	Japan	Former
8	India	Defensive
—	New Zealand	
—	Philippines	

Many of the same nations that possess chemical weapons also have active biological-weapons programs. Fewer states have actually developed biological weapons than chemical weapons because they are generally harder to produce, and their effects cannot be limited to the enemy nation. This dark picture of a region falling headlong into oblivion due to the presence of weapons of mass destruction may be contrasted with its relative peace during the 1990s.

Since the end of the war in Vietnam and the diminution of Cold War tension around the world, the Asia-Pacific region has become a much more peaceful environment than it was between 1940 and 1975. Politically speaking, the 1990s have seen that the nations of the Asia-Pacific region are relatively stable and have had fairly low incidences of military conflict.

> ➤ *Data File:* **GLOBAL**
> ➤ *Task:* **Cross-tabulation**
> ➤ *Row Variable:* **73) WAR**
> ➤ *Column Variable:* **11) REGION2**
> ➤ *View:* **Tables**
> ➤ *Display:* **Column %**

WAR   by   REGION2
Cramer's V: 0.185
Warning: Potential significance problem. Check row and column totals.

		Africa	Mid. East	Asia/Pacif	West.Hemi	Europe	TOTAL
	None	23	5	23	17	29	97
		45.1%	35.7%	57.5%	58.6%	76.3%	56.4%
	Interstate	3	3	2	2	3	13
		5.9%	21.4%	5.0%	6.9%	7.9%	7.6%
	Civil War	21	5	12	9	3	50
		41.2%	35.7%	30.0%	31.0%	7.9%	29.1%
	Independnce	2	0	0	0	0	2
		3.9%	0.0%	0.0%	0.0%	0.0%	1.2%
	Multi-type	2	1	3	1	3	10
		3.9%	7.1%	7.5%	3.4%	7.9%	5.8%
	TOTAL	51	14	40	29	38	172
		100.0%	100.0%	100.0%	100.0%	100.0%	

If you look across the top row, you see that the Asia-Pacific region has the third lowest incidence of warfare of the five regions in our comparison.[1] Nearly 58% of the countries in the Asia-Pacific region have been at peace during the period 1990–96. You can also examine the regional differences by comparing them in a bar graph.

> *Data File:* **GLOBAL**
> *Task:* **Cross-tabulation**
> *Row Variable:* **73) WAR**
> *Column Variable:* **11) REGION2**
> *View:* **Tables**
> ➤ *Display:* **Bar**

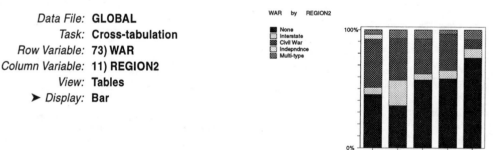

WAR   by   REGION2

■ None
▨ Interstate
▨ Civil War
▨ Independnce
▨ Multi-type

The Asia-Pacific region is nearly tied with the Western Hemisphere for the lack of warfare. It has no violent ongoing independence movements and the second lowest level of civil war. But stability and peace do not necessarily imply that the nations of this region are democratic.

---

[1] There are a few instances in this chapter where the cross-tabulation result using the GLOBAL file produces the statement "Warning: Potential significance problem." This is to alert you that the statistical significance value may not be reliable due to the small number of cases (in this case, 51 nations) used in the analysis. The likelihood of this warning message appearing will also increase as the number of cells in the table increases—the greater the number of cells, the more likely the warning message will appear. For our purposes in this chapter, we will often ignore this warning.

One factor that might explain the high level of weapons development and armament in Asia is the relatively high level of wealth obtained by states in this region.

GDP: Gross domestic product in billions of U.S. dollars

Data File: **GLOBAL**
Task: **Mapping**
➤ Variable 1: **37) GDP PPP**
➤ View: **List: Rank**

RANK	CASE NAME	VALUE
1	United States	8868
2	China	4535
3	Japan	3151
4	India	2242
5	Germany	1949
6	France	1342
7	United Kingdom	1315
8	Italy	1278
9	Brazil	1182
10	Russia	1093

As you can see from this analysis, the second (China), third (Japan), fourth (India), and tenth (Russia) largest economies in the world are located in Asia. This ranking is quite different when we examine GDP *per capita*.

GDPCAP: Gross domestic product per capita

Data File: **GLOBAL**
Task: **Mapping**
➤ Variable 1: **38) GDPCAP PPP**
➤ View: **List: Rank**

RANK	CASE NAME	VALUE
1	Luxembourg	42769
2	United States	31872
3	Norway	28433
4	Iceland	27835
5	Switzerland	27171
6	Canada	26251
7	Ireland	25918
8	Denmark	25869
9	Belgium	25443
10	Austria	25089

When GDP per capita is analyzed, Asia does not have any of its economies in the top ten. As you saw in Chapter 10, the size of an economy is usually directly related to the size of its population. Since many of the largest populations are in Asia, it makes sense that it also has some of the largest economies. Speaking of populations, let's see where the countries of Asia rank in terms of population.

POPULATION: 1998: Population in 1000s

Data File: **GLOBAL**
Task: **Mapping**
➤ Variable 1: **12) POPULATION**
➤ View: **List: Rank**

RANK	CASE NAME	VALUE
1	China	1236915
2	India	984004
3	United States	270312
4	Indonesia	212942
5	Brazil	169807
6	Russia	146861
7	Pakistan	135135
8	Bangladesh	127567
9	Japan	125932
10	Nigeria	110532

If this were an Olympic event, the countries of Asia would dominate in this category. Seven of the ten largest populations are located in Asia. China has the largest population with over 1.2 billion people, followed by India (984 million), Indonesia (213 million), Russia (146 million), Japan (125 million), Bangladesh (127 million), and Pakistan (135 million). To put this into perspective, the United States has a population of 270 million, the United Kingdom has 59 million people, and Canada has 31 million people. Or to put it yet another way, China has 40 times the number of people than Canada! There's no question that governments in largely populous nations such as China and India have different challenges than governments in Canada or the UK. Now, switch to the HISTORY file so you can examine the economic growth in Asia compared to that in the rest of the world.

The following variables indicate the 5-year average of economic growth rates between 1975 and the mid-1990s in each region of the world. For our purposes here, East Asia is defined as those nations which border the Pacific Ocean and South Asia is defined as those nations that border the Indian Ocean.

➤ *Data File:* **HISTORY**
    ➤ *Task:* **Historical Trends**
➤ *Variables:* **42) GROW.WORLD**
           41) GROW.EASIA
           43) GROW.SASIA

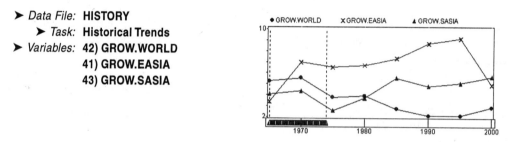

Average annual GDP growth in five-year periods: World, East Asia/Pacific, and South Asia

You can see from the analysis that East Asia and South Asia have grown at faster rates than the world average since 1980. As you'll see in the next analysis, countries in East Asia and South Asia have grown at faster rates since 1980 than the developing regions of Africa and Latin America.

    Data File: **HISTORY**
        Task: **Historical Trends**
➤ *Variables:* **41) GROW.EASIA**
           43) GROW.SASIA
           44) GROW.AFRIC
           46) GROW.LATIN

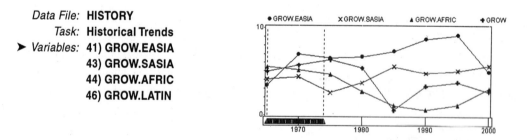

Average annual GDP growth in five-year periods: East Asia/Pacific, South Asia, sub-Saharan Africa, and Latin America/Caribbean

Africa has the slowest growth rate for the 1980s and 90s, with Latin America at only a slightly higher rate of growth. East Asia and South Asia have clearly grown the fastest in the developing world. To see the economic growth rates for individual countries, return to the GLOBAL file.

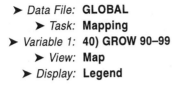

➤ *Data File:* **GLOBAL**
➤ *Task:* **Mapping**
➤ *Variable 1:* **40) GROW 90–99**
➤ *View:* **Map**
➤ *Display:* **Legend**

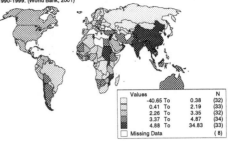

GROW 90-99 -- Average annual rate of growth in gross domestic product, 1990-1999. (World Bank, 2001)

Values		N
-40.65 To 0.38		(32)
0.41 To 2.19		(33)
2.26 To 3.35		(32)
3.37 To 4.87		(34)
4.88 To 34.83		(33)
Missing Data		(8)

The darker colors on this map (which indicate the highest growth rates) are clearly concentrated in East and South Asia for the 1990s. Let's take a closer look at the growth rates in the countries in these regions.

GROW 90–99: Average annual rate of growth in gross domestic product, 1990–1999

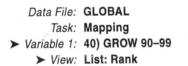

Data File: **GLOBAL**
Task: **Mapping**
➤ *Variable 1:* **40) GROW 90–99**
➤ *View:* **List: Rank**

RANK	CASE NAME	VALUE
1	Bosnia and Herzegovina	34.83
2	Equatorial Guinea	17.58
3	Lebanon	11.53
4	Kuwait	10.05
5	China	9.76
6	Maldives	7.73
7	Singapore	7.65
8	Vietnam	7.43
9	Malaysia	7.21
10	Georgia	6.88

The countries in Asia dominate this list—5 of the 10 countries with the highest annual growth rates in 1990–99 were from Asia. China led the list of Asian nations with an annual GDP growth rate of 9.76%. If you calculate this growth rate across 10 years, you realize that China's GDP grew by 104% during that period! Again, this makes you realize that countries that are experiencing massive economic growth have different challenges than those that are growing at very slow rates or have declining GDPs.

If you scroll to the bottom of this list, you see that 27 countries had *declining* GDPs over this same 10-year period. Seven countries averaged more than a 5% decline. That means their annual GDPs were sliced to one-third of what they had been just 10 years earlier! This gives you a perspective of how impressive the growth rates in many Asian countries have been, and how devastating that sustained negative economic growth can be.

There are many sectors that contribute to a nation's economic growth, including industry, the service sector, information/technology sectors, and others. Let's look at how growth in the industrial sector contributes to the growth or decline of GDPs worldwide.

Chapter 11: Newly Industrialized Countries in Asia

193

Data File: **GLOBAL**
➤ Task: **Scatterplot**
➤ Dependent Variable: **40) GROW 90–99**
➤ Independent Variable: **113) IND GROWTH**
➤ View: **Reg. Line**

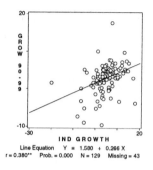
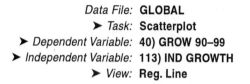

You will notice that there is a strong relationship between the industrial production growth rate and overall economic growth (r = 0.380**).

The puzzle as to why the economies of the Asia-Pacific region have grown at such a rapid rate between 1975 and the mid-1990s is very complex, but we can understand some elements of it. One of the most significant factors has been the fact that private corporations have invested huge sums of money in developing the industrial capacity of the Asia-Pacific region.

➤ Data File: **ASIA**
➤ Task: **Scatterplot**
➤ Dependent Variable: **13) GROW 90–99**
➤ Independent Variable: **14) INDUS GROW**
➤ View: **Reg. Line**

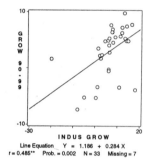

As this scatterplot shows, the relationship in Asia between industrial production growth and growth in GNP is much stronger (V = 0.485**) than found with the GLOBAL file. Notice that the graph includes countries that have experienced negative growth (i.e., those countries whose economies and industrial sectors have shrunk over the past year). When you see a scatterplot with a relationship this strong where most cases are clustered together, sometimes it's worth investigating those cases not located with the rest of the bunch. Click on the cases that have the greatest negative GDP growth rates. You should immediately notice that nearly all of these countries are from the former Soviet Union and are now in the process of making a transition to a market economy. All of them experienced negative economic and industrial growth during the period that these data were collected. Thus, we can see that political factors, such as the collapse of communism, have a direct influence on the economic patterns we witness. Now look at the cluster of dots at the top right corner of the scatterplot. Most of these countries are relatively small and have been dubbed "the Asian tigers" because of their astonishing growth rates between the late 1970s and 1990s. Ironically, in the late 1990s, these countries have also been the victims of severe economic turmoil. In Indonesia, this turmoil even resulted in a popular uprising and a change in leadership.

Another factor in the astonishing growth rates of the Asia-Pacific region has been the role of government. Initially it was thought that these countries succeeded because of their relatively low level of economic regulation. Economic regulation is the degree to which the government allows an economy to be managed by the government. On one end of the spectrum of this variable (1) are the countries that have relatively free markets. On the other end of the spectrum (3) are governments that have economies that are completely managed and regulated by the government. Do the data support the idea that unregulated markets had the highest growth rates in Asia during the period 1990–99?

Data File: **ASIA**
➤ *Task:* **ANOVA**
➤ *Dependent Variable:* **13) GROW 90–99**
➤ *Independent Variable:* **29) ECON REG2**
➤ *View:* **Graph**

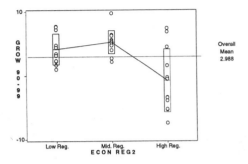

The evidence does support the hypothesis. If we look more closely at the data, our analysis does raise some questions. If you examine the cases in the lower right quadrant of the scatterplot, we again see that they consist of countries that were in the former Soviet Union. If you exclude these countries, the relationship between economic growth and economic regulation in Asia becomes fuzzy.

One theory for this relationship is that many of the nations experiencing strong economic growth also have government policies designed to protect the domestic economy. These regulations make consumer products very expensive; thus, people are much more likely to save their money than to buy these overpriced items. Let's investigate the savings levels in Asia a bit further.

Data File: **ASIA**
Task: **Scatterplot**
Dependent Variable: **13) GROW 90–99**
➤ *Independent Variable:* **16) SAVINGS**
➤ *View:* **Reg. Line**

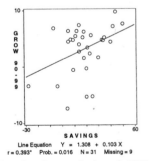

The strong relationship between a high savings rate and high levels of growth ($r = 0.393*$) suggests that government policy may have something to do with high growth rates in Asia. High levels of savings by citizens allow for a large pool of capital that business leaders and governments can invest in the domestic economy.

So far we've analyzed a few factors that explain the phenomenal growth of newly industrialized countries in Asia. In the worksheet section that follows, you will examine a few more.

WORKSHEET

NAME: _____

COURSE: _____

DATE: _____

CHAPTER

11

REVIEW QUESTIONS

Based on the first part of this chapter, answer True or False to the following items:

1. Asia has 7 of the 10 largest populations in the world.   T   F

2. Asia also has 7 of the top 10 countries in terms of annual growth rates during the 1990s.   T   F

3. Throughout the 1980s, South Asia had a faster growth rate than East Asia and the rest of the world.   T   F

4. Much of the rapid growth in Asia is attributed to the information technology sector rather than growth in industry.   T   F

5. The Asian countries that were previously part of the Soviet Union have seen rapid economic growth since their independence.   T   F

6. There is a strong, positive correlation between the savings rate in Asian countries and economic growth.   T   F

7. Because of the Hiroshima and Nagasaki bombings at the end of World War II, most Asian countries have voluntarily resisted or abandoned the development of nuclear weapons.   T   F

8. In the 1990s, the countries in the Asia-Pacific region have had comparatively low levels of interstate or intrastate war.   T   F

EXPLORIT QUESTIONS

I. Earlier in this book we used the GLOBAL file to determine that GDP per capita was inversely related to birth rates—countries with higher birth rates had lower GDP per capita. Let's see whether this holds true when we include only Asian-Pacific countries.

> ➤ Data File: **ASIA**
> ➤ Task: **Scatterplot**
> ➤ Dependent Variable: **28) BIRTHRATE**
> ➤ Independent Variable: **10) GDPCAP PPP**
> ➤ View: **Reg. Line**

Chapter 11: Newly Industrialized Countries in Asia

197

9. What is the correlation coefficient?

r = _____

10. Are these results statistically significant?

Yes   No

11. Throughout Asia, as birth rates increase, the GDP per capita decreases.

T   F

12. If Asian countries want to increase their rates of GDP per capita, they need to increase their population base.

T   F

As discussed earlier in this chapter, one factor that's attributed to economic growth in Asia is the high levels of personal savings. The more money that people save in banks, the more money that is available for loans to businesses. One theory that is said to explain the high levels of savings in certain Asian countries is that consumer goods are taxed/priced so high that people would rather save their money in the bank. Such an argument runs contrary to the sometimes cited claim that countries in Asia have a set of so-called Asian values—one of which includes being thrifty. The GLOBAL file contains a variable from the World Values Survey that indicates the percentage who think it is very important that a child learn thrift and to save money. Let's look at this item.

> ➤ *Data File:* **GLOBAL**
> ➤ *Task:* **Mapping**
> ➤ *Variable 1:* **110) KID THRIFT**
> ➤ *View:* **List: Rank**

For each case below, fill in the percentage of people in each nation who agree that it is very important that a child learn thrift and to save money.

13. South Korea _____%

14. China _____%

15. Russia _____%

16. Japan _____%

17. United States _____%

18. Canada _____%

19. United Kingdom _____%

II. With the GLOBAL file, create two scatterplots where 42) $ RICH 10% is the dependent variable for both of them. In the first scatterplot use 38) GDPCAP PPP as the independent variable, and in the second scatterplot use 15) MULTI-CULT. Based on these two analyses, answer the questions that follow.

20. As GDP per capita increases, the percentage of the national wealth controlled by 10% of the population _____ (increases/decreases).   _____

21. What is the value of r?   r = _____

22. Are the results statistically significant?   Yes   No

23. When a nation's cultural diversity increases, the percentage of the wealth controlled by 10% of the population tends to _____ (increase/decrease).   _____

24. What is the value of r?   r = _____

25. Are the results statistically significant?   Yes   No

III. Many theories could be proposed about the causal relationship between (1) culturally diverse nations, (2) the concentration of wealth by a few people, and (3) GDP per capita. For example, consider the following explanation:

> For historical and other reasons, culturally diverse countries are more likely to have one or more groups of people that control disproportionately large amounts of wealth. Because of these cultural and socioeconomic divisions within a society, the disadvantaged people have less incentive to improve their economic condition. Overall, this situation dampens the gross domestic product per capita in these culturally diverse nations. On the other hand, if a country is culturally homogeneous, there are fewer economic divisions among the population, and individuals have a fair (or equal) chance of improving their personal economic condition. Overall, this situation has a positive effect on the gross domestic product in these culturally homogeneous nations.

If the above explanation is true, we would expect to find that culturally diverse nations have lower levels of growth over time than do culturally homogeneous nations. Since we already know that some Asian countries are very homogeneous, let's see if this hypothesis holds true.

> ➤ *Data File:* **ASIA**
> ➤ *Task:* **Scatterplot**
> ➤ *Dependent Variable:* **13) GROW 90–99**
> ➤ *Independent Variable:* **8) MULTI-CULT**
> ➤ *View:* **Reg. LIne**

26. Is the correlation coefficient for this analysis in the expected direction (i.e., positive or negative)?   Yes   No

27. What is the correlation coefficient?   r = _____

28. Are the results statistically significant?   Yes   No

29. Select the [Outlier] option and remove the first outlier. What is the new correlation coefficient when the outlier is removed?   r = _____

30. Are the results statistically significant?   Yes   No

Let's try another test of the relationship between cultural diversity and economic growth using the GLOBAL file.

> *Data File:* **GLOBAL**
> *Task:* **Scatterplot**
> *Dependent Variable:* **40) GROW 90–99**
> *Independent Variable:* **15) MULTI-CULT**
> *View:* **Reg. LIne**

Once you have generated this graphic, please remove two outliers and answer the questions that follow.

31. Is the correlation coefficient for this analysis in the expected direction
(i.e., positive or negative)?   Yes   No

32. What is the correlation coefficient?   r = _____

33. Are the results statistically significant?   Yes   No

34. Does the removal of the strongest outlier change these results?   Yes   No

35. From a global perspective, would you say the hypothesis between multiculturalism
and GDP growth is supported?   Yes   No

IN YOUR OWN WORDS

In your own words, please answer the following questions.

1. From your analysis of 110) KID THRIFT, does it seem like there is such a thing as "Asian values" that drive economic growth? Are there any potential problems with drawing this conclusion from the analysis that you have done? Be sure to support your answer with evidence.

2. Which of the following hypotheses do you find more compelling? Why? Please be sure to support your answer with evidence from your analysis.

   Hypothesis 1: As levels of wealth become more equal, GDP per capita increases.

   Hypothesis 2: Societies with high levels of ethnic, cultural, and religious diversity have lower rates of economic growth.

ASIAN VALUES: POLITICAL CULTURE IN SOUTH KOREA AND JAPAN

We must ask ourselves if "Asian values" can assist us in the years of economic and socio-political uncertainty ahead. If they are relevant, they should be able to withstand the stress-test of an economic downturn.

-YB DATO' HISHAMUDDIN HUSSEIN,
MALAYSIAN GOVERNMENT MINISTER

Tasks: Cross-tabulation, Mapping, Historical Trends
Data Files: GLOBAL, ASIA, HISTORY, WVS97–S.KOREA, WVS97–JAPAN, WVS97–GERMANY

The political makeup of nations in the Asia-Pacific region is actually quite diverse compared to that of other regions.

Data File: **GLOBAL**
Task: **Cross-tabulation**
➤ *Row Variable:* **65) GOVERNMENT**
➤ *Column Variable:* **11) REGION2**
➤ *View:* **Tables**
➤ *Display:* **Column %**

GOVERNMENT by REGION2
Cramer's V: 0.324 **
Warning: Potential significance problem. Check row and column totals.

		Africa	Mid. East	Asia/Pacif	West.Hemi	Europe	TOTAL
	Old Demos	6	4	13	23	19	65
		11.8%	28.6%	32.5%	79.3%	50.0%	37.8%
	Transition	20	0	9	3	17	49
		39.2%	0.0%	22.5%	10.3%	44.7%	28.5%
	One Party	8	2	7	2	0	19
		15.7%	14.3%	17.5%	6.9%	0.0%	11.0%
	Autocratic	10	7	7	0	0	24
		19.6%	50.0%	17.5%	0.0%	0.0%	14.0%
	Civil War	7	1	4	1	2	15
		13.7%	7.1%	10.0%	3.4%	5.3%	8.7%
	TOTAL	51	14	40	29	38	172
		100.0%	100.0%	100.0%	100.0%	100.0%	

Notice that Asia seems to have a relatively even distribution of different types of regimes and relatively few democracies of the established or transitional type. If you select the Column % display, then you can see the exact percentages of each type of regime in each region. Included in the democratic category are some of the oldest democracies in the region (Australia, New Zealand, Japan, and India). The "Autocratic" category includes military governments like those in Myanmar and Brunei.

This diversity does not stop scholars and politicians in Asia and the West from asserting that there is such a thing as "Asian values" that make the nation-states of Asia distinct from all other cultures.

Asian values have been credited for the tremendous growth that the East Asian region experienced in the 1970s and 80s and the economic problems that Asia experienced during the late 1990s. In this chapter, we will examine two cases from Asia that are said to represent these values: South Korea and Japan.

SOUTH KOREA

South Korea has remained relatively independent of foreign powers for much of its history. Japan and China have always had a strong influence on the Korean peninsula, but it was not until the 20th century that Japanese domination over Korea was solidified in the brutal 40-year occupation that began in 1905 and ended with the defeat of Japan in World War II. Eight days before the surrender of the Japanese in WWII, the Soviet Union entered the war on the side of the Allied forces. At the end of the war, the United States agreed to partition Korea into North and South for occupation purposes. The territory north of the 38th parallel would be occupied by the USSR, and the south would be occupied by the United States. As tensions between the Soviet Union and the United States increased in the late 1940s, it became apparent that Korea would be partitioned in the same way that Germany was divided. This division put considerable stress on the economy. The northern part of the country was the primary industrial center whereas the south was the primary source of food for the country. Civil unrest occurred on both sides of the border. The North embraced a Stalinist model of political leadership under Kim Jong Il, and the South reverted to authoritarian government under Syngman Rhee. The tensions between the two countries resulted in war from 1949 to 1953. The United States and a United Nations force intervened on the side of the South, while newly communist China intervened on the side of the North. The tension between the two countries has not yet subsided, and the war has never officially ended. The result of this has been that both countries continue to maintain huge armies relative to the size of their population, especially North Korea.

➤ *Data File:* **ASIA**
➤ *Task:* **Mapping**
➤ *Variable 1:* **24) POP MILT**
➤ *View:* **List: Rank**

POP MILT: 1996: Members of the military per 1000 population

RANK	CASE NAME	VALUE
1	Korea, North	49.00
2	Brunei	16.67
3	Armenia	16.55
4	Singapore	15.96
5	Korea, South	14.51
6	Azerbaijan	9.18
7	Russia	8.60
8	Mongolia	8.41
9	Cambodia	8.17
10	Iran	7.76

As this list shows, North Korea maintains an army that is over three times larger than the army of the next highest country. South Korea's army makes up a smaller percentage of their population, but this smaller size is largely due to the fact that the United States has a fairly large contingency of troops and weapons in the country.

Between 1948 and 1987, South Korea was ruled by three different dictators who violated human rights, suppressed workers, and assassinated opposition leaders. In 1981, the army of South Korea killed upwards of 1,000 demonstrators in Kwangju, a southern province of the country. The conservatism of the regime has always been offset by student radicalism centered in the universities of South Korea. The students historically have opposed the autocracy of the regime, demanded the removal of U.S. troops that defend the South from the North, and supported the unification of North and South. In 1987 President Roh Tae-woo was elected president and enacted reforms that have allowed democracy to more firmly take root. He has since been replaced by a former opposition leader, Kim Dae Jung, who was once under a death sentence by an earlier autocratic government in South Korea.

JAPAN

Japan entered the 20th century with designs on the conquest of the Asia-Pacific region. It leaves the century with one of the smallest military forces in Asia, but the wealthiest economy in the region.

GDPCAP PPP: Gross domestic product per capita in Asia

Data File: **ASIA**
Task: **Mapping**
➤ *Variable 1:* **10) GDPCAP PPP**
➤ *View:* **List: Rank**

RANK	CASE NAME	VALUE
1	Japan	24898
2	Australia	24574
3	Singapore	20767
4	New Zealand	19104
5	Brunei	17600
6	Taiwan	17400
7	Korea, South	15712
8	Malaysia	8209
9	Russia	7473
10	Thailand	6132

The defeat at the hands of the United States at the end of World War II left Japan destitute and with only the faintest prospect of becoming a democracy. Not only did the nation of Japan have a strong tradition of military rule, it had very little in the way of a democratic tradition. The United States assisted Japan in writing a constitution, which was surprisingly advanced for its time. The constitution enshrines the legal rights of women and the right of unions to organize and bargain, and it forbids Japan from engaging in anything but self-defensive war.

Politics in Japan was extremely stable until the 1990s. The government was dominated by the conservative "pro-business party" called the Liberal Democratic Party (LDP). Economic success induced the Japanese people to elect and reelect the party from 1955 to 1994.

➤ *Data File:* **HISTORY**
➤ *Task:* **Historical Trends**
➤ *Variables:* **32) %LIBDEM.JA**
33) %SOCIAL.JA
34) %CLNGOV.JA

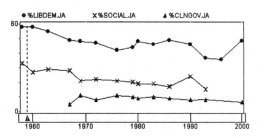

Electoral support for Liberal Democratic, Socialist, and Clean Government parties in Japan

You will notice that there were several other parties that competed for seats in the legislature over the last several decades, but it was not until financial and ethical scandals rocked the LDP in the early 1990s that the LDP loosened its grip on political power. This stability and one-party dominance of the Japanese regime led many observers to conclude that the Japanese government was not democratic. Critics of this view pointed out that elections have always been free and fair, and that the citizens of the nation preferred to return the party to power each year rather than risk a new government by other parties. Others suggested that the lack of ethnic, social, or political diversity has led the Japanese population to hold relatively similar political viewpoints. The declining percentage of support for the LDP has meant that a number of smaller parties, from the socialists to splinter groups from the LDP, have vied to control the government in a series of coalition governments. In 1994 this debate was brought to an end when the LDP was ousted from office. During the Clinton presidency (1992–2000), world leaders had to acquaint themselves with seven different prime ministers from Japan as coalition governments rose and fell. In the year 2000 the LDP returned to a more dominant position in the Japanese parliament (called the Diet). For the time being, the Japanese people seem to prefer familiarity to unstable coalition governments.

SOCIAL HARMONY IN JAPAN AND SOUTH KOREA

In the worksheet section that follows, we will focus on the countries of Japan and South Korea because they are examples of cases with a high degree of homogeneity in their populations.

➤ Data File: **ASIA**
➤ Task: **Mapping**
➤ Variable 1: **8) MULTI-CULT**
➤ View: **List: Rank**

MULTI-CULT: Multi-culturalism: odds that any 2 persons will differ in their race, religion, ethnicity (tribe), or language group

RANK	CASE NAME	VALUE
1	India	91
2	Bhutan	85
3	Tajikistan	84
4	Azerbaijan	77
5	Philippines	76
6	Fiji	75
7	Malaysia	72
7	Indonesia	72
9	Georgia	70
10	Iran	69

This variable ranks the odds that any two people will differ in the ethnic, religious, or cultural identity in a country. You'll need to scroll through to the bottom of the list to locate Japan and South Korea. These two countries have very low levels of cultural diversity. One of the often cited features of the Asian region is a set of so-called Asian values, often attributed to Confucianism and Buddhism, that make countries like Japan productive, stable, and internally harmonious. One way to determine whether or not these countries are more or less harmonious is to study the patterns of protest and demonstrations in the country to determine if they are different from those in Western countries. Korea has a very volatile social context due to its recent authoritarian political history, so examination of the levels of protest and numbers of demonstrations would not be comparable to a Western democratic nation. But on the basis of protest and riots, we can explore the evidence to see whether a country like Japan is more harmonious than the nations of other regions. One indicator of political conflict and disunity is the number of political protests that occur in a country.

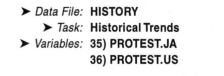

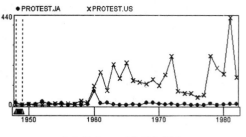

Protest in Japan and the United States

From this graph you will note that protest in Japan and the United States was relatively muted until the early 1960s when serious social unrest began to characterize American politics. During the same time in Japan, demonstrations were virtually nonexistent. Riots, which may be caused by political, economic, or social conflicts, are also a measure of the harmony or conflict that exists within a culture.

Data File: **HISTORY**
   Task: **Historical Trends**
➤ *Variables:* **37) RIOTS.JA**
   38) RIOTS.US

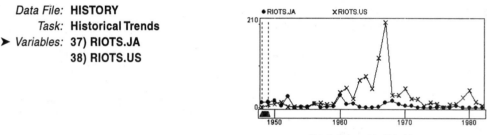

Riots in Japan and the United States

Again, it appears as though the United States has a great deal more disunity and conflict than Japan. But perhaps this is because the United States also has an extremely high level of diversity within its borders. Let's try comparing Japan to a Western country that is relatively homogeneous, such as Germany.

Data File: **HISTORY**
   Task: **Historical Trends**
➤ *Variables:* **37) RIOTS.JA**
   39) RIOTS.GM

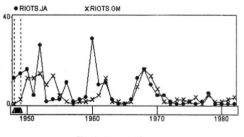

Riots in Japan and Germany

You will notice that in the previous comparison between the United States and Japan, the highest number of riots in a year was 210. This kind of comparison effectively minimizes the number of riots that can be seen in a country like Japan, which may have no more than 20 in a very riotous year. By comparing Japan and Germany, a slightly different pattern emerges. We see that in the 1950s and 60s Japan had higher levels of rioting during a couple of years than Germany did, but starting in the 1960s their patterns of rioting became relatively similar. This comparison suggests that Japan is not particularly exceptional in its level of social conflict vis-à-vis Western nations. Given this observation with regard to riots, let's reexamine protests in a comparison of Japan and Germany.

<table>
<tr><td align="right">Data File:</td><td>HISTORY</td></tr>
<tr><td align="right">Task:</td><td>Historical Trends</td></tr>
<tr><td align="right">➤ Variables:</td><td>35) PROTEST.JA</td></tr>
<tr><td></td><td>40) PROTEST.GM</td></tr>
</table>

Protest in Japan and Germany

From this we again see that Germany's and Japan's patterns of protest are relatively similar. Both had a similarly high outpouring of protest during the 1960s, but the patterns became similar through the 1970s and 80s. From this comparison of riots and protest in Japan, Germany, and the United States we discover that the United States is the exception, rather than Japan. By these measures, Japan does not seem to be any more harmonious than the Western country of Germany.

However, if we examine the level of citizen participation in demonstrations, it appears that the populations of Japan and South Korea are quite distinct from Germany.

➤ Data File: **GLOBAL**
➤ Task: **Mapping**
➤ Variable 1: **104) DEMONSTRAT**
➤ View: **List: Rank**

DEMONSTRAT: Percent who have taken part in a lawful demonstration

RANK	CASE NAME	VALUE
1	Italy	39
2	France	33
3	Sweden	30
4	Armenia	28
5	Dominican Republic	27
5	Denmark	27
5	Czech Republic	27
8	Norway	26
9	Belgium	25
9	Portugal	25

Twenty-four percent of all Germans surveyed claim that they have participated in a demonstration, but only 15% of South Koreans and 11% of Japanese citizens say as much.

Let's investigate the question of Asian values some more, but this time it's your turn.

WORKSHEET

NAME:

COURSE:

DATE:

CHAPTER
12

REVIEW QUESTIONS

Based on the first part of this chapter, answer True or False to the following items:

1. The types of governments in Asia and the Pacific are distributed relatively evenly between established democracies, transitional governments, one-party states, autocracies, and countries involved in civil wars.   T   F

2. In terms of GDP per capita in Asia, Japan is ranked first and South Korea is ranked seventh.   T   F

3. South Korea, due to its fear of an attack by North Korea, has the highest percentage of its population in the armed forces of any country in the Asia-Pacific region.   T   F

4. Japan and North Korea have more social diversity than most other Asian-Pacific countries.   T   F

5. Based on the analysis of protests and riots, Japan is more harmonious than the United States, but is similar to other culturally homogeneous Western countries, such as Germany.   T   F

EXPLORIT QUESTIONS

I.   Now let's look at the attitudes that citizens have about economic issues. We'll assume that in a harmonious society, citizens' opinions about economic issues will not vary much on the basis of class. In other words, if you were to ask "who is responsible for unemployed people?" citizens in a harmonious society would give the same answer whether they were unskilled laborers or bankers. We will use the data files for South Korea, Japan, and Germany to test this hypothesis. We know that Germany is not a harmonious society because of the class divisions that are prominent in this society. So if either Japan or South Korea is similar to the Germany, we can conclude that the country is not harmonious in its social relations on economic issues.

For each analysis, fill in the percentaged results *for the row that is specified* in the table below it. Also fill in the value for Cramer's V and indicate whether the results are statistically significant (circle Y for Yes, N for No).

Chapter 12: Asian Values: Political Culture in South Korea and Japan   209

➤ *Data Files:* **WVS97–JAPAN, WVS97–S.KOREA, and WVS9–GERMANY**
➤ *Task:* **Cross-tabulation**
➤ *Row Variable:* **BUS MGMT**
➤ *Column Variable:* **CLASS-3**
➤ *View:* **Tables**
➤ *Display:* **Column %**

Fill in the table below.

%EMP.OWN	UPPER	MIDDLE	WORKING	V =	SIGNIFICANT?
JAPAN	_____%	_____%	_____%	_____	Y N
SOUTH KOREA	_____%	_____%	_____%	_____	Y N
GERMANY	_____%	_____%	_____%	_____	Y N

6. A significant relationship between BUS MGMT and CLASS-3 in a given country means (circle one of the following)

    a. groups that agree on the same issue do not work in the same place.

    b. the different CLASS-3 groups are not in agreement on the issue of business management and the nation is therefore not "harmonious" with regard to that issue.

    c. the different CLASS-3 groups are in agreement on the issue of business management and the nation is therefore "harmonious" with regard to that issue.

    d. the countries disagree and are more likely to go to war.

7. The most harmonious country on this issue is

    a. Japan.

    b. South Korea.

    c. Germany.

8. The least harmonious country on this issue is

    a. Japan.

    b. South Korea.

    c. Germany.

9. On the business-ownership issue, which country is South Korea most similar to?

    a. Japan

    b. South Korea

    c. Germany

II. This time we'll look at the relationship between social class status and the issue of income equality. The question asks whether incomes should be made more equal or whether there should be greater incentives for individual effort.

> ➤ *Data Files:* **WVS97–JAPAN, WVS97–S.KOREA,** and **WVS97–GERMANY**
> *Task:* **Cross-tabulation**
> ➤ *Row Variable:* **INCOME EQ3**
> ➤ *Column Variable:* **CLASS-3**
> ➤ *View:* **Tables**
> ➤ *Display:* **Column %**

Fill in the table below.

INC.EQUAL	UPPER	MIDDLE	WORKING	V =	SIGNIFICANT?
JAPAN	_____%	_____%	_____%	_____	Y N
SOUTH KOREA	_____%	_____%	_____%	_____	Y N
GERMANY	_____%	_____%	_____%	_____	Y N

10. Which country is most harmonious on this issue? _____

III. Now we'll look at the relationship between social class and the issue of competition. The question asks whether competition is good because it stimulates people to work hard and to develop new ideas, or whether competition is harmful because it brings out the worst in people.

> *Data Files:* **WVS97–JAPAN, WVS97–S.KOREA** and **WVS97–GERMANY**
> *Task:* **Cross-tabulation**
> ➤ *Row Variable:* **COMPETITN**
> ➤ *Column Variable:* **CLASS-3**
> ➤ *View:* **Tables**
> ➤ *Display:* **Column %**

Fill in the table below.

%BENEFICIAL	UPPER	MIDDLE	WORKING	V =	SIGNIFICANT?
JAPAN	_____%	_____%	_____%	_____	Y N
SOUTH KOREA	_____%	_____%	_____%	_____	Y N
GERMANY	_____%	_____%	_____%	_____	Y N

11. In South Korea, the strongest differences on the value of competition are between workers in the (circle one of the following)
    a. upper class and middle class.
    b. upper class and working class.
    c. middle class and working class.

12. In Germany, the strongest differences on the value of competition are between workers in the (circle one of the following)
    a. upper class and middle class.
    b. upper class and working class.
    c. middle class and working class.

13. The most harmonious country on this issue is
    a. Japan.
    b. South Korea.
    c. Germany.

14. The least harmonious country on this issue is
    a. Japan.
    b. South Korea.
    c. Germany.

IV. Finally, look at the relationship between social class and wealth accumulation. The question asks respondents whether they think wealth can be accumulated only at the expense of others or whether wealth can grow so there is enough for everyone.

> Data Files: **WVS97–JAPAN, WVS97–S.KOREA,** and **WVS97–GERMANY**
> Task: **Cross-tabulation**
> ➤ Row Variable: **WEALTH ACC**
> ➤ Column Variable: **CLASS-3**
> ➤ View: **Tables**
> ➤ Display: **Column %**

Fill in the table below.

%EXPENSE	UPPER	MIDDLE	WORKING	V =	SIGNIFICANT?
JAPAN	_____%	_____%	_____%	_____	Y N
SOUTH KOREA	_____%	_____%	_____%	_____	Y N
GERMANY	_____%	_____%	_____%	_____	Y N

15. The belief that wealth comes at the cost of others is an issue (circle one of the following)
    a. that is really divisive only in the Germany
    b. that is really divisive only in Japan.
    c. that is really divisive only in the Germany and South Korea.
    d. that seems to divide workers in all three countries.

16. The most harmonious country on this issue is
    a. Japan.
    b. South Korea.
    c. Germany.

17. The least harmonious country on this issue is
    a. Japan.
    b. South Korea.
    c. Germany.

IN YOUR OWN WORDS

In your own words, please answer the following questions.

1. We have examined several economic issues in Japan, South Korea, and Germany to see whether or not social classes in the two Asian countries are more harmonious on economic issues than those in Germany. Based on the previous analysis, are Asian countries more harmonious on economic issues than Germany? Why might this be the case? Support your answer with evidence.

2. Does social harmony translate to relations between the sexes? Analyze the "gender gap" in Germany, Japan, and South Korea. Use the variable GENDER as the column variable and MAN'S JOB, MEN POLS, WOMEN EARN, and CONF:WOMEN as the row variables. As always, use column percentages. On the issues of men and women's roles, are men and women in Asia more harmonious in their views than men and women in Germany? On which issue is there the most harmony between genders? On which issue is there the least? Discuss your findings in the space below. Also attach up to six tables that support your analysis.

Part V

LESS DEVELOPED COUNTRIES AND THE ISLAMIC WORLD

Africa

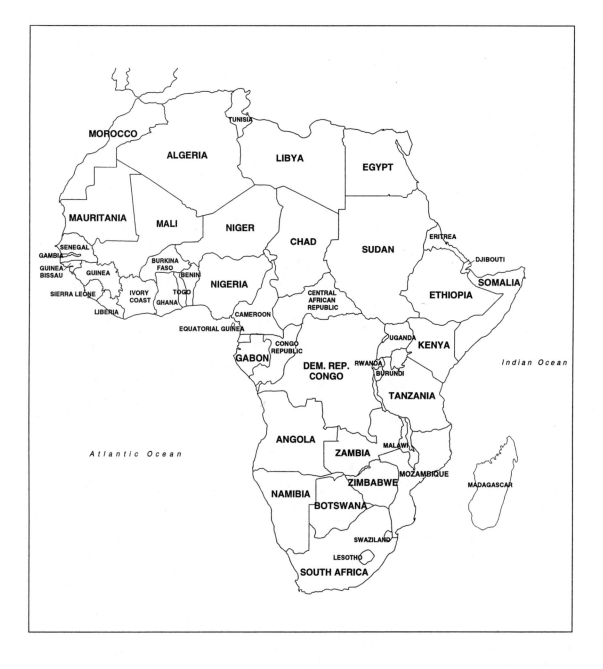

CHAPTER 13

LESS DEVELOPED COUNTRIES AND MARGINAL STATES IN AFRICA

*I go to Africa to try to make an open path for
commerce and Christianity.*

DAVID LIVINGSTONE, 1857,
BRITISH EXPLORER AND
MISSIONARY

*I who am poisoned with the blood of both,
Where shall I turn, divided to the vein?
I who have cursed the drunken officer of British rule,
how choose between this Africa and the English
tongue I love?*

DEREK WALCOTT, 1962
NOBEL LAUREATE

Tasks: Mapping, Scatterplot, Univariate, Cross-tabulation
Data Files: AFRICA, GLOBAL

INTRODUCTION TO SUB-SAHARAN AFRICA

Africa is perhaps the richest, in terms of natural resources, and most diverse continent in the world, but its history and politics are as tragic as they are complex. The continent of Africa is quite distinct from other regions of the world. The nations of Africa were colonized by European powers during the 18th and 19th centuries. The map that follows indicates the owners of colonial possessions in Africa before World War I.

➤ *Data File:* **AFRICA**
➤ *Task:* **Mapping**
➤ *Variable 1:* **24) COL.POWERS**
➤ *View:* **Map**
➤ *Display:* **Legend**

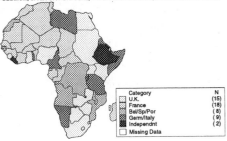

COL.POWERS -- COLONIAL POWER IN 1913: 1=UNITED KINGDOM, 2=FRANCE,
3=BELGIUM, SPAIN OR PORTUGAL, 4=GERMANY OR ITALY, 5=INDEPENDENT STATE

Category	N
U.K.	(15)
France	(18)
Bel/Sp/Por	(8)
Germ/Italy	(9)
Independnt	(2)
Missing Data	

You will notice that only two countries escaped imperialist domination and remained independent: Ethiopia and Liberia. The latter nation was resettled by ex-slaves who returned from the Americas to found their own nation.

Europeans conquered 85% of Africa during the last 20 years of the 19th century. There were at least three reasons for colonial expansion in Africa: strategic interests, land greed, and the extraction of wealth and slaves.

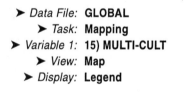

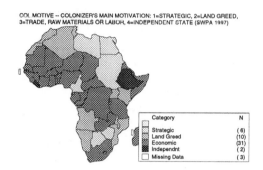

Colonized peoples of Africa were sold into slavery in Europe and America or used as slaves in their native lands to extract the wealth of their own land. Most Africans who were taken as slaves came from the western parts of Africa.

The boundaries carved out by colonizers consisted of huge land masses, rather than being organized along ethnic/tribal groups that existed at the time. As such, numerous ethnic/national groups were often combined into one country. The multiculturalism map we examined earlier in this workbook deserves another look.

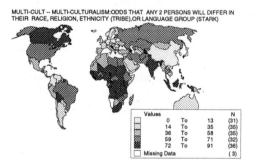

As you can see, African nations are among the most diverse nations in terms of race, ethnicity, religion, and language. This raises serious questions about our ability to describe all but a few of the countries of Africa as nation-states. You will remember from the first chapter that the nation-state is a government that has sovereignty over a territory of relatively homogeneous people. The incredible diversity, which is compounded by arbitrary borders to the nation-states of Africa, challenges the European conception of a culturally homogeneous nation-state.

Colonialism in Africa did not begin to loosen its grip until the end of World War II.

Comparative Politics

Data File: **GLOBAL**
Task: **Mapping**
➤ *Variable 1:* **71) IND PERIOD**
➤ *View:* **Map**
➤ *Display:* **Legend**

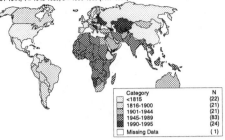

IND PERIOD -- PERIOD OF INDEPENDENCE: 1 = BEFORE 1815, 2 = 1816-1900, 3 = 1901-1944, 4 = 1945-1989, 5 = 1990-1995 (TWF 1996)

Category	N
<1815	(22)
1816-1900	(21)
1901-1944	(21)
1945-1989	(83)
1990-1995	(24)
Missing Data	(1)

As a result, most of the nations of Africa did not receive their independence until the middle to later part of the 20th century.

The study of Africa is often divided into two regions. Northern Africa is often studied in conjunction with the Islamic states of the Middle East and South Asia. Southern Africa, or sub-Saharan Africa as it is more appropriately called, is the region below the Sahara Desert which makes up approximately two-thirds of the continent of Africa.

Data File: **GLOBAL**
Task: **Mapping**
➤ *Variable 1:* **10) REGION**
➤ *View:* **Map**
➤ *Display:* **Legend**

REGION -- REGION (HDR, 1998)

Category	N
SUB-SAHARA	(43)
ARAB	(20)
ASIA/PACIF	(32)
WEST.HEMI.	(29)
EUROPE	(48)
Missing Data	

The REGION variable clearly shows these two parts of Africa. Sub-Saharan Africa is distinct from the northern part of Africa for a number of reasons. First, the religion and culture of sub-Saharan Africa differs from that of North Africa. This is clearly evident if you look at the maps showing the percentages of Muslims and Christians who live in each African country.

➤ *Data File:* **AFRICA**
➤ *Task:* **Mapping**
➤ *Variable 1:* **9) %MUSLIM**
➤ *Variable 2:* **10) %CHRISTIAN**
➤ *Views:* **Map**
➤ *Display:* **Legend**

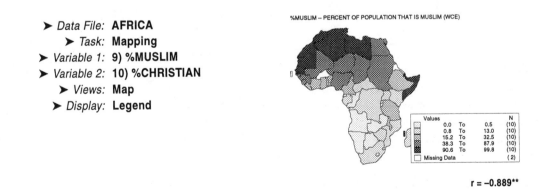

%MUSLIM -- PERCENT OF POPULATION THAT IS MUSLIM (WCE)

Values			N
0.0	To	0.5	(10)
0.8	To	13.0	(10)
15.2	To	32.5	(10)
38.3	To	87.9	(10)
90.6	To	99.8	(10)
Missing Data			(2)

r = –0.889**

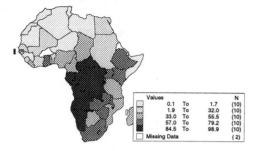

%CHRISTIAN -- PERCENT OF POPULATION THAT IS CHRISTIAN (WCE)

Values			N
0.1	To	1.7	(10)
1.9	To	32.0	(10)
33.0	To	55.5	(10)
57.0	To	79.2	(10)
84.5	To	98.9	(10)
Missing Data			(2)

Since the conquest of the Moors in the 7th century A.D., North Africa has been characterized by large populations of the Islamic faithful. And as illustrated by Dr. Livingston's quotation at the beginning of the chapter, much of the south and west of Africa was evangelized by 19th-century missionaries. Note that there is a strong negative correlation (–0.889**) between %MUSLIM and %CHRISTIAN. Where Islamic belief is strong, there is a relatively low percentage of Christians, and where Christian belief is strong, there is a relatively low percentage of Muslims.

Economically speaking, North Africa and sub-Saharan Africa are also quite distinct from one another. The variable GDP CAP 5 divides the countries of the world into five groups rank ordered according to each country's level of economic growth.

➤ *Data File:* **GLOBAL**
➤ *Task:* **Mapping**
➤ *Variable 1:* **114) GDP CAP 5**
➤ *View:* **Map**
➤ *Display:* **Legend**

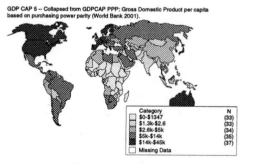

GDP CAP 5 -- Collapsed from GDPCAP PPP: Gross Domestic Product per capita based on purchasing power parity (World Bank 2001).

Category	N
$0-$1347	(33)
$1.3k-$2.6	(33)
$2.6k-$5k	(34)
$5k-$14k	(35)
$14k-$45k	(37)
Missing Data	

You will notice that Central Africa not only is the poorest region of Africa, it also is the poorest part of the world. Let's switch back to the AFRICA file and examine the same GDP per capita measure.

➤ *Data File:* **AFRICA**
➤ *Task:* **Mapping**
➤ *Variable 1:* **14) GDP CAP 5**
➤ *View:* **Map**
➤ *Display:* **Legend**

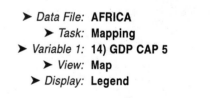

GDP CAP 5 -- Collapsed from GDPCAP PPP: Gross Domestic Product per capita based on purchasing power parity (World Bank 2001).

Category	N
$0-$1347	(26)
$1.3k-$2.6	(10)
$2.6k-$5k	(8)
$5k-$14k	(7)
Missing Data	(1)

You will notice that North Africa is wealthier than sub-Saharan Africa. Also, you will notice that South Africa and the countries that border it are wealthier than the states of Central East and West Africa. The likeliest reason for this relatively low level of economic development in Central Africa has to do with the extent to which the economy is devoted to agriculture as its primary production resource. Let's use the SCATTERPLOT task to look at the relationship between GDP per capita and the percentage of GDP derived from agriculture.

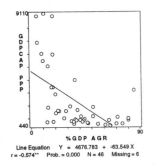

Data File: **AFRICA**
➤ Task: **Scatterplot**
➤ Dependent Variable: **17) GDPCAP PPP**
➤ Independent Variable: **15) %GDP AGR**
➤ View: **Reg. Line**

The scatterplot indicates that those countries in Africa that receive the highest percentage of their GDP from agriculture also tend to have the lowest levels of GDP per capita.

Poor economic conditions, ethnic and religious diversity, and the legacy of colonialism have combined to produce a continent characterized by unstable politics. The variable WAR categorizes each type of war according to its character.

Data File: **AFRICA**
➤ Task: **Univariate**
➤ Primary Variable: **26) WAR**
➤ View: **Pie**

WAR -- 1990-1996: TYPES OF ARMED CONFLICT: 1=NONE, 2=INTERSTATE, 3=CIVIL, 4=REGIONAL CIVIL, 5=INDEPENDENCE, 6=MULTIPLE TYPES (ALLEN, 1998)

		Freq.	%
■	1) None	23	44.2
▨	2) Interstate	3	5.8
▨	3) Civil	14	26.9
▨	4) Reg. Civil	6	11.5
▨	5) Indpndence	4	7.7
□	6) Multiple	2	3.8
	TOTAL (N)	52	100.0

Note that the majority of nation-states in Africa were involved in some type of armed conflict between 1990 and 1996. Only 44.2% of the nations in Africa were not involved in any violent conflict during these years. Interstate conflict, that is, war between nation-states, is usually the dominant form of warfare in the modern era, but in Africa pure interstate warfare accounts for only 5.8% of the violent conflict experienced between 1990 and 1996. The most dominant type of conflict during the period was civil war, which consumed 26.9% of the nations of Africa. This does not include regional civil war, which is confined to specific parts of a country. Regional civil war occurred or is ongoing in 11.5% of the countries of Africa. Wars of independence during 1990–96 occurred in 7.7% of the countries, and 3.8% of the countries suffered more than one type of warfare during this period. As a result of these conflicts, most of the parties to these conflicts have suffered tremendous tragedy in terms of the loss of life.

Data File: **AFRICA**

Task: **Univariate**

➤ Primary Variable: **27) WARDEAD**

➤ View: **Pie**

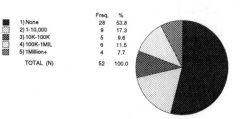

It is difficult to know how many people die from warfare. It is even more difficult to count the number of families that are affected by the loss of a family member, or to count the number of people who are severely injured in war. No one is responsible for counting these other victims, and numbers of dead are often manipulated by governments and armies for purposes of political propaganda. But awareness of the magnitude of human suffering caused by warfare is critical. It is estimated that throughout the world more than *5.6 million people died in warfare between the years of 1990 and 1995 alone!* That is a little less than 1 million people per year, and more than half of those (3.5 million) died in warfare on the African continent. The pie chart of war dead indicates that 4 out of 25 (or 7.7%) of the countries suffering the loss of life due to war lost more than 1 million people during this six-year period.

This trend has been long-standing in Africa. War uproots families, degrades health conditions, and destroys the economy. One measure of the well-being of people over time has been the infant mortality rate, which is a standard measure of the number of infant deaths per 1,000 live births. The presence of warfare is strongly associated with higher infant mortality.

➤ Data File: **GLOBAL**

➤ Task: **ANOVA**

➤ Dependent Variable: **26) INFMORTAL**

➤ Independent Variable: **74) WAR2**

➤ Views: **Graph, Means**

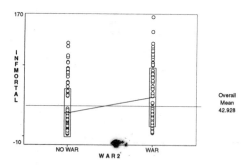

Means, Standard Deviations and Number of Cases of Dependent Var: INFMORTAL by Categories of Independent Var: WAR2
Difference of means across groups is statistically significant (Prob. = 0.000)

	N	Mean	Std.Dev.
NO WAR	96	33.030	34.007
WAR	75	55.598	41.266

From the analysis of means you can see that the infant mortality rate is nearly twice as high in countries that are experiencing warfare. Countries without warfare have an average mortality rate of 33 deaths per 1,000 live births, while countries with war in this period have a rate of 56 deaths per 1,000 live births.

The instability on the African continent has also led to the very slow growth of democracy and freedom. While there have been a few significant democratic success stories in Malawi, Mauritius, Benin, Namibia, and Botswana, most of the continent has relied on other forms of government.

➤ *Data File:* **AFRICA**
➤ *Task:* **Univariate**
➤ *Primary Variable:* **21) GOVERNMENT**
➤ *View:* **Pie**

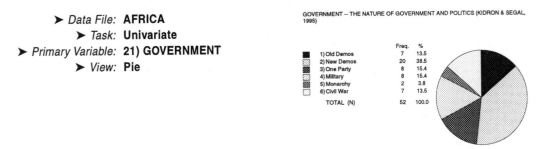

GOVERNMENT -- THE NATURE OF GOVERNMENT AND POLITICS (KIDRON & SEGAL, 1995)

		Freq.	%
■	1) Old Demos	7	13.5
▨	2) New Demos	20	38.5
▨	3) One Party	8	15.4
▨	4) Military	8	15.4
▨	5) Monarchy	2	3.8
▨	6) Civil War	7	13.5
	TOTAL (N)	52	100.0

Only 7 of the 52 African nations (13.5%) in our study may be classified as stable democratic governments. Governments in category 2 are those that are making transitions to democracy, and while they may succeed in their endeavor, most of them have fairly limited hope of doing so in the near future. We can examine the second category of transition states in terms of their political rights and civil liberties to determine nations' prospects for democracy.[1]

Data File: **AFRICA**
➤ *Task:* **Cross-tabulation**
➤ *Row Variable:* **29) POL RIGHT2**
➤ *Column Variable:* **21) GOVERNMENT**
➤ *View:* **Tables**
➤ *Display:* **Column %**

POL RIGHT2　by　GOVERNMENT
Cramer's V: 0.413
Warning: Potential significance problem.　Check row and column totals.

		GOVERNMENT						
		Old Demos	New Demos	One Party	Military	Monarchy	Civil War	TOTAL
POL RIGHT2	Low (1-4)	4	11	7	7	2	7	38
		66.7%	55.0%	87.5%	100.0%	100.0%	87.5%	74.5%
	High(5-7)	2	9	1	0	0	1	13
		33.3%	45.0%	12.5%	0.0%	0.0%	12.5%	25.5%
	Missing	1	0	0	0	0	0	1
	TOTAL	6	20	8	7	2	8	51
		100.0%	100.0%	100.0%	100.0%	100.0%	100.0%	

As you'll recall, a higher number indicates nation-states that have high levels of individual political rights; a low number indicates those that have low levels of political freedom. Here we see that over half of newly democratic countries (55.0%) have low levels of political freedom. While this may seem disappointing, this category at least fares better than all other government types in Africa in terms of political rights.

Let's do a similar analysis, using a variable for civil liberties.

---

[1] There are a few instances in this chapter where the cross-tabulation result using the AFRICA file produces the statement "Warning: Potential significance problem." This is to alert you that the statistical significance value may not be reliable due to the small number of cases (in this case, 51 nations) used in the analysis. The likelihood of this warning message appearing will also increase as the number of cells in the table increases—the greater the number of cells, the more likely the warning message will appear. For our purposes in this chapter, we will often ignore this warning.

Data File: **AFRICA**

Task: **Cross-tabulation**

➤ Row Variable: **31) CIVIL LIB2**

➤ Column Variable: **21) GOVERNMENT**

➤ View: **Tables**

➤ Display: **Column %**

CIVIL LIB2   by   GOVERNMENT
Cramer's V: 0.424
Warning: Potential significance problem. Check row and column totals.

		GOVERNMENT						
		Old Demos	New Demos	One Party	Military	Monarchy	Civil War	TOTAL
CIVIL LIB2	Low (1-4)	4	14	8	7	2	8	43
		66.7%	70.0%	100.0%	100.0%	100.0%	100.0%	84.3%
	High(5-7)	2	6	0	0	0	0	8
		33.3%	30.0%	0.0%	0.0%	0.0%	0.0%	15.7%
	Missing	1	0	0	0	0	0	1
	TOTAL	6	20	8	7	2	8	51
		100.0%	100.0%	100.0%	100.0%	100.0%	100.0%	

This analysis of civil liberties reveals a slightly more discouraging result. Only 30% of the new democracies have ratings of 5 or above in this analysis. Although we won't do it here, a different analysis reveals that 35% of the cases are classified at a promising rate of 4.

Clearly, the nation-states of Africa are struggling in many ways, but the analysis of political variables shows a more mixed picture than the stereotype of Africa suggests. In the worksheet section that follows, you will examine the relationship between a number of social problems and policies to combat these problems.

WORKSHEET

NAME:

COURSE:

DATE:

CHAPTER
13

Workbook exercises and software are copyrighted. Copying is prohibited by law.

REVIEW QUESTIONS

Based on the first part of this chapter, answer True or False to the following items:

1. Africa is the most culturally diverse continent in the world.   T   F

2. One of the reasons scholars divide the study of Africa between Saharan and sub-Saharan Africa is that there are significant cultural differences between the two regions.   T   F

3. There are also significant economic differences between Saharan and sub-Saharan Africa.   T   F

4. A majority of African states that are in the "transitional" category have good ratings in the area of civil liberties.   T   F

5. Only a few areas were colonized in Africa, in part because the vast Saharan region had little in the way of natural resources.   T   F

6. Applying the term *nation-state* to the countries of Africa is problematic because most of them aren't composed of relatively homogeneous people.   T   F

EXPLORIT QUESTIONS

I. The variable %FEM.LEGIS indicates the percentage of parliamentary seats held by females. We have data for 46 of the 52 African countries.

> ➤ *Data File:* **AFRICA**
> ➤ *Task:* **Mapping**
> ➤ *Variable 1:* **12) %FEM.LEGIS**
> ➤ *View:* **List: Rank**

Write down the five top countries and list the percentage of parliamentary seats held by females.

Chapter 13: Less Developed Countries and Marginal States in Africa   227

COUNTRY	% OF SEATS
_____	_____
_____	_____
_____	_____
_____	_____
_____	_____

II. Why do you think there is so much variation in the percentage of parliamentary seats held by women? Let's explore two hypotheses: (1) African countries with high rates of female education will be more likely to have higher percentages of women holding parliamentary seats; (2) in countries where women hold higher percentages of parliamentary seats, we can also expect to find higher rates of women in professional occupations.

> Data File: **AFRICA**
> ➤ Task: **Scatterplot**
> ➤ Dependent Variable: **12) %FEM.LEGIS**
> ➤ Independent Variable: **13) M/F EDUC.**
> ➤ View: **Reg. Line**

7. What is the correlation coefficient for this scatterplot?   r = _____

8. Are these results statistically significant?   Yes   No

9. Do these results support the hypothesis that as education rates for women increase, so will their participation in the political system?   Yes   No

10. Now remove one outlier. Which case did you remove?   _____

> Data File: **AFRICA**
> Task: **Scatterplot**
> Dependent Variable: **12) %FEM.LEGIS**
> ➤ Independent Variable: **11) %FEM.PROF.**
> ➤ View: **Reg. Line**

11. What is the correlation coefficient for this scatterplot?   r = _____

12. Are these results statistically significant?   Yes   No

13. Does the rate of female professionals seem to be related to the percentage of women in the legislature?   Yes   No

III. Now let's look at the relationship between literacy and the role of women in positions of social and political leadership in Africa. The variable FEM MINIST gives the percentage of the government's cabinet seats held by women. The variable IL FEM >15 measures the rate of illiteracy among women over the age of 15.

> Data File: **AFRICA**
> Task: **Scatterplot**
> ➤ Dependent Variable: **35) FEM MINIST**
> ➤ Independent Variable: **33) IL:FEM>15**
> ➤ View: **Reg. Line**

14. What is the correlation coefficient for this scatterplot?   r = _____

15. Are these results statistically significant?   Yes   No

16. Does the rate of female political leadership seem to be related to the illiteracy level of women over age 15?   Yes   No

IV. The most pressing health problem in the world is the proliferation of the AIDS virus. The variable AIDS/HIV measures the percentage of the population with AIDS/HIV. Before we can consider what might be an effective strategy, we must understand the problems. Is illiteracy or GDP associated with HIV/AIDS in Africa? What about government spending on health?

> ➤ Data File: **GLOBAL**
> ➤ Task: **Mapping**
> ➤ Variable 1: **115) AIDS/HIV**
> ➤ View: **Rank**

17. How many African nations are in the top ten nations with HIV/AIDS?   _____

> ➤ Data File: **AFRICA**
> ➤ Task: **Scatterplot**
> ➤ Dependent Variable: **38) HIV/AIDS1**
> ➤ Independent Variable: **34) IL:FEM<25**
> ➤ View: **Reg. Line**

18. The scatterplot suggests that

     a.   as illiteracy among women under 25 increases, the percentage of those with HIV/AIDS decreases.

     b.   as illiteracy among women under 25 increases, the percentage of those with HIV/AIDS increases.

     c.   as literacy among women under 25 increases, the percentage of those with HIV/AIDS increases.

     d.   as literacy among women under 25 increases, the percentage of those with HIV/AIDS decreases.

     e.   both a and c are true.

Now let's see if HIV/AIDS is associated with levels of wealth in African nation-states.

> Data File: **AFRICA**
> Task: **Scatterplot**
> Dependent Variable: **38) HIV/AIDS1**
> ➤ Independent Variable: **17) GDPCAP PPP**
> ➤ View: **Reg. Line**

19. What is the correlation coefficient for this scatterplot? r = _____

20. Are these results statistically significant? Yes No

21. Does GDP per capita seem to be related to the HIV/AIDS rate? Yes No

Now let's examine the role that health expenditure and international aid plays in the number of HIV/AIDS cases, but before we start on the analysis let's be sure that we understand the variables that we are working with. Please match the variable in the list below with its best description by placing the variable number in the blank provided.

0) NO SUCH VARIABLE

36) HEALTH EXP

38) HIV/AIDS1

39) HIV/AIDS2

40) HIV/AIDS3

43) AID CAP

DESCRIPTION   **VARIABLE NUMBER**

22. The number of childhood (ages 0–14) HIV/AIDS cases: _____

23. The percentage of the adult population (ages 15–49) with HIV/AIDS: _____

24. The number of female (ages 15–49) HIV/AIDS cases: _____

25. Government health expenditure in dollars: _____

26. Health expenditure per capita (PPP US$): _____

27. International aid per capita: _____

Now examine the relationship between HIV/AIDS cases and health expenditure for each variable relationship.

> Data File: **AFRICA**
> Task: **Scatterplot**
> ➤ Dependent Variables: **38) HIV/AIDS1**
>   **39) HIV/AIDS2**
>   **40) HIV/AIDS3**
> ➤ Independent Variable: **36) HEALTH EXP**
> ➤ View: **Reg. Line**

28. 36) HEALTH EXP and 38) HIV/AIDS1   r = _____   Significant?   Yes   No

29. 36) HEALTH EXP and 39) HIV/AIDS2   r = _____   Significant?   Yes   No

30. 36) HEALTH EXP and 40) HIV/AIDS3   r = _____   Significant?   Yes   No

Now examine the relationship between HIV/AIDS cases and international aid for each variable relationship.

> | | |
> | --- | --- |
> | Data File: | **AFRICA** |
> | Task: | **Scatterplot** |
> | Dependent Variables: | **38) HIV/AIDS1** |
> | | **39) HIV/AIDS2** |
> | | **40) HIV/AIDS3** |
> | ➤ Independent Variable: | **43) AID CAP** |
> | ➤ View: | **Reg. Line** |

31. 43) AID CAP and 38) HIV/AIDS1   r = _____   Significant?   Yes   No

32. 43) AID CAP and 39) HIV/AIDS2   r = _____   Significant?   Yes   No

33. 43) AID CAP and 40) HIV/AIDS3   r = _____   Significant?   Yes   No

IN YOUR OWN WORDS

In your own words, please answer the following questions.

1. Summarize the results of your analysis of HIV/AIDS. Which factors (literacy, GDP per capita, health spending, and international aid per capita) are associated with a lower number of cases of HIV/AIDS? From this analysis, would you conclude that enough is being done to confront the HIV/AIDS crisis in Africa? Be sure to support your answer with evidence. Print out three scatterplots that support your analysis.

2. What are the key features of the movement of refugees in Africa? Is it state weakness, war, health, or economic problems? Using the two variables 44) REFUGEES and 46) ASYLUM as dependent variables, write a paragraph that analyzes the movement of refugees in Africa. You may use any variable in the AFRICA data file that you think might be associated with the movement of refugees in Africa. Print out the two best explanations and attach them to this worksheet. The variable REFUGEES indicates the number of refugees from a given country. The variable ASYLUM indicates the number of refugees that are now residing in the country.

CHAPTER **14**

SOCIAL CAPITAL IN NIGERIA AND SOUTH AFRICA

People are people through other people.
XHOSA PROVERB OFTEN QUOTED
BY ARCHBISHOP DESMOND TUTU

Tasks: Mapping, Univariate, Historical Trends, Cross-tabulation
Data Files: GLOBAL, HISTORY, WVS97–NIGERIA, WVS97–S.AFRICA

SOCIAL CAPITAL IN NIGERIA AND SOUTH AFRICA

One of the leading reasons for the violence and instability experienced in this region is the suspicion and fear bred by a legacy of colonial rule, violence, and mistrust between indigenous Africans and their colonizers. European colonizers often used one ethnic group against another to divide and conquer the continent. Not every African ethnic group was at peace before the Europeans' conquest of the continent, but the pattern of pitting one group against the other exacerbated latent political conflicts between the various ethnic groups in each country. This is perhaps one reason that Nigerians and South Africans have a very difficult time trusting others in their respective countries.

➤ *Data File:* **GLOBAL**
➤ *Task:* **Mapping**
➤ *Variable 1:* **109) TRUST?**
➤ *View:* **List: Rank**

TRUST?: Percent who say, "Most people can be trusted."

RANK	CASE NAME	VALUE
1	Norway	65
2	Sweden	60
3	Denmark	58
4	Netherlands	55
5	China	52
5	Canada	52
7	Finland	48
8	Ireland	47
9	Iceland	44
10	Japan	42

If you scroll down the table you will notice that both South Africans and Nigerians have some of the lowest levels of trust among their citizens. They rank 48th and 50th out of the 61 countries surveyed on this question for the World Values Survey. Social trust of fellow citizens is one indicator of what Robert Putnam refers to as "social capital."[1] Social capital is the reserve of goodwill and trust citizens

---

[1] Robert Putnam, *Making Democracy Work: Civic Traditions in Modern Italy* (Princeton, NJ: Princeton University Press, 1993).

have toward one another that allows them to engage in democratic behaviors. In a study of Italy, Putnam theorizes that democracy works best when citizens with different backgrounds and perspectives can trust one another. On the face of it, this makes sense. If you generally trust people, you will be more inclined to tolerate election results that do not work in your favor. While you may not agree with the decisions of your government, if you trust that people will not harm you, you are much more likely to allow them to govern if they are properly chosen by the community as a whole. Social capital in and of itself, though, does not necessarily precede democratic behavior. Democracy is usually very risky business if you are part of a group that feels threatened, so a track record of benevolent government and loyal opposition can help to build the social capital necessary for democracy. In this exercise and the worksheet section that follows, we will examine social capital and political development in Nigeria and South Africa.

NIGERIA

Although Europeans were involved in the West African slave trade from the 16th century, the British Empire controlled what is now present-day Nigeria from 1886. Nigeria consisted not only of small tribes but of nations and empires as well until the European conquest. More than 250 ethnic groups reside in Nigeria, but at least three large groups have dominated the political landscape in Nigeria since independence: the *Hausa-Fulani*, *Igbo*, and *Yoruba*.

Prior to the time of the British conquest, the Hausa-Fulani had established an extensive empire in Northern Nigeria. This was a nation devoted to the practice of Islam, whose Hausa branch had a long history of domination and empire between A.D. 1000 and 1200. The Fulanis dominated in the period of British conquest, but the two groups became so intertwined that the two are generally referred to as the Hausa-Fulani. The Hausa-Fulani succeeded in remaining relatively insulated from British domination. The British allowed them a degree of autonomy in self-government and, unlike the southern part of the country, did not allow Christian proselytizing in the North.

The Igbo (pronounced "eebo") and the Yoruba reside in the southern part of the nation. Unlike the Hausa-Fulani, the Igbo were politically decentralized and independent. They had settled widely throughout the country and were integrally involved in the early military governments in Nigeria. They are described by other groups as "pushy" and "aggressive." The Igbo have also been very adept at appropriating Western education, commerce, and political practices. Unlike the Hausa-Fulani, the Igbo were very receptive to Christian missionary efforts and are also said to be strongly egalitarian.

The Yoruba live in the southwestern part of the country in and around the capital, Lagos. The Yoruba have a long tradition of promoting commerce in the context of their network of city-states and have had highly stratified societies and relatively authoritarian political structures. Like the Igbo, the Yoruba have been very receptive to Western missionaries and schools imported to the region during the 19th and 20th centuries.

For political reasons, it is very difficult to get an exact count by ethnicity (see Table 14.1). Each group is interested in overrepresenting its numbers so that it may lay claim to a greater share of political power, so the only two estimates we have are unreliable. The 1963 census and the 2001 CIA estimates have very similar results, but these results differ from most scholarly samples of the Nigerian population.

Comparative Politics

Table 14.1. Ethnic Identities in Nigeria, 1963–2001

Group	1963 Census	CIA Estimate 2001
Hausa-Fulani	29.5	29%
Yoruba	20.3	21%
Igbo	16.6	18%
Other	33.6	32%

The 1973 and 1991 Nigerian censuses did not even ask a question about ethnicity. The World Values Survey did attempt such a question, but that is complicated because it also gave the respondents the option of indicating they were "Nigerian first and a member of an ethnic group second."

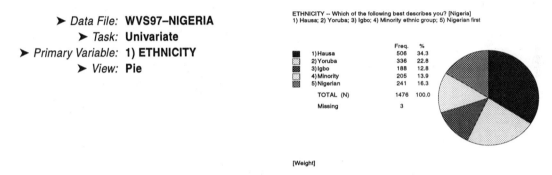

➤ *Data File:* **WVS97–NIGERIA**
➤ *Task:* **Univariate**
➤ *Primary Variable:* **1) ETHNICITY**
➤ *View:* **Pie**

ETHNICITY -- Which of the following best describes you? [Nigeria]
1) Hausa; 2) Yoruba; 3) Igbo; 4) Minority ethnic group; 5) Nigerian first

		Freq.	%
■	1) Hausa	506	34.3
	2) Yoruba	336	22.8
	3) Igbo	188	12.8
	4) Minority	205	13.9
	5) Nigerian	241	16.3
	TOTAL (N)	1476	100.0
	Missing	3	

[Weight]

You will notice that only 16.3% indicated that they were "Nigerian first." Also note that the percentage of people who identify themselves as Hausa-Fulani was high (34.3%) relative to the census taken in 1963, and that the percentage of Igbo (12.8%) was relatively low compared to census estimates. Only the percentage of Yoruba (22.8%) is close to the census estimates. Interpreting such data is complicated by the question, and the potential conclusions are many: that there are fewer Igbo and Hausa-Fulani in Nigeria; that more Hausa-Fulani were included in this sample; or that the Igbo are more identified with the nation of Nigeria, so their numbers in terms of ethnicity merely *appear* to be lower.

SOUTH AFRICA

South Africa is also an extremely diverse nation. Prior to European settlement, it was dominated by two large ethnic groups, the *Xhosa* and the *Zulu*, although several smaller groups existed. The nation's indigenous diversity was further complicated by the immigration of two European groups. Dutch South Africans, along with some German and French Protestants, immigrated to the continent in the beginning of the 17th century. This group refers to themselves as *Afrikaaners*. Over the next 200 years, British settlers began to immigrate to the coastal areas of present-day South Africa. This immigration resulted in conflicts between the two European groups. This conflict finally erupted into full-scale warfare in the early 20th century. By 1910 the British government established a "commonwealth government" which recognized the British monarch as head of state, (as the governments still do in Canada and Australia). The government became independent from the British Commonwealth in 1934 and established itself as the Republic of South Africa. During the next ten years, white South Africans, led by the Afrikaaners, became increasingly fearful of their minority status vis-à-vis the large indigenous African majority. While the results that follow do not exactly match the census data shown in Table 14.2, you can see that the racial composition in South Africa is politically favorable to an indigenous African majority.

> *Data File:* **WVS97–S.AFRICA**
> *Task:* **Univariate**
> *Primary Variable:* **1) ETHNIC GRP**
> *View:* **Pie**

ETHNIC GRP --

		Freq.	%
■	1) Caucasian	236	15.8
▨	2) Black	1095	73.3
▨	3) S. Asian	38	2.6
▨	4) Coloured	125	8.4
	TOTAL (N)	1495	100.0

[Weight]

Table 14.2. 1990 Census

Asian	3.0%
Black	70.3%
Coloured	11.1%
White	15.8%
English 6.3%	
Afrikaaner 9.5%	

The sample data from the World Values Survey show that blacks make up 73.3% of the population, while whites constitute only 15.8% of the population. So-called coloureds, who are bi-racial, make up 8.4% of this sample, and South Asians (mostly from India) account for the remaining 2.6% of the population. One weakness of this variable is that it does not measure the ethnic diversity in African society very well. There are many ethnic groups that make up the ethnic designation (black) and a few that make up the white. A second ethnic variable asked respondents to indicate their ethnicity.

> *Data File:* **WVS97–S.AFRICA**
> *Task:* **Univariate**
> *Primary Variable:* **2) ETHNIC**
> *View:* **Bar - Freq.**

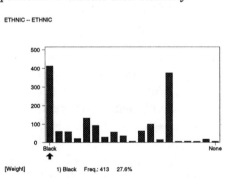

ETHNIC -- ETHNIC

[Weight]   1) Black   Freq.: 413   27.6%

Click on the bar or use the arrow keys to move from category to category on the bar graph.

As you can see, a plurality of the population (27.6%) identifies itself as black. But as you move to the right, you see that individuals identify themselves as being a part of many other ethnic groups. The two largest indigenous ethnic groups in the sample are Zulu (8.9%) and Xhosa (6.2%). Many blacks would consider themselves as originating from one or both of these two groups, but they identify their current ethnicity as black. Specific ethnic identities are not the exclusive domain of blacks in South Africa. Whites also see themselves as distinct. As you move to the right, you will see that 4.3% of the sample consider themselves English South African, 6.7% consider themselves Afrikaans South African (originating from Holland), and 1.1% say that they are Afrikaaner.

From the numbers, one can see that many white South Africans would be fearful of majoritarian democracy. As a result of this fear, the white government instituted the *apartheid* policy, designed to exclude nonwhites from the political process, and segregated housing, education, and other public facilities. This policy served to hinder the human development of blacks compared to that of whites living in South Africa. For example, this next analysis compares the infant mortality rate for blacks in South Africa with the rate for whites.

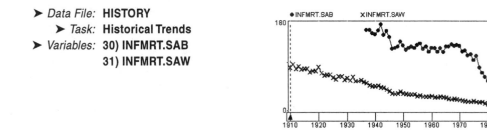

> ➤ Data File: **HISTORY**
> ➤ Task: **Historical Trends**
> ➤ Variables: **30) INFMRT.SAB**
> **31) INFMRT.SAW**

Infant mortality of blacks and whites in South Africa

Although both rates of infant mortality declined throughout the 20th century, the gap between white and black infant mortality remained substantial. When this World Values Survey was conducted in South Africa, apartheid had been abolished for three years. In 1994 apartheid was abolished and a truly representative democratic government was established.

TRUST AND POLITICAL DEVELOPMENT

In addition to ethnicity, religion is a divisive factor in both Nigeria and South Africa.

> ➤ Data File: **WVS97–NIGERIA**
> ➤ Task: **Cross-tabulation**
> ➤ Row Variable: **2) WH RELIG**
> ➤ Column Variable: **1) ETHNICITY**
> ➤ View: **Tables**
> ➤ Display: **Column %**

WH RELIG   by   ETHNICITY
Weight Variable: WEIGHT2
Cramer's V: 0.322 **

		ETHNICITY						
		Hausa	Yoruba	Igbo	Minority	Nigerian	Missing	TOTAL
WH RELIG	Catholic	4	62	68	33	33	0	200
		0.8%	18.8%	37.7%	16.3%	14.1%		13.7%
	Protestant	3	31	26	18	34	1	111
		0.5%	9.5%	14.4%	8.7%	14.2%		7.6%
	Pentecostl	2	45	33	49	28	0	157
		0.4%	13.7%	18.2%	24.2%	11.9%		10.8%
	Muslim	383	159	4	82	120	0	748
		75.6%	48.2%	2.3%	40.9%	51.0%		51.5%
	Cherubim	114	9	25	13	7	0	168
		22.6%	2.7%	13.9%	6.5%	2.9%		11.6%
	Other	0	23	24	7	14	2	68
		0.0%	7.1%	13.5%	3.4%	5.9%		4.7%
	Missing	1	6	9	4	5	1	25
	TOTAL	506	330	179	201	236	3	1452
		100.0%	100.0%	100.0%	100.0%	100.0%		

There is a very strong, significant relationship between religious affiliation and group identity. You will notice that the Hausa-Fulani are overwhelmingly Islamic (75.6%), whereas only 2.3% of the Igbo affiliate with Islam. The Igbo are mostly Catholic, but there are also Igbo who affiliate with mainline and Pentecostal Protestant denominations. The Yoruba are mostly Islamic, and they are evenly divided between the different types of Christian denominations. What is perhaps most interesting about this is that people who identify themselves as "Nigerian first" are mostly Islamic (51%) and, like the Yoruba, evenly divided between the Christian religious groups.

In South Africa, the majority of the population is affiliated with the Dutch Reformed Church and a few other Protestant denominations. But there are a few Catholics and other denominations represented.

➤ Data File: **WVS97–S.AFRICA**
➤ Task: **Cross-tabulation**
➤ Row Variable: **3) WH RELIG**
➤ Column Variable: **1) ETHNIC GRP**
➤ View: **Tables**
➤ Display: **Column %**

WH RELIG   by   ETHNIC GRP
Weight Variable: WEIGHT2
Cramer's V: 0.478 **

		ETHNIC GRP				
		White	Black	S. Asian	Coloured	TOTAL
WH RELIG	None	36	118	2	2	158
		15.6%	11.2%	5.0%	1.8%	11.0%
	Catholic	15	163	1	17	196
		6.4%	15.5%	2.7%	14.3%	13.6%
	Protestant	170	530	4	89	794
		74.0%	50.4%	11.7%	73.0%	55.0%
	Hindu	0	0	24	0	24
		0.0%	0.0%	62.6%	0.0%	1.6%
	Other	9	241	7	13	270
		3.9%	22.9%	18.0%	10.9%	18.8%
	Missing	6	43	1	3	53
	TOTAL	230	1052	38	122	1442
		100.0%	100.0%	100.0%	100.0%	

In South Africa, a clear majority of whites worship in the context of the Protestant denominations. Blacks affiliate to a lesser extent with Protestantism, but are also likely to be affiliated with the Catholic Church. South Asians are predominantly Hindu while 73.0% percent of coloureds affiliate with Protestant churches. Clearly, in both countries there are significant differences between ethnic groups and their religious affiliations.

If we want to understand whether religious or ethnic differences are more likely to be the source of mistrust in Nigeria and South Africa, then we must conduct an analysis that examines trust in terms of ethnic and religious differences.

➤ Data File: **WVS97–NIGERIA**
➤ Task: **Cross-tabulation**
➤ Row Variable: **3) TRUST PEOP**
➤ Column Variable: **1) ETHNICITY**
➤ View: **Tables**
➤ Display: **Column %**

TRUST PEOP   by   ETHNICITY
Weight Variable: WEIGHT2
Cramer's V: 0.115 **

		ETHNICITY						
		Hausa	Yoruba	Igbo	Minority	Nigerian	Missing	TOTAL
TRUST PEOP	Can trust	84	45	48	48	34	0	258
		19.5%	14.4%	27.4%	24.7%	15.5%		19.5%
	Be careful	345	264	128	146	183	1	1067
		80.5%	85.6%	72.6%	75.3%	84.5%		80.5%
	Missing	77	27	12	10	24	2	153
	TOTAL	429	309	176	195	217	3	1325
		100.0%	100.0%	100.0%	100.0%	100.0%		

In general, most Nigerians feel as though it is difficult to trust others. However, there are significant differences between ethnic groups on this point. The Igbo are the most trusting relative to the other groups, and the Yoruba are the least trusting.

➤ *Data File:* **WVS97–S.AFRICA**
➤ *Task:* **Cross-tabulation**
➤ *Row Variable:* **4) TRUST PEOP**
➤ *Column Variable:* **1) ETHNIC GRP**
➤ *View:* **Tables**
➤ *Display:* **Column %**

TRUST PEOP   by   ETHNIC GRP
Weight Variable: WEIGHT2
Cramer's V: 0.095 **

| | | ETHNIC GRP | | | | |
		Caucasian	Black	S. Asian	Coloured	TOTAL
TRUST PEOP	Can trust	29	215	3	16	263
		12.6%	20.4%	9.2%	12.6%	18.2%
	Be careful	203	835	33	108	1179
		87 4%	79 6%	90 8%	87 4%	81.8%
	Missing	4	46	2	2	53
	TOTAL	232	1049	37	123	1441
		100.0%	100.0%	100.0%	100.0%	

As in Nigeria, most South Africans do not trust others. Only 18.2% of the whole South African population indicate that they trust others. Blacks are the most trusting, whites and coloureds are the next most trusting. Asians are in the lowest categories of trust. Are there differences when we analyze trust according to religion? What about South Africa, where Desmond Tutu, archbishop of the Anglican Church in South Africa, led Christians and other South Africans in the anti-apartheid movement?

Data File: **WVS97–S.AFRICA**
Task: **Cross-tabulation**
Row Variable: **4) TRUST PEOP**
➤ *Column Variable:* **3) WH RELIG**
➤ *View:* **Tables**
➤ *Display:* **Column %**

TRUST PEOP   by   WH RELIG
Weight Variable: WEIGHT2
Cramer's V: 0.074

| | | WH RELIG | | | | | | | |
		None	Catholic	Protestant	Muslim	Hindu	Other	Missing	TOTAL
TRUST PEOP	Can trust	29	41	126	2	2	54	8	254
		19.3%	22.2%	16.5%	9.5%	9.9%	21.8%		18.3%
	Be careful	123	143	639	15	21	195	43	1135
		80.7%	77.8%	83.5%	90.5%	90.1%	78.2%		81.7%
	Missing	6	12	28	1	1	4	1	53
	TOTAL	152	184	765	16	23	249	53	1390
		100.0%	100.0%	100.0%	100.0%	100.0%	100.0%		

In the analysis of social trust in South Africa, there appears to be little significant difference between religious groups.

➤ *Data File:* **WVS97–NIGERIA**
➤ *Task:* **Cross-tabulation**
➤ *Row Variable:* **3) TRUST PEOP**
➤ *Column Variable:* **2) WH RELIG**
➤ *View:* **Tables**
➤ *Display:* **Column %**

TRUST PEOP   by   WH RELIG
Weight Variable: WEIGHT2
Cramer's V: 0.098 *

| | | WH RELIG | | | | | | | |
		Catholic	Protestant	Pentecostl	Muslim	Cherubim	Other	Missing	TOTAL
TRUST PEOP	Can trust	48	19	28	111	39	11	2	256
		26.8%	18.2%	19.4%	16.8%	25.2%	16.9%		19.6%
	Be careful	132	85	117	548	116	55	16	1052
		73.2%	81.8%	80.6%	83.2%	74.8%	83.1%		80.4%
	Missing	19	7	12	90	14	4	6	153
	TOTAL	180	105	145	658	154	66	25	1308
		100.0%	100.0%	100.0%	100.0%	100.0%	100.0%		

Because of a weaker correlation in this analysis of Nigeria, it seems as though religion is not as significant a source of mistrust of other people as ethnicity. So far, it seems that ethnicity is a more significant source of division in Nigeria and South Africa than religion.

The Nigerian survey was conducted during the five-year reign of military dictator Sani Abacha. Abacha succeeded the brutal dictatorship of Ibrahim Babangida, a Gwari leader from the north of Nigeria. Ethnic loyalties still superseded national loyalty in Nigeria, and this makes it very difficult for democracy to flourish. In 1999, former General Olusegun Obasanjo, a Yoruba who has ties to the Hausa-Fulani, was elected President of Nigeria in the first fair elections since 1976. The ethnic and/or regional identity of the political leader may actually influence the feelings that members of specific ethnic groups have about their level of trust in government. When this survey was conducted, Abacha, with strong ties to the Hausa-Fulani, was in power. How did this fact influence confidence in government?

Data File: **WVS97–NIGERIA**
Task: **Cross-tabulation**
➤ Row Variable: **4) CONF:GOVT**
➤ Column Variable: **1) ETHNICITY**
➤ View: **Tables**
➤ Display: **Column %**

CONF:GOVT   by   ETHNICITY
Weight Variable: WEIGHT2
Cramer's V: 0.277 **

| | | ETHNICITY | | | | | | |
		Hausa	Yoruba	Igbo	Minority	Nigerian	Missing	TOTAL
C O N F : G O V T	Great deal	173	7	11	30	64	0	286
		48.3%	3.6%	7.7%	19.5%	31.7%		27.0%
	A lot	64	11	21	27	25	0	148
		17.9%	5.4%	15.0%	17.3%	12.3%		14.0%
	Not much	66	64	44	44	62	0	281
		18.4%	31.5%	32.1%	28.8%	30.4%		26.5%
	None	55	122	63	53	52	0	344
		15.4%	59.5%	45.2%	34.3%	25.6%		32.5%
	Missing	147	131	50	51	38	3	421
	TOTAL	359	205	138	153	203	3	1058
		100.0%	100.0%	100.0%	100.0%	100.0%		

As you can see, there is a significant difference in the level of trust in government between the Hausa-Fulani and other groups. While overall there is very low confidence in government, it is lowest among those who classify themselves as Yoruba and highest among the northern Hausa-Fulani. Perhaps the differences in Nigerians' level of confidence in government has more to do with their religious identity.

Data File: **WVS97–NIGERIA**
Task: **Cross-tabulation**
Row Variable: **4) CONF:GOVT**
➤ Column Variable: **2) WH RELIG**
➤ View: **Tables**
➤ Display: **Column %**

CONF:GOVT   by   WH RELIG
Weight Variable: WEIGHT2
Cramer's V: 0.197 **

| | | WH RELIG | | | | | | | |
		Catholic	Protestant	Pentecostl	Muslim	Cherubim	Other	Missing	TOTAL
C O N F : G O V T	Great deal	10	10	8	251	2	4	0	285
		8.8%	14.3%	7.1%	36.9%	15.1%	7.3%		27.3%
	A lot	21	11	10	99	1	5	1	146
		17.5%	15.3%	9.6%	14.6%	5.3%	8.3%		14.0%
	Not much	34	26	41	159	4	12	5	276
		29.3%	35.8%	38.4%	23.4%	27.3%	22.0%		26.4%
	None	52	25	47	170	8	35	8	337
		44.3%	34.5%	44.9%	25.1%	52.4%	62.4%		32.3%
	Missing	83	40	51	70	154	14	11	421
	TOTAL	117	72	106	679	15	56	25	1044
		100.0%	100.0%	100.0%	100.0%	100.0%	100.0%		

Religious differences are also significant in the analysis of confidence in government. Muslims tend to trust government more than most of the Christian denominations. Christian denominations have the least trust in government. What about South Africa?

Comparative Politics

► Data File: **WVS97–S.AFRICA**
► Task: **Cross-tabulation**
► Row Variable: **5) CONF:GOVT**
► Column Variable: **1) ETHNIC GRP**
► View: **Tables**
► Display: **Column %**

CONF:GOVT by ETHNIC GRP
Weight Variable: WEIGHT2
Cramer's V: 0.249 **

		ETHNIC GRP				
		Caucasian	Black	S. Asian	Coloured	TOTAL
C O N F : G O V T	Great deal	12	416	7	12	447
		5.3%	41.8%	20.4%	10.7%	32.7%
	A lot	67	375	16	36	493
		30.4%	37.6%	44.7%	31.9%	36.1%
	Not much	87	148	12	50	296
		39.5%	14.8%	32.0%	44.8%	21.7%
	None	55	58	1	14	128
		24.9%	5.9%	2.8%	12.6%	9.4%
	Missing	15	99	2	14	129
	TOTAL	221	997	36	111	1365
		100.0%	100.0%	100.0%	100.0%	

Ethnicity has a significant relationship with confidence in the South African political system. Blacks in South Africa appear to have the highest level of confidence, whereas whites and coloureds have the lowest. For the most part, these groups appear to be much more confident in their government than the citizens of Nigeria are. Does religion show as significant a difference in the level of confidence in government between religious groups?

Data File: **WVS97–S.AFRICA**
Task: **Cross-tabulation**
Row Variable: **5) CONF:GOVT**
► Column Variable: **3) WH RELIG**
► View: **Tables**
► Display: **Column %**

CONF:GOVT by WH RELIG
Weight Variable: WEIGHT2
Cramer's V: 0.064

		WH RELIG						
		None	Catholic	Protestant	Hindu	Other	Missing	TOTAL
C O N F : G O V T	Great deal	45	60	215	5	105	18	429
		31.0%	33.8%	30.1%	22.3%	40.4%		32.6%
	A lot	54	65	264	10	82	20	474
		37.2%	36.6%	36.9%	43.6%	31.5%		36.0%
	Not much	35	41	160	7	47	8	289
		24.0%	22.9%	22.4%	31.3%	18.1%		21.9%
	None	11	12	76	1	26	3	126
		7.7%	6.7%	10.6%	2.7%	10.1%		9.5%
	Missing	13	18	80	1	11	5	129
	TOTAL	145	177	714	22	259	53	1317
		100.0%	100.0%	100.0%	100.0%	100.0%		

The relationship between confidence in the political system and religion is not as strong as the relationship between confidence in government and ethnicity, and there are some interesting differences. All of the main Christian religious groups appear to have relatively more confidence in government than do people of the Hindu faith.

We have already established several things in the preliminary part of this chapter. First, compared to other countries, Nigerians and South Africans have low levels of trust in fellow citizens. Second, compared to South Africans, Nigerians have low levels of trust toward other citizens. Third, the distrust in Nigeria seems to be somewhat related to religious differences (the Islamic Nigerians are more trusting than most other religious groups). Fourth, the Hausa-Fulani are more trusting of fellow citizens than are the Igbo or Yoruba.

If South Africans and Nigerians are to build strong democracies, groups within these societies must work to overcome their mistrust and suspicion of one another.

Workbook exercises and software are copyrighted. Copying is prohibited by law.

REVIEW QUESTIONS

Based on the first part of this chapter, answer True or False to the following items:

1. Nigerians have a lower level of trust in fellow citizens than do South Africans.   T   F

2. Most Hausa-Fulani are Islamic.   T   F

3. The lack of trust between people within the countries of South Africa and Nigeria
    is primarily rooted in religious differences.   T   F

4. In both Nigeria and South Africa, the differences between people in their overall
    confidence in government are ethnic and religious.   T   F

EXPLORIT QUESTIONS

I.   One of the things discussed in this chapter is that if states are going to be democratic, their citizens
     need to trust others in their society. Let's see if we can understand more about interethnic relations in
     Nigeria. Then we'll see if ethnic groups in South Africa differ in terms of trust.

     Use the WVS97–NIGERIA data file and then the WVS97–S.AFRICA file to perform the series of
     cross-tabulations indicated. For each result, fill in the percentaged results *for the row that is specified*
     in the table below. Note that you are also asked to fill in the "total percent" for that row (which indi-
     cates the overall percentage of the respondents who gave that answer to the survey question).
     Finally, indicate whether the results are statistically significant (circle Y for Yes, N for No).

     NIGERIA SURVEY

     > *Data File:* **WVS97–NIGERIA**
     > *Task:* **Cross-tabulation**
     > *Row Variables:* **6) NB:RACE; 7) NB:MUSLIMS, 8) NB:AIDS; 9) NB:CHRIST**
     > *Column Variable:* **1) ETHNICITY**
     > *View:* **Tables**
     > *Display:* **Column %**

     Fill in the table below.

	HAUSA	YORUBA	IGBO	NIGERIAN	TOTAL	SIGNIFI-CANT?
6) NB:RACE % Yes	_____%	_____%	_____%	_____%	_____%	Y N
7) NB:MUSLIMS % Yes	_____%	_____%	_____%	_____%	_____%	Y N
8) NB:AIDS % Yes	_____%	_____%	_____%	_____%	_____%	Y N
9) NB:CHRIST % Yes	_____%	_____%	_____%	_____%	_____%	Y N

5. Which ethnic group in Nigeria is least likely to want to live next door to a person of a different race?   _____

6. Which ethnic group in Nigeria is least likely to mind living next door to a person of a different race?   _____

7. Overall, which ethnic group trusts Muslims the least?   _____

8. Overall, which ethnic group trusts Muslims the most?   _____

9. Which group makes the least desirable neighbor across all ethnic groups?   _____

10. Overall, which ethnic group trusts Christians the least?   _____

11. Overall, which ethnic group trusts Christians the most?   _____

12. Does there seem to be a relationship between ethnicity and social trust in Nigeria?   Yes   No

SOUTH AFRICA SURVEY

➤ *Data File:* **WVS97–S.AFRICA**
➤ *Task:* **Cross-tabulation**
➤ *Row Variables:* **7) NB:RACE; 8) NB:AIDS; 9) NB:BLK; 10) NB:WHITE; 11) NB:CLRD; 12) NB:IND**
➤ *Column Variable:* **1) ETHNIC GRP**
➤ *View:* **Tables**
➤ *Display:* **Column %**

Fill in the table below.

	WHITE	BLACK	ASIAN	COLORED	TOTAL	SIGNIFI-CANT?
7) NB:RACE %Yes	_____%	_____%	_____%	_____%	_____%	Y N
8) NB:AIDS %Yes	_____%	_____%	_____%	_____%	_____%	Y N
9) NB:BLK %Yes	_____%	_____%	_____%	_____%	_____%	Y N
10) NB:WHITE %Yes	_____%	_____%	_____%	_____%	_____%	Y N
11) NB:CLRD %Yes	_____%	_____%	_____%	_____%	_____%	Y N
12) NB:IND %Yes	_____%	_____%	_____%	_____%	_____%	Y N

Let's say that living next door to someone of a different race is an indicator of trust. Consider the following questions:

13. In South Africa, which ethnic group is least trusting of blacks? _____

14. In South Africa, which ethnic group is least trusting of whites? _____

15. In South Africa, which ethnic group is least trusting of coloureds? _____

16. In South Africa, which ethnic group is least trusting of Indians? _____

17. Based on these results, which ethnic group in South Africa appears to have the least trust among its own ethnic group? _____

18. Overall, which ethnic group is least trusted in South Africa? _____

19. Overall, does there seem to be a relationship between ethnicity and social trust in South Africa? Yes   No

II. Another significant issue involved in state-building, or the promotion of strong democracies, is the legitimacy of the government. This can be undermined by corruption, bribery, and self-interested leadership. Thus, stable government will be more likely to endure where government officials resist bribery, corruption, or ruling in the interest of a few. Often leaders and civil servants in governments will seek to give one group an advantage over other groups. Groups that are oppressed by unjust governments may also be more willing to engage in violent behavior than citizens whose governments treat them fairly. Let's examine the extent to which ethnicity or religion may affect citizens' views on bribery, corruption, and governing in Nigeria and South Africa. For each result, fill in the percentaged results for the row that is specified in the table below. Also, indicate whether the results are statistically significant (circle Y for Yes, N for No).

NIGERIA SURVEY (ethnicity)

➤ *Data File:* **WVS97–NIGERIA**
➤ *Task:* **Cross-tabulation**
➤ *Row Variables:* **10) BRIBERY; 11) CORRUPTION; 12) WHO RULES?**
➤ *Column Variable:* **1) ETHNICITY**
➤ *View:* **Tables**
➤ *Display:* **Column %**

Fill in the table below.

	HAUSA	YORUBA	IGBO	NIGERIAN	V =	SIGNIFI-CANT?
10) BRIBERY %Never	_____%	_____%	_____%	_____%	_____	Y N
11) CORRUPTION %All	_____%	_____%	_____%	_____%	_____	Y N
12) WHO RULES? %All	_____%	_____%	_____%	_____%	_____	Y N

20. Do ethnic groups in Nigeria differ significantly in all three areas?   Yes   No

21. Which ethnic group is least likely to think bribery is never justified?   _____

22. Which ethnic group is most likely to think bribery is never justified?   _____

23. Which ethnic group is least likely to believe that all politicians are involved in corruption?   _____

24. Which ethnic group is most likely to think the government rules for the benefit of all citizens?   _____

25. Which ethnic group is least likely to think the government rules for the benefit of all citizens?   _____

NIGERIA SURVEY (religion)

Data File:	**WVS97–NIGERIA**
Task:	**Cross-tabulation**
Row Variables:	**10) BRIBERY; 11) CORRUPTION; 12) WHO RULES?**
➤ *Column Variable:*	**2) WH RELIG**
➤ *View:*	**Tables**
➤ *Display:*	**Column %**

Fill in the table below.

	CATHOLIC	PROT.	PENT	MUSLIM	CHERUBIM	SIGNIFI-CANT?
10) BRIBERY %Never	_____%	_____%	_____%	_____%	_____%	Y N
11) CORRUPTION %All	_____%	_____%	_____%	_____%	_____%	Y N
12) WHO RULES? %All	_____%	_____%	_____%	_____%	_____%	Y N

26. Do religious groups in Nigeria differ significantly in all three areas?   Yes   No

27. Which religious group is most likely to think bribery is never justified?   _____

28. Which religious group is least likely to believe that all politicians are involved in corruption?   _____

29. Which religious group is most likely to believe that all politicians are involved in corruption?   _____

30. Which religious group is most likely to think the government rules for the benefit of all citizens?   _____

31. Which religious group is least likely to think the government rules for the benefit of all citizens?   _____

Now use the WVS97–S.AFRICA file to do the same analysis.

SOUTH AFRICA SURVEY (ethnicity)

➤ *Data File:*	**WVS97–S.AFRICA**
➤ *Task:*	**Cross-tabulation**
➤ *Row Variables:*	**13) BRIBERY; 14) CORRUPTION; 15) WHO RULES?**
➤ *Column Variable:*	**1) ETHNIC GRP**
➤ *View:*	**Tables**
➤ *Display:*	**Column %**

Fill in the table below.

	WHITE	BLACK	ASIAN	COLORED	SIGNIFICANT?
13) BRIBERY %Never	_____%	_____%	_____%	_____%	Y N
14) CORRUPTION %All	_____%	_____%	_____%	_____%	Y N
15) WHO RULES? %All	_____%	_____%	_____%	_____%	Y N

32. Do ethnic groups in South Africa differ significantly in all three areas? Yes   No

33. Which ethnic group is most likely to think bribery is never justified? _____

34. Which ethnic group is least likely to believe that all politicians are involved in corruption? _____

35. Which ethnic group is most likely to think the government rules for the benefit of all citizens? _____

36. Which ethnic group is least likely to think the government rules for the benefit of all citizens? _____

SOUTH AFRICA SURVEY (religion)

Data File:	**WVS97–S.AFRICA**
Task:	**Cross-tabulation**
Row Variables:	**13) BRIBERY; 14) CORRUPTION; 15) WHO RULES?**
➤ Column Variable:	**3) WH RELIG**
➤ View:	**Tables**
➤ Display:	**Column %**

Fill in the table below.

	NONE	CATHOLIC	PROTESTANT	HINDU	OTHER	SIGNIFI-CANT?
13) BRIBERY % Never	_____%	_____%	_____%	_____%	_____%	Y N
14) CORRUPTION % All	_____%	_____%	_____%	_____%	_____%	Y N
15) WHO RULES? % All	_____%	_____%	_____%	_____%	_____%	Y N

37. Do religious groups in South Africa differ significantly in all three areas?   Yes   No

38. Which religious group is most likely to think bribery is never justified?   _____

39. Which religious group is least likely to believe that all politicians are involved
    in corruption?   _____

40. Which religious group is most likely to believe that all politicians are involved
    in corruption?   _____

IN YOUR OWN WORDS

In your own words, please answer the following questions.

1. Assume that people in South Africa vote solely on the basis of the ethnicities they trust. If all ethnic groups in South Africa were of equal size, which ethnic groups would probably do poorly in national elections? Explain your answer in a short paragraph using the data you obtained in this analysis. (Hint: Do not rely on the "Total %""column for your answer. Since ethnic groups would be of equal size, you need to average the scores for each row and then compare those results.)

2. Based on the analyses in the last part of the chapter and Part I of the worksheets, does ethnicity or religion better explain the differences in citizens' trust in Nigeria? in South Africa? Compare and contrast these two countries in your answer. If there is a difference between the two countries, try to explain why this might be the case.

3. In a brief paragraph, discuss whether you think ethnicity or religion plays a bigger role in South Africa and Nigeria in terms of one's view toward corruption, bribery, and governing. Also discuss why you think the ethnic group least opposed to bribery, least inclined to believe that government leaders are corrupt, and most inclined to believe that government rules in the interest of all feels this way.

Central and South America

MEXICO

Gulf of Mexico

THE BAHAMAS

CUBA

DOM. REP.

JAMAICA

BELIZE HAITI

HONDURAS

GUATEMALA

NICARAGUA

EL SALVADOR

PANAMA

COSTA RICA

TRINIDAD & TOBAGO

VENEZUELA

GUYANA

SURINAME

FRENCH GUIANA

COLOMBIA

ECUADOR

PERU

BRAZIL

Pacific Ocean

BOLIVIA

PARAGUAY

CHILE

URUGUAY

ARGENTINA

Atlantic Ocean

CHAPTER **15**

AUTHORITY PATTERNS IN MEXICO AND BRAZIL

We are building this nation, as in putting pieces of broken glass together.

JEAN-BERTRANDE ARISTIDE, 1995,
FORMER PRESIDENT, HAITI

Tasks: Mapping, Historical Trends, Cross-tabulation, Univariate, Correlation, Scatterplot
Data Files: GLOBAL, LATIN, HISTORY, WVS97–BRAZIL, WVS97–MEXICO, WVS97all, WVS97–USA

Unlike most other regions in our study, the Americas are relatively homogeneous from a cultural and linguistic perspective. Had Europe not colonized this so-called New World, this region would likely be far more diverse than it is today. Let's examine cultural diversity in South America using the GLOBAL file.

> *Data File:* **GLOBAL**
> *Task:* **Mapping**
> *Variable 1:* **15) MULTI-CULT**
> *View:* **Map**
> *Display:* **Legend**

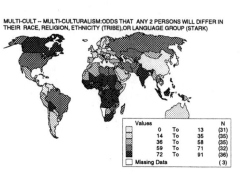

MULTI-CULT -- MULTI-CULTURALISM:ODDS THAT ANY 2 PERSONS WILL DIFFER IN THEIR RACE, RELIGION, ETHNICITY (TRIBE),OR LANGUAGE GROUP (STARK)

Values			N
0	To	13	(31)
14	To	35	(35)
36	To	58	(35)
59	To	71	(32)
72	To	91	(36)
Missing Data			(3)

Countries in South and Central America are much less diverse than those in Africa, but not quite as homogeneous as European nations. The exceptional countries are those highlighted in brown, such as Bolivia and Suriname, which have very large, diverse indigenous populations. European colonizers decimated the indigenous populations with warfare and disease, so now with a few exceptions, most of the inhabitants of this continent speak Spanish, or Portuguese, or English. The nations that colonized South and Central America are very different from those that colonized Africa. We can see the pattern of colonizing nations by examining the LATIN file.

> *Data File:* **LATIN**
> *Task:* **Mapping**
> *Variable 1:* **19) COLONIZE**
> *View:* **Map**
> *Display:* **Legend**

Category	N
Spain	(20)
Portugal	(1)
Britain	(3)
France	(2)
Netherland	(1)
Missing Data	

The Americas were the first region to be colonized by Europeans. Beginning in the 15th century, the Spanish and Portuguese kingdoms competed fiercely to secure the most land in the New World. Before all of the land had even been fully explored, the pope managed to prod the Portuguese and the Spanish into a treaty dividing up "all heathen lands 500 miles to the west of the Azores islands." This left Spain with most of the land in the Americas and Portugal with the region that is present-day Brazil. The British laid claim to North America. In 1519, Hernando Cortes arrived in Mexico from Cuba and began the brutal conquest of the Aztec empire. Farther south, Francisco Pizarro conquered Peru for Spain in 1531. Both efforts at conquest took years, and the native peoples lost hundreds of thousands of lives during the violent wars and counter-rebellions. Spain and Portugal dominated the Southwestern Hemisphere through the beginning of the 19th century. Between 1800 and 1825, the world witnessed the first collapse of a global empire. During this remarkable period of time, the empires of Spain, Britain, and Portugal all lost hold of most of their New World possessions.

IND DATE: Year of independence

Data File: **LATIN**
Task: **Mapping**
> *Variable 1:* **17) IND DATE**
> *View:* **List: Rank**

RANK	CASE NAME	VALUE
1	Belize	1981
2	Suriname	1975
3	Bahamas	1973
4	Barbados	1966
4	Guyana	1966
6	Trinidad & Tobago	1962
6	Jamaica	1962
8	Panama	1903
9	Cuba	1902
10	Dominican Republic	1844

As you can see from the ranking, all but a few of the major countries in South America were "liberated" between 1810 and 1828. This 18-year period also corresponds to the demise of the Spanish empire, which began more than 100 years earlier with the defeat of the Spanish fleet in 1688. Caribbean island possessions of Spain, such as Cuba, were retained much longer because they were easier to hold than the vast land masses of South and Central America. Six of the 27 countries in the southern part of the Americas—Suriname, Dominican Republic, Haiti, Jamaica, Guyana, and Belize—were colonized by Britain, France, and the Netherlands. These colonies were held until after World War II in a pattern similar to what was done in Africa and Asia. Knowledge of this pattern of independence helps us to understand the historical trend of independence.

➤ *Data File:* **HISTORY**
    ➤ *Task:* **Historical Trends**
➤ *Variables:* **3) IND/DECADE**

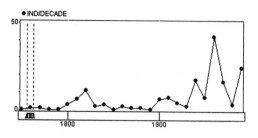

Number of independent nations each decade

If you scroll through the event file, you will notice that the Latin American wars of independence correspond to a sharp rise in the number of countries that became independent in the early 1820s.

The original colonizers came to the Americas seeking gold, but what they found instead were vast tracts of rich pasture land that became important in the plantation and ranching economies that developed during the 19th and 20th centuries.

➤ *Data File:* **GLOBAL**
    ➤ *Task:* **Mapping**
➤ *Variable 1:* **6) %MEAD-PAST**
      ➤ *View:* **Map**
    ➤ *Display:* **Legend**

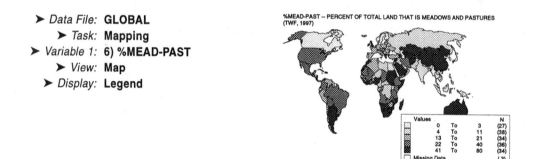

Argentina, Paraguay, Uruguay, Mexico, and much of Central America developed an extensive agricultural economy during the 19th century.

In addition to farmland, the forests of South America have proven to be one of the most valuable resources of the region.

Data File: **GLOBAL**
    Task: **Mapping**
➤ *Variable 1:* **7) %FOR-WOOD**
    ➤ *View:* **Map**
    ➤ *Display:* **Legend**

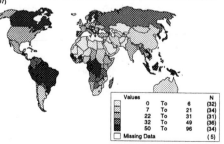

These natural resources and abundant land led most countries to organize themselves for agricultural production. While not as extensive as in Africa or Asia, a considerable percentage of the labor force in South and Central America still works in the agricultural sector of the economy.

> *Data File:* **LATIN**
>> *Task:* **Mapping**
> *Variable 1:* **13) %GDP AGR**
> *Variable 2:* **10) GDPCAP PPP**
>> *Views:* **Map**
>> *Display:* **Legend**

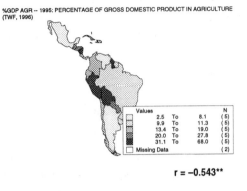

%GDP AGR -- 1995: PERCENTAGE OF GROSS DOMESTIC PRODUCT IN AGRICULTURE (TWF, 1996)

Values			N
2.5	To	8.1	(5)
9.9	To	11.3	(5)
13.4	To	19.0	(5)
20.0	To	27.8	(5)
31.1	To	68.0	(5)
Missing Data			(2)

r = –0.543**

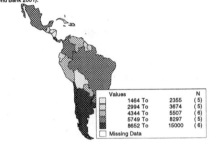

GDPCAP PPP -- Gross Domestic Product per capita based on purchasing power parity (World Bank 2001).

Values			N
1464	To	2355	(5)
2994	To	3674	(5)
4344	To	5507	(6)
5749	To	8297	(5)
8652	To	15000	(6)
Missing Data			

This continued organization of life around agricultural production is one of the factors that has been responsible for the continued poverty of the region. You will notice that the more a country's economy is agriculturally based, the more likely it is to be poor. The poorest countries have been those that have had difficulty making the transition to industry.

The life of a peasant farmer in South and Central America is extremely difficult. We can use the LATIN file to see the pattern of land ownership.

LANDOWNERS: 80 percent of total farmland is owned by:
1 = up to 55% of the farms, 2 = up to 30% of the farms,
3 = less than 20% of the farms

> *Data File:* **LATIN**
>> *Task:* **Mapping**
> *Variable 1:* **20) LANDOWNERS**
>> *View:* **List: Rank**

RANK	CASE NAME	VALUE
1	El Salvador	<20%
1	Guatemala	<20%
1	Dominican Republic	<20%
1	Ecuador	<20%
5	Chile	<30%
5	Colombia	<30%
5	Peru	<30%
8	Uruguay	<55%
8	Panama	<55%
8	Mexico	<55%

In El Salvador, Guatemala, Dominican Republic, and Ecuador, more than 80% of the farmland is owned by less than 20% of the farmers. Eighty percent of the land is owned by less than 30% of the farmers in Chile, Colombia, and Peru. This pattern of ownership means that many farmers are left to subsist on hillside plots or plots too small to produce enough for their families while wealthy farmers control vast tracts of fertile land. In the past, this disparity of land ownership has led to more serious consequences in the distribution of overall wealth. The variable 14) $ RICH 10% describes how much of a nation's income is received by the richest 10% of the population.

$ RICH 10%: Percentage of national income received by the richest 10 percent

Data File: **LATIN**
Task: **Mapping**
➤ Variable 1: **14) $ RICH 10%**
➤ View: **List: Rank**

RANK	CASE NAME	VALUE
1	Ecuador	51.5
2	Honduras	50.6
3	Brazil	48.3
4	Panama	44.2
5	Colombia	43.5
6	Guatemala	42.1
7	Dominican Republic	41.7
8	Mexico	40.6
9	Costa Rica	39.8
10	Venezuela	35.7

The first thing you will notice is that in a few countries 10% of the population receives more than half of the national income. This means that in a country like Ecuador, 90% of the people divide up 48.5% of the national income.

In spite of these difficulties, South and Central America are increasingly characterized by growing political and economic stability. In the period 1990–96, the Americas in the Western Hemisphere experienced a relatively low incidence of war compared to Africa and the Middle East.[1]

➤ Data File: **GLOBAL**
➤ Task: **Cross-tabulation**
➤ Row Variable: **73) WAR**
➤ Column Variable: **11) REGION2**
➤ View: **Tables**
➤ Display: **Column %**

WAR by REGION2
Cramer's V: 0.185
Warning: Potential significance problem. Check row and column totals.

		Africa	Mid. East	Asia/Pacif	West.Hemi	Europe	TOTAL
WAR	None	23	5	23	17	29	97
		45.1%	35.7%	57.5%	58.6%	76.3%	56.4%
	Interstate	3	3	2	2	3	13
		5.9%	21.4%	5.0%	6.9%	7.9%	7.6%
	Civil War	21	5	12	9	3	50
		41.2%	35 7%	30.0%	31.0%	7.9%	29.1%
	Indepndnce	2	0	0	0	0	2
		3.9%	0.0%	0.0%	0.0%	0.0%	1.2%
	Multi-type	2	1	3	1	3	10
		3.9%	7.1%	7.5%	3.4%	7.9%	5.8%
	TOTAL	51	14	40	29	38	172
		100.0%	100.0%	100.0%	100.0%	100.0%	

---

[1] As in Chapters 3, 8, 11, and 13, there are a few instances in this chapter where the cross-tabulation result using the GLOBAL or LATIN file produces the statement "Warning: Potential significance problem." This is to alert you that the statistical significance value may not be reliable due to the small number of countries used in the analysis. The likelihood of this warning message appearing will also increase as the number of cells in the table increases—the greater the number of cells, the more likely the warning message will appear. For our purposes in this chapter, we will often ignore this warning.

You will notice that the Western Hemisphere (South America + Central America + Mexico, the United States, and Canada) had a relatively high level of peace in the region. However, the wars that did exist during the period 1990–96 were civil in character. Most of these wars were holdovers from repressive authoritarian governments of the 1960s and 70s and the revolutionary movements that opposed them. The variable 31) GOVT 1978 in the LATIN file indicates the type of government each country had in the 1970s.

➤ *Data File:* **LATIN**
  ➤ *Task:* **Mapping**
➤ *Variable 1:* **31) GOVT 1978**
➤ *Variable 2:* **23) INSURGENCY**
  ➤ *Views:* **Map**
  ➤ *Display:* **Legend**

GOVT 1978 -- TYPE OF GOVERNMENT IN 1978 (FITW, 1979) 1=DEMOCRATIC OR NEWLY DEMOCRATIC; 2=MILITARY DICTATORSHIP OR ONE PARTY SYSTEM

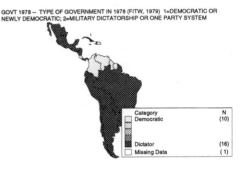

Category	N
Democratic	(10)
Dictator	(16)
Missing Data	(1)

r = 0.355*

INSURGENCY -- INSURGENCIES DURING 1975-1995: 1=NONE, 2=MINOR INSURGENCY, 3=MAJOR INSURGENCY (SWPA, 1997)

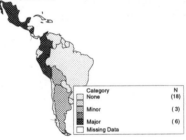

Category	N
None	(18)
Minor	(3)
Major	(6)
Missing Data	

You will notice that most of the continent was governed by nondemocratic regimes in 1978. This resulted in a number of insurgencies, or civil wars, against these governments.

Most countries with insurgency movements within them also had repressive political regimes in the 1970s. This violent, and often highly ideological, conflict resulted in serious abuses of human rights that continue to this day in spite of the fact that most countries have now embraced democracy. The HUMAN RTS variable indicates the type of human rights abuses perpetrated by a government.

    Data File: **LATIN**
      ➤ *Task:* **Univariate**
➤ *Primary Variable:* **24) HUMAN RTS**
       ➤ *View:* **Pie**

HUMAN RTS -- ABUSE OF HUMAN RIGHTS: 1=NONE, 2=MISTREATMENT BY POLICE, 3=ARBITRARY ARREST/DETENTION, 4=TORTURE, 5=EXTRAJUDICIAL EXECUTIONS (SWPA, 1997)

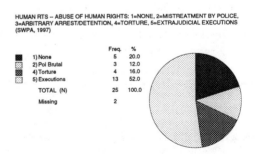

	Freq.	%
1) None	5	20.0
2) Pol Brutal	3	12.0
4) Torture	4	16.0
5) Executions	13	52.0
TOTAL (N)	25	100.0
Missing	2	

As you can see, the legacy of authoritarianism and violent conflict in South American countries has persisted beyond the 1970s. Only 20% of countries in South America do not have complaints of some sort against their government. Fifty-two percent of all governments in the 1990s continue to use extra-judicial executions, which are executions without a trial. These same governments often use torture, arbitrary arrest, and harassment to silence their political opponents. While violent conflict may at one time have been ideologically inspired, violence in South and Central America is now often related to the drug trade.

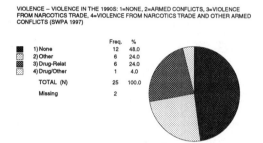

Data File:	**LATIN**
Task:	**Univariate**
➤ Primary Variable:	**25) VIOLENCE**
➤ View:	**Pie**

VIOLENCE -- VIOLENCE IN THE 1990S: 1=NONE, 2=ARMED CONFLICTS, 3=VIOLENCE FROM NARCOTICS TRADE, 4=VIOLENCE FROM NARCOTICS TRADE AND OTHER ARMED CONFLICTS (SWPA 1997)

		Freq.	%
■	1) None	12	48.0
▨	2) Other	6	24.0
▤	3) Drug-Relat	6	24.0
▦	4) Drug/Other	1	4.0
	TOTAL (N)	25	100.0
	Missing	2	

Forty-eight percent of countries in South and Central America experienced no organized violence, but almost one-third of the countries that now do experience some type of organized violence experience this as a direct result of the drug trade. In spite of these difficulties, the overwhelming trend is toward multiparty democracy and away from authoritarian forms of political organization.

Data File:	**LATIN**
➤ Task:	**Mapping**
➤ Variable 1:	**32) GOVERNMENT**
➤ View:	**Map**

GOVERNMENT -- GOVERNMENT: THE NATURE OF GOVERNMENT AND POLITICS (KIDRON & SEGAL, 1995)

You will notice that there are now no governments in Central and South America directly controlled by military dictators. In fact, the least democratic governments are the one-party states of Cuba and Mexico. This is not to say that many of the new democracies don't also struggle in the efforts to become more democratic. But it is astonishing to see so much change between 1978 and the present.

Scholars have debated whether international conflicts, such as the Cold War, were responsible for these wars or whether authoritarianism is endemic to South American culture. While the specific form of government is no longer authoritarian, the political culture continues to be very traditional and quite conducive to authoritarian forms of political and social organization.

AUTHORITY IN BRAZIL AND MEXICO

One leading scholar of comparative politics has suggested that authority patterns in politics mirror authority patterns found at other social levels. Political scientist Harry Eckstein argued that one of the reasons democracy failed in Germany during the 1920s was that the organization of political parties, churches, labor unions, and even the family remained hierarchical and authoritarian despite having an extremely democratic political system. That citizens' social organization remained very authoritarian despite the fact that the government became democratic eventually undermined democracy in Germany and led to the popular embrace of national socialism under Hitler. The same hypothesis that applied to Germany could be tested in the context of South and Central America. We will examine two countries Brazil and Mexico) with different political histories to determine whether or not "authority patterns" in society reflect democratic or authoritarian tendencies.

BRAZIL

Brazil has a fascinating political history that extends from Portuguese colonial domination to monarchy, military dictatorship, and democracy. Perhaps the most influential figure in Brazilian history, General Getulio Vargas seized power from 1930 to 1945 and mixed heavy-handed authoritarian political rule with populist handouts for the labor unions and working class. In the wake of Vargas' rule, authoritarian militarism coupled with populism has dominated elite thought and practice. Throughout the 1960s and 70s, a military junta dominated the political life of Brazil. As long as this regime produced prosperity, Brazilians endured political oppression and denial of civil liberties. Between 1965 and 1973, Brazil grew at a rapid pace by borrowing heavily. However, an economic crisis in the early 1970s began to shake the legitimacy of the military junta, and the military decided that it would engage in a gradual process of reform. The junta allowed an indirect democratic election in 1985, and a direct popular election in 1989.

Political instability and heavy borrowing by military and civilian governments have led to a debt crisis of severe proportions in Brazil.

➤ *Data File:* **GLOBAL**
➤ *Task:* **Mapping**
➤ *Variable 1:* **44) EXT.DEBT**
➤ *View:* **Map**
➤ *Display:* **Legend**

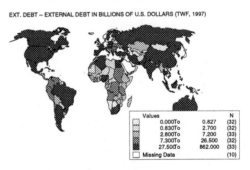

EXT. DEBT -- EXTERNAL DEBT IN BILLIONS OF U.S. DOLLARS (TWF, 1997)

Values		N
0.000To	0.827	(32)
0.830To	2.700	(32)
2.800To	7.200	(33)
7.300To	26.500	(32)
27.50To	862.000	(33)
Missing Data		(10)

Thanks to this legacy, Brazil is now the third highest external debtor in the world. Neither the military nor the civilian governments managed the economy very well between the late 1940s and the early 1990s, which only increased poverty and human suffering.

In rankings of civil liberties, Brazil still has some room for improvement.

Data File: **GLOBAL**
Task: **Mapping**
➤ Variable 1: **59) CIV LIBS**
➤ View: **Map**
➤ Display: **Find case: Brazil**

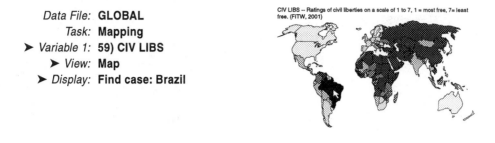

CIV LIBS -- Ratings of civil liberties on a scale of 1 to 7, 1 = most free, 7= least free. (FITW, 2001)

BRAZIL (3)

Brazil is given a rating of 3 on civil liberties because of the role that the police and the military still play in the harassment of civilians. In 1992 alone, the Sao Paulo police killed 1,470 people, accounting for one-third of all homicides in the state. Despite all of these problems, the government has endured democratic transition of power from one president to the next without serious problems since 1985.

MEXICO

The current constitutional government of Mexico dates back to the 1910 revolution against the dictator Porfirio Diaz. While Mexican mythology indicates that the revolution was an uprising of the poor masses, it was in fact orchestrated by liberal elites. By the end of the revolution, popular heroes of the revolution like Pancho Villa and Emiliano Zapata were assassinated and elite control was restored to benefit middle- and upper-class industrialists. Beginning in the 1930s, Mexico experienced the rule of a succession of authoritarian presidents from the single party that consolidated power after the revolution. Until the year 2000 the PRI (*Partido Revolucionario Institucional*) dominated the political landscape, winning every presidential election since 1929. Using its vast financial resources, dominance of state-owned media, and often corrupt election practices, the PRI has been able to effectively neutralize opposition to its hand-picked successors to the previous presidents.

In recent years the dominance of the PRI in the political system began to erode. In 1994 a small group of disciplined Indians living in the impoverished state of Chiapas seized control of some small towns and declared war against the "corrupt government." This action drew international attention to the lack of democratic competition and the corruption of the Mexican political system that shamed President Carlos Salinas de Gortari into instituting election reforms. Political parties that sought to challenge the PRI also drew attention to corruption in local areas where PRI votes exceeded the number of eligible voters in a region. The PRI candidate for president—Ernesto Zedillo— received 48.9% of the votes in the 1994 election (dubbed the cleanest in Mexican history by election observers). Three years after the election, the World Values Survey picked up on this downward trend in the PRI fortunes.

> *Data File:* **WVS97–MEXICO**
> *Task:* **Univariate**
> *Primary Variable:* **1) PARTY #1**
> *View:* **Bar - Freq.**

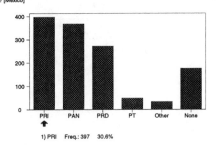

PARTY #1 -- If there were a national election tomorrow, for which party on this list would you vote? [Mexico]

1) PRI   Freq.: 397   30.6%

In 1997 only 30.6% of the population supported the PRI. By 2000 PAN (translated Party of National Action) presidential candidate Vincente Fox Quesada overthrew the longest standing streak of party dominance in the Western Hemisphere with his victory in the election. Fox, a former executive for Coca-Cola, is committed to market reform and is currently initiating significant reform in the Mexican political and economic systems.

AUTHORITY PATTERNS

The fact that Mexicans desire change more urgently than citizens of more advanced industrial democracies is apparent in the analysis of a question from the World Values Survey. People in each country were asked whether or not they thought that society should be changed by revolutionary action or defended at all costs.

> *Data File:* **WVS97all**
> *Task:* **Cross-tabulation**
> *Row Variable:* **6) SOCIET CHG**
> *Column Variable:* **1) COUNTRY**
> *View:* **Tables**
> *Display:* **Column %**

SOCIET CHG   by   COUNTRY
Cramer's V: 0.261 **

| | | COUNTRY | | | | | | | | |
		Germany	USA	Japan	Russia	S Korea	Mexico	Turkey	Nigeria	TOTAL
SOCIET CHG	Radical	83	68	29	198	146	173	390	811	1898
		4.2%	4.8%	3.5%	10.9%	12.5%	12.8%	21.2%	31.6%	14.7%
	Reform	1722	1059	593	1511	644	783	1010	1350	8672
		87.1%	75.3%	72.6%	82.9%	55.2%	57.9%	55.0%	52.5%	67.0%
	Defend	171	279	195	114	376	397	436	409	2377
		8.7%	19.8%	23.9%	6.3%	32.2%	29.3%	23.7%	15.9%	18.4%
	Missing	50	136	237	217	83	157	71	199	1150
	TOTAL	1976	1406	817	1823	1166	1353	1836	2570	12947
		100.0%	100.0%	100.0%	100.0%	100.0%	100.0%	100.0%	100.0%	

In the analysis of this cross-tabulation you can see that Koreans, Mexicans, Turks, and Nigerians most strongly desire radical change. This pattern suggests a relatively high degree of dissatisfaction with political authority in these four countries. What is the source of this dissatisfaction?

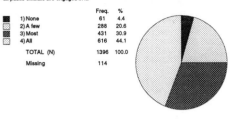

> *Data File:* **WVS97–MEXICO**
> *Task:* **Univariate**
> *Primary Variable:* **2) CORRUPTION**
> *View:* **Pie**

One of the sources of dissatisfaction with political authority is the widespread corruption of the government and those who work for the government. Of the Mexican population sampled, 44.1% believes that all public officials engage in corruption. Only 4.4% are willing to say that none of the public officials participate in corrupt activities. What is the state of public perception of corruption in Brazil?

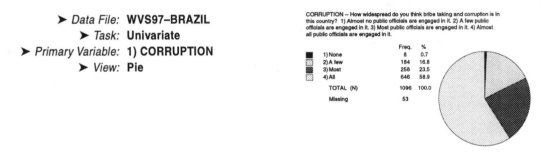

> *Data File:* **WVS97–BRAZIL**
> *Task:* **Univariate**
> *Primary Variable:* **1) CORRUPTION**
> *View:* **Pie**

Public suspicion of corruption may be high in Mexico, but in Brazil it is even higher. A full 58.9% of the population believes that all public officials are corrupt. Less than 1% of the population is even willing to say that no one in public life is corrupt.

Another way to examine popular attitudes toward the authority of government is to assess the extent to which citizens express the opinion that people should have more respect for authority. In this analysis we will compare Mexico and Brazil to the United States.

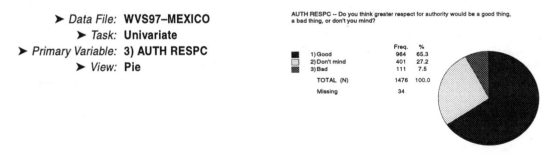

> *Data File:* **WVS97–MEXICO**
> *Task:* **Univariate**
> *Primary Variable:* **3) AUTH RESPC**
> *View:* **Pie**

In the analysis of respect for authority in Mexico, we see that a majority (65.3%) think that respect for authority is generally a good thing.

➤ *Data File:* **WVS97–BRAZIL**
➤ *Task:* **Univariate**
➤ *Primary Variable:* **2) AUTH RESPC**
➤ *View:* **Pie**

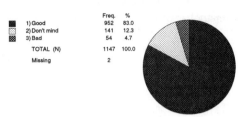

AUTH RESPC -- Do you think greater respect for authority would be a good thing, a bad thing, or don't you mind?

	Freq.	%
1) Good	952	83.0
2) Don't mind	141	12.3
3) Bad	54	4.7
TOTAL (N)	1147	100.0
Missing	2	

In Brazil 83% of the population think that respect for authority is good, but let's compare both Mexico's and Brazil's percentages to that of the United States.

➤ *Data File:* **WVS97-USA**
➤ *Task:* **Univariate**
➤ *Primary Variable:* **13) AUTH RESPC**
➤ *View:* **Pie**

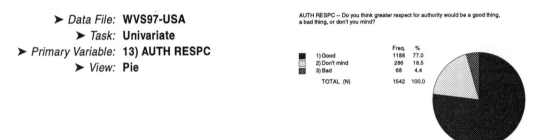

AUTH RESPC -- Do you think greater respect for authority would be a good thing, a bad thing, or don't you mind?

	Freq.	%
1) Good	1188	77.0
2) Don't mind	286	18.5
3) Bad	68	4.4
TOTAL (N)	1542	100.0

Interpreting these results is tricky, but it is clear that in the United States, more people believe that respect for authority is a good thing than those who live in Mexico. But it is possible that this difference is due to the fact that Americans think the lack of respect for authority among its own citizens is a serious problem. It is also possible that Mexicans are reacting to a legacy of too much respect for authority. It is also clear that Brazilians have the highest level of respect for authority. Whether this is the legacy of military dominance or some other factor needs further exploration.

Another variable that might help us to understand citizens' respect for authority is the extent to which the citizens of a country would fight for their country if called on.

➤ *Data File:* **WVS97–MEXICO**
➤ *Task:* **Univariate**
➤ *Primary Variable:* **4) FIGHT WAR?**
➤ *View:* **Pie**

FIGHT WAR? -- Of course, we all hope that there will not be another war, but if it were to come to that, would you be willing to fight for your country?

	Freq.	%
1) Yes	889	73.0
2) No	329	27.0
TOTAL (N)	1218	100.0
Missing	292	

In Mexico a clear majority of citizens would respond to the call to fight for their country. What about Brazilians?

Comparative Politics

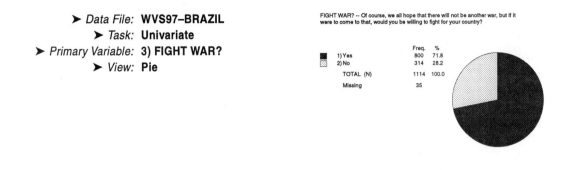

➤ *Data File:* **WVS97–BRAZIL**
➤ *Task:* **Univariate**
➤ *Primary Variable:* **3) FIGHT WAR?**
➤ *View:* **Pie**

FIGHT WAR? -- Of course, we all hope that there will not be another war, but if it were to come to that, would you be willing to fight for your country?

		Freq.	%
■	1) Yes	800	71.8
▨	2) No	314	28.2
	TOTAL (N)	1114	100.0
	Missing	35	

Brazil is nearly the same as Mexico. Does the United States have the same level of support?

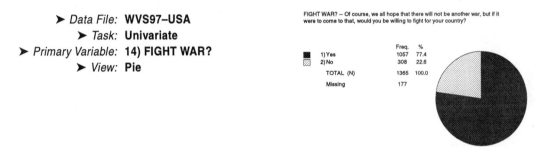

➤ *Data File:* **WVS97–USA**
➤ *Task:* **Univariate**
➤ *Primary Variable:* **14) FIGHT WAR?**
➤ *View:* **Pie**

FIGHT WAR? -- Of course, we all hope that there will not be another war, but if it were to come to that, would you be willing to fight for your country?

		Freq.	%
■	1) Yes	1057	77.4
▨	2) No	308	22.6
	TOTAL (N)	1365	100.0
	Missing	177	

In the United States a very large percentage of the population appears willing to fight if called on. Again we see that U.S. citizens appear just as inclined to be the "authoritarians" as Brazilians and Mexicans. In either case, it seems that citizens of Brazil and Mexico are more dissatisfied with their social circumstances than most countries in our comparison. In the worksheet section you will examine the extent to which citizens from Mexico and Argentina have confidence in their social and political institutions.

WORKSHEET

NAME: _____

COURSE: _____

DATE: _____

CHAPTER
15

REVIEW QUESTIONS

Based on the first part of this chapter, answer True or False to the following items:

1. Most of the Americas were first colonized by Britain.   T   F

2. The liberation of Latin America occurred at the same time as the American Revolution.   T   F

3. The Spanish colonies of the New World were "liberated" by the British and French.   T   F

4. There were more military dictatorships in South and Central America during the 1970s than there are today.   T   F

5. In recent years, government use of torture and summary executions have not been a problem in South and Central America.   T   F

6. Brazilian history has featured political leadership that is both authoritarian and populist.   T   F

7. Because of their authoritarian heritage, citizens of Mexico and Brazil seem to have a higher level of respect for authority than people in the United States.   T   F

8. Mexicans are more likely than Brazilians to believe that their politicians are corrupt.   T   F

9. Mexicans are more likely to fight for their country than are Brazilians.   T   F

10. Americans are less likely to fight for their country than are Mexicans or Brazilians.   T   F

EXPLORIT QUESTIONS

As discussed in the previous chapter, most governments in Latin America have become democratic over the past 20 years. However, these countries have also struggled to solve their most pressing problems, which often stem from the elite abuse of power and position to gain material advantages. The organization Transparency International studies corruption in government and has generated an index that measures the degree of corruption in a society. Open the GLOBAL file and look at the variable description for 72) NO CORRUPT.

11. Write down the main description of this variable.

_____

_____

_____

12. What would be the value for a country without any corruption?   Value = _____

13. What would be the value for a country that is completely corrupt?   Value = _____

> ➤ *Data File:* **GLOBAL**
> ➤ *Task:* **Mapping**
> ➤ *Variable 1:* **72) NO CORRUPT**
> ➤ *View:* **List: Rank**

14. What is the TI rating and ranking for corruption in Brazil?

          RATING   **RANKING**

       _____   _____

15. What is the TI rating and ranking for corruption in Mexico?

          RATING   **RANKING**

       _____   _____

16. Describe any regional patterns that exist for this variable.

II. So far in this workbook the SCATTERPLOT and MAPPING tasks have been used to produce correlation coefficients (r) between two variables. However, sometimes it is desirable to correlate three or more variables at a time. ExplorIt's CORRELATION task allows you to select several variables at once and then it produces a table that shows the correlation coefficients for each pair of variables. Of course, the correlation results for any pair of variables will match those produced with the MAPPING and SCATTERPLOT tasks. The CORRELATION task simply saves several steps and allows you to view several correlation results in one table.

Use ExplorIt's CORRELATION task to examine the extent to which corruption is associated with economic inequality and voter turnout in the Western Hemisphere. Since the GLOBAL data file is being used, the analysis will need to be limited to the Western Hemisphere using the [Subset] option.

Data File: **GLOBAL**
➤ Task: **Correlation**
➤ Variables: **72) NO CORRUPT**
43) INEQUALITY
42) $ RICH 10%
57) %TURNOUT
➤ Subset Variable: **10) REGION**
➤ Subset Category: **Include: West. Hemisphere**

Indicate the correlation coefficient for each of the following variables and NO CORRUPT.

17. INEQUALITY   r = _____

18. $ RICH 10%   r = _____

19. %TURNOUT   r = _____

20. Nations in the Western Hemisphere that have low levels of economic inequality
tend to have more corruption.   T   F

21. Nations in the Western Hemisphere in which higher percentages of the national
wealth are received by the richest 10% of the population tend to have high
levels of corruption.   T   F

22. Western Hemisphere countries with high levels of corruption tend to have low levels
of voter turnout.   T   F

III. Use the SCATTERPLOT task to repeat the analysis between NO CORRUPT and %TURNOUT.
Continue to limit the analysis to the Western Hemisphere using the [Subset] option.

Data File: **GLOBAL**
➤ Task: **Scatterplot**
➤ Dependent Variable: **72) NO CORRUPT**
➤ Independent Variable: **57) %TURNOUT**
➤ Subset Variable: **10) REGION**
➤ Subset Category: **Include: West. Hemisphere**
➤ View: **Reg. Line**

Now identify the outlier by clicking on the [Outlier] option and then select the [Remove] option.

23. What is the outlier?   _____

Identify the next outlier and remove this case too.

24. What is the second outlier?   _____

25. The two outliers are located in North America.   T   F

26. The cases remaining in the analysis are from South and Central America.   T   F

IV. You have been hired as a consultant to help the president of Brazil to avert what seems to be an impending coup. She urgently needs to reduce corruption and improve the image of government agencies. The Brazilian president would like to target the government agencies that seem most corrupt to the overall population, especially those who are in favor of military rule (a junta). The four areas to be examined are the military, the police force, the parties, and the government as a whole. The survey you administered in Brazil includes a series of questions that assess the confidence rates for the various government agencies. Use these data to determine the agencies in which people have a great deal of confidence and no confidence. Also examine which agencies the supporters of military rule have the most confidence and the least confidence in.

You will need to use the WVS97–BRAZIL file and the CROSS-TABULATION task to complete this series of analyses. The variable 13) JUNTA will be the independent variable (the column variable) in each analysis. The dependent variables (row variables) are listed below. For each result, fill in the percentages (use column percentaging) for the row that is specified in the table below. Note that you are also asked to fill in the "total percent" for that row (which indicates the overall percentage of respondents who gave that answer to the survey question). Finally, indicate whether the results are statistically significant (circle Y for Yes, N for No).

> ➤ *Row Variables:*   **4) CONF:ARMY**
>   **5) CONF:COPS**
>   **6) CONF:PARL**
>   **7) CONF:LEGAL**

Fill in the table below.

%NONE	GOOD	BAD	TOTAL	V =	SIGNIFI-CANT?
4) CONF:ARMY					
% Great deal	_____%	_____%	_____%	_____	Y N
% None	_____%	_____%	_____%		
5) CONF:COPS					
% Great deal	_____%	_____%	_____%	_____	Y N
% None	_____%	_____%	_____%		
6) CONF:PARL					
% Great deal	_____%	_____%	_____%	_____	Y N
% None	_____%	_____%	_____%		
7) CONF:LEGAL					
% Great deal	_____%	_____%	_____%	_____	Y N
% None	_____%	_____%	_____%		

27. Overall, in which two agencies do people in Brazil have the lowest level of confidence (none)?   _____

_____

28. Overall, in which of the four agencies do people have a great deal of confidence?   _____

29. In which two agencies do supporters of military government in Brazil have the least confidence?   _____

_____

30. In which agency do supporters of military government in Brazil have the most confidence?

31. In which agency do opponents of military government in Brazil have the most confidence?   _____

32. In all four areas, Brazilian opinion on military rule makes a difference in terms of perceived confidence. Each result is statistically significant.   T   F

33. In terms of support for military government, the area having the greatest differences in confidence levels is the police.   T   F

V. Your consultant work for Brazil was so well received that the president of Mexico hired you to do the same work in his country. Follow the instructions provided in the previous question, but keep in mind that the Mexican president is interested in leading a program of military reform. He is most interested in appealing to his constituents who have deep suspicions about the military. [Use 14) JUNTA as the column variable.]

Fill in the table below.

%NONE	GOOD	BAD	TOTAL	V =	SIGNIFI-CANT?
5) CONF:ARMY					
% Great deal	_____%	_____%	_____%	_____	Y N
% None	_____%	_____%	_____%		
6) CONF:COPS					
% Great deal	_____%	_____%	_____%	_____	Y N
% None	_____%	_____%	_____%		

%NONE	GOOD	BAD	TOTAL	V =	SIGNIFI-CANT?
7) CONF:PARL					
% Great deal	_____%	_____%	_____%	_____	Y N
% None	_____%	_____%	_____%		
8) CONF:LEGAL					
% Great deal	_____%	_____%	_____%	_____	Y N
% None	_____%	_____%	_____%		

34. Overall, in which two agencies do people in Mexico have the lowest level of confidence (i.e., none)?

_____

_____

35. Overall, in which of the four agencies do people have a great deal of confidence (i.e., great deal)?

_____

36. In which two agencies do supporters of military government in Mexico have the least confidence?

_____

_____

37. In which agency do supporters of military government in Mexico have the most confidence?

_____

38. In which agency do opponents of military government in Mexico have the most confidence?

_____

39. In all four areas, Mexican opinion on military rule makes a difference in terms of perceived confidence. Each result is statistically significant.   T   F

40. In terms of support for military government, the area having the greatest differences in confidence levels is the parliament.   T   F

VI. A software mogul has agreed to donate substantial amounts of money to Mexico and Brazil to promote small businesses in local neighborhoods. He's unsure which aid agency or organization in each country should be used to distribute the money, so he hires you to determine which ones people in each country respect the most. Specifically, he wants you to research public opinion on the women's movement, unions, the church, the civil service, and major companies. There's one more issue. Because of a public relations snafu that resulted in the software mogul being criticized for never seeking the advice of women, he has instructed you to rely heavily on the public opinion of women in Mexico and Brazil.

You will need to use the CROSS-TABULATION task to complete this series of analyses. The variable GENDER will be the independent variable (the column variable) in each analysis. The dependent variables (row variables) are listed below. For each result, fill in the percentages (use column percentaging) *for the row that is specified* in the table below. Note that you are also asked to fill in the "total percent" for that row. Finally, indicate whether the results are statistically significant (circle Y for Yes, N for No).

➤ *Row Variables:* **CONF:CHRCH**
CONF:UNION
CONF:CIVIL
CONF:COMP
CONF:WOMEN

BRAZIL

Fill in the table below.

%NONE	MALE	FEMALE	TOTAL	V =	SIGNIFICANT?
8) CONF:CHRCH					
% Great deal	____%	____%	____%	_____	Y N
% None	____%	____%	____%		
9) CONF:UNION					
% Great deal	____%	____%	____%	_____	Y N
% None	____%	____%	____%		
10) CONF:CIVIL					
% Great deal	____%	____%	____%	_____	Y N
% None	____%	____%	____%		
11) CONF:COMP					
% Great deal	____%	____%	____%	_____	Y N
% None	____%	____%	____%		
12) CONF:WOMEN					
% Great deal	____%	____%	____%	_____	Y N
% None	____%	____%	____%		

41. Overall, in which two institutions do people in Brazil have the least confidence (i.e., none)?

_____

_____

42. Overall, in which organization do people have the most confidence (i.e., great deal)?

_____

43. Do women and men differ in terms of the organization or agency in which they have the most confidence?

Yes   No

44. If the money were to be distributed to these organizations or agencies according to the amount of confidence women have in them, what would the order be? What would the order be if only men were consulted?

	WOMEN	MEN
MOST CONFIDENCE	1. _____	_____
	2. _____	_____
	3. _____	_____
	4. _____	_____
LEAST CONFIDENCE	5. _____	_____

MEXICO

Fill in the table below.

%NONE	MALE	FEMALE	TOTAL	V =	SIGNIFICANT?
9) CONF:CHRCH					
% Great deal	_____%	_____%	_____%	_____	Y N
% None	_____%	_____%	_____%		
10) CONF:UNION					
% Great deal	_____%	_____%	_____%	_____	Y N
% None	_____%	_____%	_____%		

%NONE	MALE	FEMALE	TOTAL	V =	SIGNIFICANT?
11) CONF:CIVIL					
% Great deal	_____%	_____%	_____%	_____	Y N
% None	_____%	_____%	_____%		
12) CONF:COMP					
% Great deal	_____%	_____%	_____%	_____	Y N
% None	_____%	_____%	_____%		
13) CONF:WOMEN					
% Great deal	_____%	_____%	_____%	_____	Y N
% None	_____%	_____%	_____%		

45. Overall, in which two institutions do people in Mexico have the least
confidence (i.e., none)?   _____

                                                                       _____

46. Overall, in which organization do people have the most confidence
(i.e., great deal)?   _____

47. Do women and men differ in terms of the organization or agency in which they
have the most confidence?   Yes   No

48. If the money were to be distributed to these organizations or agencies according to the
amount of confidence women have in them, what would the order be? What would the order
be if only men were consulted?

	WOMEN	MEN
MOST CONFIDENCE	1. _____	_____
	2. _____	_____
	3. _____	_____
	4. _____	_____
LEAST CONFIDENCE	5. _____	_____

Chapter 15: Authority Patterns in Mexico and Brazil

IN YOUR OWN WORDS

In your own words, please answer the following questions.

1. If the Brazilian president had to pick one agency to improve in order to avert a military coup, which one should she pick? Why? What would be her second choice? Be sure to support your answers with evidence.

2. If the president of Mexico were to draw on one institution to help him in his reform of the military, which one should he draw on? Why? What would be his second choice? Be sure to support your answers with evidence.

3. After receiving your preliminary report, the software mogul decides he wants three agencies/organizations in each country to utilize the grants. These grants will be distributed across three groups according to a 50%-30%-20% split respective to your ranking. However, you must select the same rank order for both nations. Which three organizations would you choose, and which order would you select? Explain your rationale for both.

The Islamic World

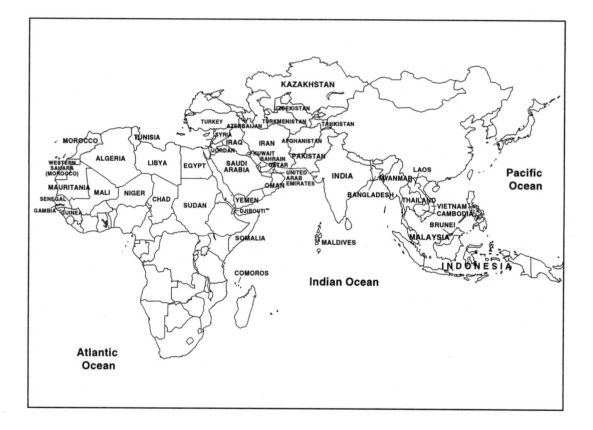

KAZAKHSTAN

UZBEKISTAN

TURKEY   TURKMENISTAN   TAJIKISTAN
AZERBAIJAN
SYRIA
MOROCCO   TUNISIA   IRAQ   IRAN   AFGHANISTAN
JORDAN
WESTERN   ALGERIA   LIBYA   EGYPT   KUWAIT   PAKISTAN
SAHARA   BAHRAIN
(MOROCCO)   SAUDI   QATAR   LAOS   Pacific
ARABIA   UNITED   INDIA   MYANMAR   Ocean
MAURITANIA   MALI   NIGER   ARAB
OMAN   EMIRATES
SENEGAL   CHAD   BANGLADESH   THAILAND
GAMBIA   GUINEA   SUDAN   YEMEN   VIETNAM
CAMBODIA
DJIBOUTI   BRUNEI
SOMALIA   MALDIVES   MALAYSIA

COMOROS   Indian Ocean   INDONESIA

Atlantic
Ocean

CHAPTER **16**

ISLAM AND POLITICS IN PAKISTAN AND TURKEY

*Islamic fundamentalists in Arab countries preach
their ideology because they consider Islam the
elevator to take power.*

HASSAN II, 1995,
KING OF MOROCCO

Tasks: Mapping, Cross-tabulation, Univariate, Scatterplot, ANOVA
Data Files: GLOBAL, WVS97all, WVS97–PAKISTAN, WVS97–TURKEY

In 1979 Islamic fundamentalists overthrew the shah of Iran and established a theocratic government, or Islamic Republic, rooted in the theological principles outlined in the holy book of Islam, the Qur'an (or Koran). Western observers were taken by surprise by the militancy of the students who were the vanguard of the Islamic revolution in Iran. As a result of this event, countries where Islam dominates the religious landscape are increasingly understood as a separate type of political system. The Islamic world consists of states that govern themselves by Islamic law, or have a large majority of the population who are Islamic believers.

Let's use the WORLDS.7 variable in the GLOBAL data file to examine the Islamic countries throughout the world. To include only Islamic countries in the following map, use ExplorIt's [Subset] option, as described below.

➤ *Data File:* **GLOBAL**
➤ *Task:* **Mapping**
➤ *Variable 1:* **80) WORLDS.7**
➤ *Subset Variable:* **80) WORLDS.7**
➤ *Subset Category:* **Include: 5) Islamic**
➤ *View:* **Map**

WORLDS.7 -- CLASSIFICATION OF COUNTRIES INTO "SEVEN WORLDS" OR
CATEGORIES: 1 = LIBERAL DEMOCRACY, 2 = COMMUNIST/POST-COMMUNIST, 3 =

[Subset]

The option for selecting a subset variable is located on the same screen you use to select other variables. For this example, additionally select 80) WORLDS.7 for the subset variable. A window will appear that shows you the categories of the subset variable. Select 5) Islamic as your subset category and choose the [Include] option. Then click [OK] and continue as usual. With this particular subset selected, the results will be limited to countries in the Islamic world. The subset selection continues until you do one of the following: exit the task, delete the subset variable, or use the [Clear All] button to clear all variables.

279

This map includes only those countries that have a large percentage of Islamic adherents *and* a political system that is influenced by the Koran. You will notice that most of these countries are concentrated in North Africa, the Middle East, and parts of South Asia. Look at the percentage of the population for all countries that are Islamic believers.

Data File: **GLOBAL**
Task: **Mapping**
➤ Variable 1: **83) %MUSLIM**
➤ View: **Map**
➤ Display: **Legend**

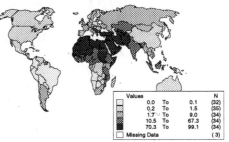

%MUSLIM -- % of the population that is Muslim. (WCE, 2001)

Values			N
0.0	To	0.1	(32)
0.2	To	1.5	(35)
1.7	To	9.0	(34)
10.5	To	67.3	(34)
70.3	To	99.1	(34)
Missing Data			(3)

Note: Before selecting the %MUSLIM variable, use the [Clear All] button to remove the subset selected in your previous analysis.

Once again we see that the concentrations of Islamic believers are found in North Africa and almost all of South Asia. If you use the [List: Rank] option to view the specific percentages for nations, you see that the population in more than 14 countries is greater than 95% Muslim; 40 countries are at least 50% Muslim. There is also a high concentration of Islamic believers in the republics of the former USSR. If Islamic revival in other parts of the world is any indication of the future of the southern republics of the former Soviet Union, then we can expect that these states will also develop an "Islamic" character.

The study of Islamic states as a distinct political phenomenon is antithetical to Western notions of religion and politics. John McCormick notes that the Judeo-Christian understanding of religion and politics is that they are separate realms:

"Render . . . unto Caesar the things which are Caesar's and unto God the things that are God's" (Matthew 22:21) . . . is a principle that most liberal democracies follow. For many Muslims, by contrast, Islam is the state, there is no separation of state (*dawla*) and religion (*din*) (in theory at least), and all Muslims are part of a larger entity . . . that transcends race and national borders.

McCormick and other scholars of this region suggest that Westerners see political Islam as being more analogous to an ideology than a religion because Islam has a complete body of law for ordering society. As a result, you will notice that the states of the Islamic world tend to be distinct from other categories of states around the world. For example, examine the type of governments that are found in Islamic nations.[1]

---

[1] There are a few instances in this chapter where the cross-tabulation result using the GLOBAL file produces the statement "Warning: Potential significance problem." This is to alert you that the statistical significance value may not be reliable due to the small number of cases used in the analysis. The likelihood of this warning message appearing will also increase as the number of cells in the table increases—the greater the number of cells, the more likely the warning message will appear. For our purposes in this chapter, we will often ignore this warning.

Comparative Politics

Data File: **GLOBAL**
➤ Task: **Cross-tabulation**
➤ Row Variable: **65) GOVERNMENT**
➤ Column Variable: **80) WORLDS.7**
➤ View: **Tables**
➤ Display: **Column %**

GOVERNMENT by WORLDS.7
Cramer's V: 0.494 **
Warning: Potential significance problem. Check row and column totals.

| | WORLDS.7 | | | | | | | |
	Lib Democ	Comm/P-Com	NICs	LDCs	Islamic	Marginal	Micro	TOTAL
Old Demos	24	0	15	16	3	2	5	65
	100.0%	0.0%	71.4%	44.4%	11.5%	8.0%	83.3%	37.8%
Transition	0	22	4	10	2	10	1	49
	0.0%	64.7%	19.0%	27.8%	7.7%	40.0%	16.7%	28.5%
One Party	0	8	1	4	5	1	0	19
	0.0%	23.5%	4.8%	11.1%	19.2%	4.0%	0.0%	11.0%
Autocratic	0	0	1	6	14	3	0	24
	0.0%	0.0%	4.8%	16.7%	53.8%	12.0%	0.0%	14.0%
Civil War	0	4	0	0	2	9	0	15
	0.0%	11.8%	0.0%	0.0%	7.7%	36.0%	0.0%	8.7%
TOTAL	24	34	21	36	26	25	6	172
	100.0%	100.0%	100.0%	100.0%	100.0%	100.0%	100.0%	

If you look down the column labeled Islamic, you see that 53.8% of all nation-states having Islamic political systems are autocratic. By far, this is the highest percentage of any world classification. The next highest category, less developed countries, is only about 17% autocratic. The second most common category for Islamic states is one-party states (19%), and there are very few that are democracies or in transition to democracies.

The "autocratic" categorization of Islamic states hides the fact that there is a lot of variety in their political and legal systems. If we limit our analysis to those nation-states with majority Islamic populations, we can see that there is still a lot of political variety within these nations.

Data File: **GLOBAL**
➤ Task: **Univariate**
➤ Primary Variable: **68) ISLAMPOL**
➤ View: **Pie**

ISLAMPOL -- POLITICAL SYSTEM OF THE ISLAMIC WORLD (TWF, 2001)

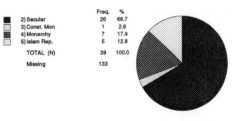

		Freq.	%
■	2) Secular	26	66.7
▨	3) Const. Mon	1	2.6
▧	4) Monarchy	7	17.9
▨	5) Islam Rep.	5	12.8
	TOTAL (N)	39	100.0
	Missing	133	

The Islamic political model is distinct from other models of politics in that it does not even seem to aspire to democratic forms of organization. But even in this unique category, the models of government are numerous. Secular Islamic states (66.7% of states with majority Muslim populations) seek to marginalize the Islamic faith and moderate its hold on politics while often retaining many of the legal requirements of the faith.

Another obvious form is monarchy, which comprises 20.5% of states if you combine absolute monarchies and constitutional monarchies. It should be noted that the Islamic countries are the only countries in the world to retain absolute monarchy as a form of political organization. Finally, in the latter part of the 20th century several countries organized themselves as Islamic Republics. Most of these are concentrated in South Asia. Let's look at this same variable using the MAPPING task. Perhaps there is a regional pattern to the political organization of the Islamic states.

ISLAMPOL -- POLITICAL SYSTEM OF THE ISLAMIC WORLD (TWF, 2001)

Data File: **GLOBAL**
➤ Task: **Mapping**
➤ Variable 1: **68) ISLAMPOL**
➤ View: **Map**
➤ Display: **Legend**

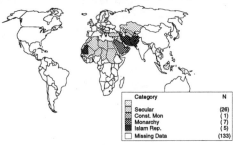

Category	N
Secular	(26)
Const. Mon	(1)
Monarchy	(7)
Islam Rep.	(5)
Missing Data	(133)

There doesn't seem to be much of a pattern, although three of the five Islamic Republics (Pakistan, Iran, and Afghanistan) are clustered together in South Asia. The most recent nation to declare itself an Islamic Republic, Afghanistan, is still in the midst of a civil war between forces that advocate a more secular form of political organization (among other things) and a movement called the Taliban who advocate an unequivocally Islamic approach to politics. The latter group wants all legal norms and structures of the country to conform to Islamic law, which is derived from the Koran. The Koran outlines a structure for holy living in the context of culture, economy, politics, and the family.

There are essentially three types of legal systems that Islamic countries have adopted: those that are European in nature, those that are strictly Islamic, and those that include aspects of both. Let's examine the legal systems of Islamic countries, while retaining the map showing the political system.

Data File: **GLOBAL**
Task: **Mapping**
Variable 1: **68) ISLAMPOL**
➤ Variable 2: **69) ISLAMLEGAL**
➤ View: **Map**
➤ Display: **Legend**

ISLAMPOL -- POLITICAL SYSTEM OF THE ISLAMIC WORLD (TWF, 2001)

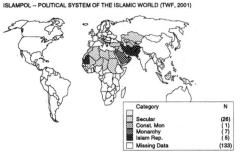

Category	N
Secular	(26)
Const. Mon	(1)
Monarchy	(7)
Islam Rep.	(5)
Missing Data	(133)

r = 0.563**

ISLAMLEGAL -- LEGAL SYSTEM OF THE ISLAMIC WORLD (TWF, 2001)

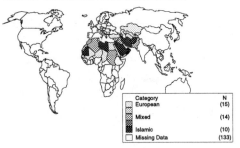

Category	N
European	(15)
Mixed	(14)
Islamic	(10)
Missing Data	(133)

As the legend for the legal systems map shows, 15 countries with majority Islamic populations have adopted a European legal system, 14 have a mixed legal system, and 10 have an Islamic legal system. Unsurprisingly, 4 of the 5 states that have Islamic political systems also have Islamic legal systems. Many of the absolute monarchies, such as Saudi Arabia and the United Arab Emirates, also abide by Islamic law. On the other hand, the secular political systems like Egypt and Turkey abide by European legal traditions. But what is responsible for these differences? Let's check to see if the type of legal system is at all related to the percentage of Muslims in a society.

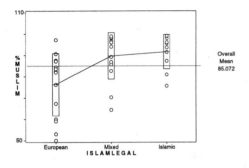

> Data File: **GLOBAL**
> ➤ Task: **ANOVA**
> ➤ Dependent Variable: **83) %MUSLIM**
> ➤ Independent Variable: **69) ISLAMLEGAL**
> ➤ View: **Graph**

Mixed and Islamic legal systems are associated with the presence of a larger Muslim population. If you click on the [Statistics:Means] button, you will see the mean population of Muslims in a country for each legal system. In European systems, you see that the average population of Muslims is 76.3%. Mixed systems have 89.7% Muslims, and Islamic legal systems have 91.7%. The differences in mean Muslim population between these three types of legal systems are significant.

Islam teaches the freedom of religion, political expression, and association. Let's examine how Islamic countries rate in these areas using the FREEDOM variable in the GLOBAL data file. The FREEDOM variable combines the measures for civil liberties and political rights into one measure having three categories: not free, partly free, and free.

> Data File: **GLOBAL**
> ➤ Task: **Cross-tabulation**
> ➤ Row Variable: **75) FREEDOM**
> ➤ Column Variable: **80) WORLDS.7**
> ➤ View: **Tables**
> ➤ Display: **Column %**

FREEDOM   by   WORLDS.7
Cramer's V: 0.529 **

		WORLDS.7							
		Lib Democ	Comm/P-Com	NICs	LDCs	Islamic	Marginal	Micro	TOTAL
FREEDOM	FREE	24	12	15	10	0	3	4	68
		100.0%	35.3%	71.4%	27.8%	0.0%	12.5%	80.0%	40.2%
	PART FREE	0	9	6	18	6	9	1	49
		0.0%	26.5%	28.6%	50.0%	24.0%	37.5%	20.0%	29.0%
	NOT FREE	0	13	0	8	19	12	0	52
		0.0%	38.2%	0.0%	22.2%	76.0%	50.0%	0.0%	30.8%
	Missing	0	0	0	0	1	1	1	3
	TOTAL	24	34	21	36	25	24	5	169
		100.0%	100.0%	100.0%	100.0%	100.0%	100.0%	100.0%	

The Islamic countries included in this data file have the lowest ratings for civil liberties and political rights. As this table shows, three-quarters of all Islamic countries are classified as "not free." Only 24% of the Islamic countries are in the "partly free" category, and none of the Islamic countries are considered "free." Note also that Islamic states have a lower level of freedom than do nation-states categorized as less developed countries and marginal states.

What about war? Are Islamic countries more likely or less likely to be involved in wars than other regions of the world?

Data File: **GLOBAL**
Task: **Cross-tabulation**
➤ *Row Variable:* **73) WAR**
➤ *Column Variable:* **80) WORLDS.7**
➤ *View:* **Tables**
➤ *Display:* **Column %**

WAR   by   WORLDS.7
Cramer's V: 0.229
Warning: Potential significance problem. Check row and column totals.

		Lib Democ	Comm/P-Com	NICs	LDCs	Islamic	Marginal	Micro	TOTAL
WAR	None	19	21	12	22	9	8	6	97
		79.2%	61.8%	57.1%	61.1%	34.6%	32.0%	100.0%	56.4%
	Interstate	2	4	0	3	4	0	0	13
		8.3%	11.8%	0.0%	8.3%	15.4%	0.0%	0.0%	7.6%
	Civil War	2	7	7	10	10	14	0	50
		8.3%	20.6%	33.3%	27.8%	38.5%	56.0%	0.0%	29.1%
	Indepndnce	0	0	0	0	1	1	0	2
		0.0%	0.0%	0.0%	0.0%	3.8%	4.0%	0.0%	1.2%
	Multi-type	1	2	2	1	2	2	0	10
		4.2%	5.9%	9.5%	2.8%	7.7%	8.0%	0.0%	5.8%
	TOTAL	24	34	21	36	26	25	6	172
		100.0%	100.0%	100.0%	100.0%	100.0%	100.0%	100.0%	

In spite of the pan-Islamic ideal of a brotherhood of all Islamic countries, Islamic countries have experienced more interstate conflict than any other region in the world. Between 1990 and 1996, 16% of Islamic states were involved in interstate conflict. Wars between Iran and Iraq and between Iraq and Kuwait explain much of this conflict, but the region is still not very secure, and a common faith in Islam has not helped it to overcome its conflicts. Civil wars have also plagued these countries. Afghanistan, Algeria, Sudan, Turkey, Iraq, and Egypt have all suffered tremendous loss of life as a result of internal strife.

If Islamic countries have higher levels of war, this must have an impact on their gross domestic product. You would expect that Islamic countries spend a greater percentage of their government budgets on armed forces. Let's see if this is the case.

Data File: **GLOBAL**
➤ *Task:* **Scatterplot**
➤ *Dependent Variable:* **53) MIL/BUDGET**
➤ *Independent Variable:* **83) %MUSLIM**
➤ *View:* **Reg. Line**

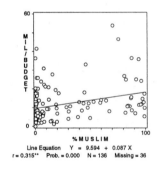

Line Equation   Y = 9.594 + 0.087 X
r = 0.315**   Prob. = 0.000   N = 136   Missing = 36

The correlation between government spending on the armed forces and the percentage of Muslims is moderately strong (r = 0.315**). Notice the cases located above the regression line and on the right side of the screen. These dots represent Islamic states that spend a lot of their budget for military purposes. If you click on these dots, you immediately notice that most are oil-producing nations. Thus, they have a great deal of money to spend on defense and are distinctly above the norm. Conversely, if you click on the cases located below the regression line and on the right side of the screen, you find Islamic countries that are not oil producers. This scatterplot suggests that oil production may, in fact, play a more important role in military spending than does the religious character of Islamic nation-states.

One issue that has received a great deal of attention in the international media is the treatment that women have received in Islamic countries. Many international organizations argue that Islam treats women in a degrading fashion, limits their personal freedom, and even justifies acts of violence and torture toward women. The Islamic faithful counter that Western standards are used unfairly in the evaluation of women in Islamic countries. They claim that women are treated as special creations of God, who are not subjected to the pornography, obscenity, and immorality commonly found in the West. Some Islamic scholars even claim that poor treatment of women in many Islamic countries is not the fault of Islam, which treats all people with dignity, but is brought on by poverty and ignorance. We cannot resolve this debate here, but we can analyze the plight of women in Islamic states and compare it to the plight of women in other poor states (such as the marginal states) to see if they are worse off. We will hypothesize that unequal treatment of women is not due to the religious character of countries but, rather, to their level of development.

To examine this relationship, we'll use the "gender equity index," which combines a number of factors (such as education, employment opportunities, equal treatment) in the assessment of women's equality in a nation.

Data File: **GLOBAL**
➤ Task: **Mapping**
➤ Variable 1: **97) GENDER EQ**
➤ View: **Map**
➤ Display: **Legend**

GENDER EQ -- 1995: GENDER-RELATED DEVELOPMENT INDEX (GDI) (HDR, 1998)

Values			N
0.165 To	0.376		(32)
0.399 To	0.617		(32)
0.620 To	0.714		(33)
0.718 To	0.826		(32)
0.834 To	0.940		(33)
Missing Data			(10)

For this index, 0 is the lowest possible score and 1.0 is the highest score. The higher the score, the more equally women have developed. What we want to do is look at the relationship between the gender equity index and the WORLDS.7 variable.

Data File: **GLOBAL**
➤ Task: **ANOVA**
➤ Dependent Variable: **97) GENDER EQ**
➤ Independent Variable: **80) WORLDS.7**
➤ View: **Graph**

Overall Mean 0.629

Carefully examine the graph line and think about how you might summarize the relationship between these two variables. What does this graph tell us? We can now easily compare different groups of countries. In this graph you can see that the first category, liberal democracies, has the highest level of gender equity. The average score for communist and postcommunist countries is below the liberal democracies and slightly below newly industrialized countries. And now for the purpose of this analysis: notice that Islamic countries have a higher average level of gender equity than marginal states and LDCs. You can also look at these mean values themselves in the form of a table.

Data File: **GLOBAL**
Task: **ANOVA**
Dependent Variable: **97) GENDER EQ**
Independent Variable: **80) WORLDS.7**
➤ *View:* **Means**

Means, Standard Deviations and Number of Cases of Dependent Var: GENDER EQ by Categories of Independent Var: WORLDS.7
Difference of means across groups is statistically significant (Prob. = 0.000)

	N	Mean	Std.Dev.
Lib Democ	24	0.901	0.028
Comm/P-Com	32	0.688	0.103
NICs	20	0.754	0.095
LDCs	36	0.498	0.161
Islamic	23	0.572	0.156
Marginal	22	0.387	0.182
Micro	5	0.715	0.162

If you are continuing from the previous example, select the [Means] button.

This table shows the actual mean value of gender equity within each category of the independent variable (Seven Worlds). As we can see, liberal democracies have the highest score, 0.901. The marginal states have the lowest mean gender equity score, 0.387. The Islamic nations are far below the liberal democracies, with a mean gender equity score of 0.572, but they are higher than LDCs and marginal states. Finally, the differences between these states are significant.

The study of Islamic states as a distinctive group of countries is in a relatively early stage in political science. In the worksheet section, you will look at some of the first political science in those states.

WORKSHEET

NAME: _____

COURSE: _____

DATE: _____

CHAPTER

16

REVIEW QUESTIONS

Based on the first part of this chapter, answer True or False to the following items:

1. Most Islamic nations are in North Africa, South Asia, and the Middle East.   T   F

2. One reason that Islamic conceptions of politics are different from those of the West is that Islamic teaching does not separate religion and the state.   T   F

3. Due to the basic principles outlined in the Koran, the majority of Islamic states are democratic or in transition to democracy.   T   F

4. Absolute monarchy is the most common political system in countries with a majority of Muslims.   T   F

5. Although Islam teaches respect for human rights, Islamic countries tend to violate this teaching and have among the worst ratings for freedom in the world.   T   F

6. Of the countries in the Seven Worlds classification, Islamic states are the least likely to have been at peace between 1990 and 1996.   T   F

7. Countries with high percentages of Muslims spend a higher percentage of their government budgets on defense than those countries with lower percentages of Muslims.   T   F

8. The differences in gender equity across the various types of countries are statistically significant.   T   F

EXPLORIT QUESTIONS

I. In the preliminary part of this chapter, we saw that Islamic, marginal, and less developed countries have the lowest scores on the gender equity scale. These findings suggest that economic development and political instability may contribute more to the low levels of equality for women than the religious character of the country. But a gender equity index is just one variable that can be used to test this theory. Let's examine a few other items that assess gender equality in nation-states.

Chapter 16: Islam and Politics in Pakistan and Turkey

➤ *Data File:* **GLOBAL**
➤ *Task:* **ANOVA**
➤ *Dependent Variable:* **95) %FEM.LEGIS**
➤ *Independent Variable:* **80) WORLDS.7**
➤ *View:* **Graph**

9. Based on the ANOVA graphic alone, do countries appear to differ significantly in the percentage of women who are represented in the national legislature?   Yes   No

10. List the type of country that has the highest level of women's representation in the legislature.   _____

Data File: **GLOBAL**
Task: **ANOVA**
Dependent Variable: **95) %FEM.LEGIS**
Independent Variable: **80) WORLDS.7**
➤ *View:* **Means**

11. List the type of country that has the lowest level of women's representation in the legislature. Also indicate the mean (i.e., average) percentage of women in the legislature for that type.   Country Type _____

                              Mean Percentage _____

12. Are the differences between types of nations and the levels of women's representation in the legislature statistically significant?   Yes   No

13. Since Islamic countries have lower rates of female representation in the legislature than marginal countries and less developed countries, this suggests that the religious character of countries may play an important role in gender equity.   T   F

14. Based on these results, one might conclude that (circle one of the following)

     a. economic development appears to be more important than religious character in determining the level of female representation in the legislature.

     b. the religious character of nation-states appears to be more important than economic development in determining the level of female representation in the legislature.

     c. both the religious character of nation-states and their level of economic development seem to have an impact on the level of female representation in the legislature.

II. One issue of concern to many in the West is the percentage of women in Islamic countries who have their external sexual organs cut away as a means to discourage sexual activity. Since this practice, known as sexual mutilation, occurs almost exclusively on the continent of Africa, our Seven Worlds variable won't be of much use in this analysis. Instead, use the SCATTERPLOT task to examine the relationship between 101) %SEX MUTIL and the three variables listed below. For each analysis, fill in the correlation coefficient, indicate whether the results are statistically significant, and show the direction of the relationship (whether it's positive or negative).

Data File: **GLOBAL**
➤ Task: **Scatterplot**
➤ Dependent Variable: **101) %SEX MUTIL**
➤ Independent Variable: **83) %MUSLIM** [Repeat analysis with **38) GDPCAP PPP, 84) %CHRISTIAN**]
➤ View: **Reg. Line**

When you conduct the analysis of 83) %MUSLIM and 38) GDPCAP PPP, please remove four outliers from the analysis and then answer the questions. Fill in the information below.

	CORRELATION COEFFICIENT	SIGNIFICANT?	DIRECTION OF RELATIONSHIP
15. 83) %MUSLIM	r = _____	Y N	Positive Negative
16. 38) GDPCAP PPP	r = _____	Y N	Positive Negative
17. 84) %CHRISTIAN	r = _____	Y N	Positive Negative

18. Countries with higher percentages of Muslims tend to have higher rates of women who have been sexually mutilated.   T   F

19. Countries with high rates of GDP per capita have high rates of sexual mutilation. This suggests that the level of economic development plays an important role in terms of sexual mutilation.   T   F

20. Countries with higher rates of GDP per capita tend to have slightly lower rates of sexual mutilation. However, these results are not statistically significant.   T   F

21. Countries with higher percentages of Christians tend to have lower rates of sexual mutilation of women.   T   F

III. So far we have examined the role of religion and women at what is referred to as the "aggregate level" of analysis. This means that we have examined the percentage of women in a given country who are in the legislature, but we have not examined the results of questions asked of actual men and women in an Islamic society. For years this data was very difficult to obtain, but in the latest release of the World Values Survey we have the results of surveys conducted in Pakistan and Turkey. This has allowed political scientists to begin to get some answers to a number of questions that we have had about religion and politics in the Islamic world. First, let's see how important religion is across a variety of nation-states.

➤ Data File: **WVS97all**
➤ Task: **Cross-tabulation**
➤ Row Variable: **8) RELI IMPT?**
➤ Column Variable: **1) COUNTRY**
➤ View: **Tables**
➤ Display: **Column %**

22. Which two nation-states have the highest percentage of citizens who say that religion is very important?

                COUNTRIES   **PERCENTAGE**

                _____   _____

                _____   _____

23. Which two nation-states have the highest percentage of citizens who say that religion is not at all important?

                COUNTRIES   **PERCENTAGE**

                _____   _____

                _____   _____

24. Now use the data files from Pakistan (WVS97–PAKISTAN) and Turkey (WVS97+TURKEY) to determine which society is more secularized. Use the variable RELI IMPT? Which society is more secular? Please give your reason for coming to this conclusion.

IV. One of the issues that many of the Islamic faithful are concerned about is the encroachment of Western secular culture on Islamic values and the corruption of the young. Let's examine whether or not these concerns are well founded. Do the young consider religion to be as important as the old do? Is watching TV associated with lower levels of religious salience?

          ➤ *Data Files:*   **WVS97–PAKISTAN**
                           WVS97–TURKEY
              ➤ *Task:*   **Cross-tabulation**
       ➤ *Row Variable:*   **RELI IMPT?**
   ➤ *Column Variables:*   **AGE GROUP**
                           WATCH TV (Pakistan only)
              ➤ *View:*   **Tables**
           ➤ *Display:*   **Column %**

Fill in the table below.

AGE GROUP

	18–24	25–34	35–44	45–54	55+	V=	SIGNIFI-CANT?
PAKISTAN 4) RELI IMPT? % Very	_____%	_____%	_____%	_____%	_____%	_____	Y N
TURKEY 3) RELI IMPT? % Very	_____%	_____%	_____%	_____%	_____%	_____	Y N

WATCH TV

	NO TV	1–2 HRS	2–3 HRS	3+ HRS	V=	SIGNIFI-CANT?
PAKISTAN 4) RELI IMPT? % Very	_____%	_____%	_____%	_____%	_____	Y N

Interpret the results of these analyses in the *In Your Own Words* section.

V. Islam does generally limit the opportunities for the advancement of women, but do women also endorse these limitations? Let's analyze the role that gender plays in attitudes toward gender roles.

> ➤ *Data Files:* **WVS97–PAKISTAN**
> **WVS97–TURKEY**
> ➤ *Task:* **Cross-tabulation**
> ➤ *Row Variables:* **EDUC BOYS**
> **MAN'S JOB**
> **TALK POLIT**
> **MEN POLS**
> ➤ *Column Variable:* **GENDER**
> ➤ *View:* **Tables**
> ➤ *Display:* **Column %**

Fill in the table below.

PAKISTAN

	MALE	FEMALE	V=	SIGNIFICANT?
5) EDUC BOYS				
% Strongly agree	_____%	_____%	_____	Y N
% Strongly disagree	_____%	_____%		

PAKISTAN (cont.)

	MALE	FEMALE	V=	SIGNIFICANT?
6) MAN'S JOB				
% Agree	_____%	_____%	_____	Y N
% Disagree	_____%	_____%		
7) TALK POLIT				
% Frequently	_____%	_____%	_____	Y N
% Never	_____%	_____%		
8) MEN POLS				
% Strongly agree	_____%	_____%	_____	Y N
% Strongly disagree	_____%	_____%		

TURKEY

	MALE	FEMALE	V=	SIGNIFICANT?
4) EDUC BOYS				
% Strongly agree	_____%	_____%	_____	Y N
% Strongly disagree	_____%	_____%		
5) MAN'S JOB				
% Agree	_____%	_____%	_____	Y N
% Disagree	_____%	_____%		
6) TALK POLIT				
% Frequently	_____%	_____%	_____	Y N
% Never	_____%	_____%		
7) MEN POLS				
% Strongly agree	_____%	_____%	_____	Y N
% Strongly disagree	_____%	_____%		

IN YOUR OWN WORDS

In your own words, please answer the following questions.

1. Write a brief paragraph that summarizes the results of your analysis of sexual mutilation. In terms of sexual mutilation of women, indicate whether the religious character of a nation-state or its economic development plays a more important role.

2. Discuss the role that age and television watching may (or may not) play in the process of secularization. Be sure to support your comments with evidence.

3. Review the results from the analyses of Pakistan and Turkey. In a brief paragraph, evaluate the following hypothesis: There is no relationship between the gender of an individual and that individual's support for more limited opportunities for women in education, the economy, and politics. Use evidence from your analysis to support your conclusions.

APPENDIX: VARIABLE NAMES AND SOURCES

Note for MicroCase Users: These data files may be used with MicroCase. If you are moving variables from these files into other MicroCase files, or vice versa, you may need to reorder the cases. Also note that files that have been modified in MicroCase will not function properly in Student ExplorIt.

◆ DATA FILE: AFRICA ◆

1) COUNTRY
2) AREA
3) POPULATION
4) POP GROWTH
5) LIFE EXPCT
6) HUM DEVLP3
7) EDUCATION
8) MULTI-CULT
9) %MUSLIM
10) %CHRISTIAN
11) FEM.PROF.
12) %FEM.LEGIS
13) M/F EDUC.
14) GDP CAP 5
15) %GDP AGR
16) GDP

17) GDPCAP PPP
18) ECON GROW
19) ECON DEVEL
20) FREE3
21) GOVERNMENT
22) IND DATE
23) IND PERIOD
24) COL.POWERS
25) COL.MOTIVE
26) WAR
27) WARDEAD
28) POL RIGHTS
29) POL RIGHT2
30) CIVIL LIBS
31) CIVIL LIB2
32) EDUC INDEX

33) IL:FEM>15
34) IL:FEM<25
35) FEM MINIST
36) HEALTH EXP
37) FEMECON1
38) HIV/AIDS1
39) HIV/AIDS2
40) HIV/AIDS3
41) MALARIA1
42) TUBERC1
43) AID CAP
44) REFUGEES
45) WAR2
46) ASYLUM

◆ DATA FILE: ASIA ◆

1) COUNTRY
2) AREA
3) POPULATION
4) POP GROWTH
5) LIFE EXPCT
6) HUM DEVLP3
7) EDUCATION
8) MULTI-CULT
9) GDP PPP
10) GDPCAP PPP
11) ECON GROW
12) ECON DEVEL

13) GROW 90–99
14) INDUS GROW
15) ECON REG
16) SAVINGS
17) $ RICH 10%
18) FREE3
19) GOVERNMENT
20) IND DATE
21) IND PERIOD
22) NUKES
23) MISSILES
24) POP MILT

25) ARMDFORCES
26) KID THRIFT
27) NATL PRIDE
28) BIRTHRATE
29) ECON REG2
30) MIL/GNI
31) WORLDS.7
32) CHEM ARMS
33) BIOL ARMS
34) COMMUNIST

◆ DATA FILE: CSES–GERMANY ◆

1) PARTY VOTE
2) LT-RT-3
3) SEX
4) EDUCATION
5) RELIGION

6) CH.ATTEND
7) UNION?
8) VOTED?
9) OPINION
10) VOTE MATER

11) WHO POWER
12) CONTACT
13) POL KNOW
14) GERMWT3
15) EAST/WEST

◆ DATA FILE: CSES–UK ◆

1) PARTY VOTE
2) LT-RT-3
3) SEX
4) EDUCATION
5) RELIGION2

6) CH.ATTEND
7) UNION?
8) VOTED?
9) OPINION
10) VOTE MATER

11) WHO POWER
12) CONTACT
13) POL KNOW
14) BRITWT

◆ DATA FILE: EUROPE ◆

1) COUNTRY
2) AREA
3) POPULATION
4) POP GROWTH
5) LIFE EXPCT
6) HUM DEVLP3
7) EDUCATION
8) MULTI-CULT
9) C.CONFLICT
10) GDP
11) GDPCAP PPP
12) GROW 90–99
13) FREE 3
14) GOVERNMENT
15) GOVERNMEN2
16) IND DATE
17) IND PERIOD
18) LEFT/RIGHT
19) INJUSTICE
20) COLD WAR
21) NATO

22) EUROPE
23) CENSORSHIP
24) CAP PUNISH
25) #PARTIES
26) #PARTIES2
27) ELECTSYSTM
28) ELECTSYST2
29) %TURNOUT
30) %TURNOUT2
31) %EXT.LEFT
32) STS.EXLEFT
33) %SOCIALIST
34) STS.SOCIAL
35) %SOC.DEM
36) STS.SOCDEM
37) %GREEN
38) STS.GREEN
39) %LIBERAL
40) STS.LIBERL
41) %CENTER
42) STS.CENTER

43) %CH.DEM
44) STS.CHDEM
45) %CONSERVAT
46) STS.CONSRV
47) %EXT.RIGHT
48) STS.EXRICH
49) %REGIONAL
50) STS.REGION
51) %OTHER
52) STS.OTHER
53) FREEDOM
54) COMMUNIST
55) FREE2001
56) REGULATION
57) COMM TYPE
58) POL RIGHTS
59) CIV LIBS
60) POL RIGHT2
61) CIV LIBS2

◆ DATA FILE: GLOBAL ◆

1) COUNTRY
2) AREA
3) COASTLINE
4) % ARABLE
5) %PERM CROP
6) %MEAD-PAST
7) %FOR-WOOD
8) %OTHERLAND
9) %IRRIGATED
10) REGION
11) REGION2
12) POPULATION
13) POP GROWTH
14) DENSITY
15) MULTI-CULT
16) EDUC INDEX
17) PUB EDUCAT
18) IL:MALE>15
19) IL:FEM>15
20) ILLITERACY
21) IL:FEM<25
22) IL:MALE<25
23) IL: YOUTH
24) BIRTHRATE
25) FERTILITY
26) INFMORTAL
27) MORTAL<5
28) CONTRACEPT
29) DEATHRATE
30) IM:DPT
31) IM:MEASLES
32) LIFE FEM.
33) LIFE MALE
34) LIFEEXPCT2
35) CALORIES
36) QUAL. LIFE
37) GDP PPP
38) GDPCAP PPP
39) GDPCAP PP3

40) GROW 90–99
41) GDP/AREA
42) $ RICH 10%
43) INEQUALITY
44) EXT. DEBT
45) FREE2001
46) REGULATION
47) CARS/1000
48) PC/1000
49) TV/1000
50) NEWS/CP
51) CELL PHONE
52) POP MILT
53) MIL/BUDGET
54) MIL/GNI
55) ARMY/TEACH
56) ARMY/DOCTR
57) %TURNOUT
58) C.CONFLICT
59) CIV LIBS
60) CIV LIBS2
61) POL RIGHTS
62) POL RIGHT2
63) ELECTSYSTM
64) ELECSYSTM2
65) GOVERNMENT
66) COMMUNIST
67) COMM TYPE
68) ISLAMPOL
69) ISLAMLEGAL
70) IND DATE
71) IND PERIOD
72) NO CORRUPT
73) WAR
74) WAR2
75) FREEDOM
76) FREEDOM2
77) NUKES
78) CAP PUNISH

79) THREEWORLD
80) WORLDS.7
81) HUMAN DEV.
82) ECON DEVEL
83) %MUSLIM
84) %CHRISTIAN
85) %CATHOLIC
86) %HINDU
87) %BUDDHIST
88) %JEWISH
89) JEHOV.WITN
90) MORMONS
91) %MUSLIM>50
92) FEM. PROF
93) FEM.MANAGE
94) FEM.OFFICE
95) %FEM.LEGIS
96) %FEM.HEADS
97) GENDER EQ
98) M/F EDUC.
99) F/M EMPLOY
100) ABORTION
101) SEX MUTIL
102) GEM
103) BOYCOTT?
104) DEMONSTRAT
105) SIT-INS
106) PETITON?
107) P. INTEREST
108) TALK POL.
109) TRUST?
110) KID THRIFT
111) WORK PRIDE
112) URBAN %
113) IND GROWTH
114) GDP CAP 5
115) HIV/AIDS

◆ DATA FILE: HISTORY ◆

1) DATE
2) IND NATION
3) IND/DECADE
4) %COMMGM
5) %COMMFR

6) %COMMSW
7) %SOCIALFR
8) %LABOURUK
9) %SOCDEMSW
10) %SOCDEMGM

11) %GREENFR
12) %GREENSW
13) %GREENGM
14) %FREEDEMGM
15) %LIBRLSW

Appendix: Variable Names and Sources

◆ DATA FILE: HISTORY cont'd ◆

16) %LIBDEMUK
17) STS.LIB.UK
18) %CENTERFR
19) %CENTERSW
20) %CHDEMSW
21) %CHDEMGM
22) %CONSERVFR
23) %CONSERVSW
24) %CONSERVUK
25) %EXRIGHTFR
26) %EXRIGHTGM
27) INFMRT.USW

28) INFMRT.MAU
29) INFMRT.EGY
30) INFMRT.SAB
31) INFMRT.SAW
32) %LIBDEM.JA
33) %SOCIAL.JA
34) %CLNGOV.JA
35) PROTEST.JA
36) PROTEST.US
37) RIOTS.JA
38) RIOTS.US
39) RIOTS.GM

40) PROTEST.GM
41) GROW.EASIA
42) GROW.WORLD
43) GROW.SASIA
44) GROW.AFRIC
45) GROW.MEAST
46) GROW.LATIN
47) GROW.EU/CA
48) GR:RUSSIA
49) GR:POLAND

◆ DATA FILE: LATIN ◆

1) COUNTRY
2) AREA
3) POPULATION
4) POP GROWTH
5) LIFE EXPCT
6) HUM DEVLP3
7) EDUCATION
8) MULTI-CULT
9) GDP PPP
10) GDPCAP PPP
11) ECON GROW
12) ECON DEVEL

13) %GDP AGR
14) $ RICH 10%
15) FORESTLAND
16) FREE3
17) IND DATE
18) IND PERIOD
19) COLONIZE
20) LANDOWNERS
21) PAST LAND
22) LANDDISPUT
23) INSURGENCY
24) HUMAN RTS

25) VIOLENCE
26) TERRORISM
27) POL RIGHTS
28) POL RIGHT2
29) CIVIL LIBS
30) CIVIL LIB2
31) GOVT 1978
32) GOVERNMENT
33) DEBT PAYMT
34) EXT. DEBT

◆ DATA FILE: WVS97all ◆

1) COUNTRY
2) WORLDS.7
3) TRUST PEOP

4) LT-RT-3
5) INCOME EQ2
6) SOCIET CHG

7) CORRUPTION
8) RELI IMPT?

◆ DATA FILE: WVS97–AUSTRALIA ◆

1) GENDER
2) LT-RT-3
3) SOCIET CHG
4) IMPORTS
5) IMMIGRANTS

6) PV:GOVT
7) ABORT-3
8) PROST-3
9) SIGN PETN
10) DEMONSTR

11) CLASS-3
12) WATCH TV
13) WEIGHT2

◆ DATA FILE: WVS97–BRAZIL ◆

1) CORRUPTION
2) AUTH RESPCT
3) FIGHT WAR?
4) CONF:ARMY
5) CONF:COPS

6) CONF:PARL
7) CONF:LEGAL
8) CONF:CHRCH
9) CONF:UNION
10) CONF:CIVIL

11) CONF:COMP
12) CONF:WOMEN
13) JUNTA
14) GENDER

◆ DATA FILE: WVS97–GERMANY ◆

1) PRE-1989
2) INCOME3
3) GENDER
4) LT-RT-3
5) AGE GROUP
6) CLASS
7) SOCIET CHG
8) IMPORTS
9) IMMIGRANTS
10) PV:GOVT

11) ABORT-3
12) PROST-3
13) SIGN PETN
14) DEMONSTR
15) CLASS-3
16) WATCH TV
17) PARTY #1
18) ENV:TAX
19) CONF:EURO
20) CONF: WOMEN

21) PV: ESCAPE
22) BUS MGMT
23) INCOME EQ3
24) COMPETITN
25) WEALTH ACC
26) MAN'S JOB
27) MEN POLS
28) WOMEN EARN
29) DEM:ECONOM

◆ DATA FILE: WVS97–JAPAN ◆

1) INCOME3
2) LT-RT-3
3) AGE GROUP
4) GENDER
5) SOCIET CHG
6) IMPORTS
7) IMMIGRANTS
8) PV:GOVT

9) ABORT-3
10) PROST-3
11) SIGN PETN
12) DEMONSTR
13) CLASS-3
14) WATCH TV
15) BUS MGMT
16) WEALTH ACC

17) INCOME EQ3
18) COMPETITN
19) MAN'S JOB
20) MEN POLS
21) WOMEN EARN
22) CONF:WOMEN
23) WEIGHT2

◆ DATA FILE: WVS97–MEXICO ◆

1) PARTY #1
2) CORRUPTION
3) AUTH RESPC
4) FIGHT WAR?
5) CONF:ARMY

6) CONF:COPS
7) CONF:PARL
8) CONF:LEGAL
9) CONF:CHRCH
10) CONF:UNION

11) CONF:CIVIL
12) CONF:COMP.
13) CONF:WOMEN
14) JUNTA
15) GENDER

◆ DATA FILE: WVS97–NIGERIA ◆

1) ETHNICITY
2) WH RELIG
3) TRUST PEOP
4) CONF:GOVT
5) JUNTA

6) NB:RACE
7) NB:MUSLIMS
8) NB:AIDS
9) NB:CHRIST
10) BRIBERY

11) CORRUPTION
12) WHO RULES?
13) WEIGHT2

◆ DATA FILE: WVS97–PAKISTAN ◆

1) GENDER
2) AGE GROUP
3) WATCH TV

4) RELI IMPT?
5) EDUC BOYS
6) MAN'S JOB

7) TALK POLIT
8) MEN POLS
9) WEIGHT2

◆ DATA FILE: WVS97–POLAND ◆

1) CORRUPTION
2) PRE REGIME
3) NOW REGIME
4) FUT REGIME
5) BUS OWN

6) BUS MGMT
7) DEM:ECONOM
8) AGE GROUP
9) TOWN SIZE
10) CONF:EURO

11) DEM:BETTER
12) ORDER-FREE
13) PRE-REGIM2

◆ DATA FILE: WVS97–RUSSIA ◆

1) CORRUPTION
2) PRE REGIME
3) NOW REGIME
4) FUT REGIME
5) AGE GROUP

6) BUS OWN
7) BUS MGMT
8) DEM:ECONOM
9) TOWN SIZE
10) CONF:EURO

11) DEMOCRACY
12) AUTOCRAT
13) DEM:BETTER
14) ORDER-FREE
15) PRE-REGIM2

◆ DATA FILE: WVS97–S.AFRICA ◆

1) ETHNIC GRP
2) ETHNIC
3) WH RELIG
4) TRUST PEOP
5) CONF:GOVT
6) AUTOCRAT

7) NB:RACE
8) NB:AIDS
9) NB:BLK
10) NB:WHTE
11) NB:CLRD
12) NB:IND

13) BRIBERY
14) CORRUPTION
15) WHO RULES?
16) WEIGHT2

◆ DATA FILE: WVS97–S.KOREA ◆

1) GENDER
2) CLASS-3
3) BUS MGMT
4) INCOME EQ3

5) COMPETITN
6) WEALTH ACC
7) MAN'S JOB
8) MEN POLS

9) WOMEN EARN
10) CONF:WOMEN

◆ DATA FILE: WVS97–SWEDEN ◆

1) GENDER
2) SOCIET CHG
3) IMPORTS
4) IMMIGRANTS
5) PV:GOVT
6) LT-RT-3

7) ABORT-3
8) PROST-3
9) SIGN PETN
10) DEMONSTR
11) CLASS-3
12) WATCH TV

13) PARTY #1
14) CONF:EURO
15) CONF:WOMEN
16) ENV:TAX
17) PV:ESCAPE

◆ DATA FILE: WVS97–TURKEY ◆

1) GENDER
2) AGE GROUP
3) RELI IMPT?

4) EDUC BOYS
5) MAN'S JOB
6) TALK POLIT

7) MEN POLS

◆ DATA FILE: WVS97–UK ◆

1) PARTY VOTE
2) LT-RT-3
3) SEX
4) EDUCATION
5) RELIGION

6) CH.ATTEND
7) UNION?
8) VOTED?
9) OPINION
10) VOTE MATER

11) WHO POWER
12) CONTACT
13) POL KNOW
14) BRITWT

◆ DATA FILE: WVS97–USA ◆

1) GENDER
2) LT-RT-3
3) SOCIET CHG
4) IMPORTS
5) IMMIGRANTS
6) PV:GOVT

7) ABORT-3
8) PROST-3
9) SIGN PETN
10) DEMONSTR
11) CLASS-3
12) WATCH TV

13) AUTH RESPC
14) FIGHT WAR?
15) BUS OWN
16) BUS MGMT

SOURCES

AFRICA

The data in AFRICA are from a variety of sources. The variable description for each variable uses the following abbreviations to indicate the source.

ALLEN: Paul Allen, *Student Atlas of World Politics* 3rd Edition, Connecticut: Dushkin/McGraw-Hill, 1998.

FITW: *Freedom in the World*, published annually by Freedom House.

HDR: *Human Development Report*, published annually by the United Nations Development Program.

KIDRON & SEGAL: *State of the World Atlas*, 5th Edition, London: Penguin, 1995.

SAUS: *Statistical Abstract of the United States*, published annually by the U.S. Department of Commerce.

SWPA: Dan Smith, *The State of War and Peace Atlas*, 1st Edition, London: Penguin, 1997.

STARK: Coded and calculated by Rodney Stark.

TWF: *The World Factbook*, published annually by the Central Intelligence Agency.

TWW: *The World's Women*, published by the United Nations, 1995.

WCE: *World Christian Encyclopedia*, David B. Barrett, editor, Oxford University Press, 1982.

WDI: *World Development Indicators*, published annually by the World Bank.

ASIA

The data in ASIA are from a variety of sources. The variable description for each variable uses the following abbreviations to indicate the source.

ALLEN: Paul Allen, *Student Atlas of World Politics* 3rd Edition, Connecticut: Dushkin/McGraw-Hill, 1998.

CNS: Center for Non-proliferation Studies, Monterey Institute for International Studies. http://cns.miis.edu.

FITW: *Freedom in the World*, published annually by Freedom House.

HDR: *Human Development Report*, published annually by the United Nations Development Program.

KIDRON & SEGAL: *State of the World Atlas*, 5th Edition, London: Penguin, 1995.

SAUS: *Statistical Abstract of the United States*, published annually by the U.S. Department of Commerce.

SWPA: Dan Smith, *The State of War and Peace Atlas*, 1st Edition, London: Penguin, 1997.

STARK: Coded and calculated by Rodney Stark.

TWF: *The World Factbook*, published annually by the Central Intelligence Agency.

WDI: *World Development Indicators*, published annually by the World Bank.

WDR: *World Development Report*, published annually by the World Bank.

CSES

The data in all files with the prefix CSES come from data collected by the Comparative Study of Electoral Systems Study Group. COMPARATIVE STUDY OF ELECTORAL SYSTEMS, MODULE 1, 1996–2001 [Computer file]. Comparative Study of Electoral Systems, Center for Political Studies, Institute for Social Research, Ann Arbor, Michigan. Thanks to David Howell, Director of Studies. Selected variables have been collapsed or recoded by the author.

EUROPE

The data in EUROPE are from a variety of sources. The variable description for each variable uses the following abbreviations to indicate the source.

AI: *Amnesty International Report,* published annually.

EU: European Union at IU, Department of West European Studies at Indiana University. http://www.indiana.edu/~unionet/memberst.htm.

FITW: *Freedom in the World*, published annually by Freedom House.

HDR: *Human Development Report*, published annually by the United Nations Development Program.

HF: *The Index of Economic Freedom*, published annually by The Heritage Foundation and The Wall Street Journal.

IDEA: Institute for Democracy and Electoral Assistance. Turnout data are from the institute's *Global Report on Political Participation*. (Stockholm, 1997). Electoral system data and coding are from *The International Handbook of Electoral System Design* (Stockholm, 1997).

KIDRON & SEGAL: *State of the World Atlas*, 5th Edition, London: Penguin, 1995.

LE ROY: Coded and calculated by Michael K. Le Roy. The number of parties is coded and calculated by counting the number of parties that received greater than 5% at the last election.

NATO: "Euro-Atlantic Partnership Council Member Countries, January, 1998," http://www.nato.int/pfp/partners.htm.

P&E: Parties and Elections in Europe, Wolfram Nordsieck, University of Dusseldorf, Germany. http://www.parties-and-elections.de/indexe.html. Coding into party categories from the Extreme Left to Extreme Right by Michael K. Le Roy.

SAUS: *Statistical Abstract of the United States*, published annually by the U.S. Department of Commerce.

STARK: Coded and calculated by Rodney Stark.

TWF: *The World Factbook*, published annually by the Central Intelligence Agency.

WDI: *World Development Indicators*, published annually by the World Bank.

WVS: World Values Study Group. WORLD VALUES SURVEY, 1981–1984, 1990–1993, AND 1995–1997 [Computer files]. ICPSR version. Ann Arbor, MI: Institute for Social Research (producer), 2000. Ann Arbor, MI: Inter-university Consortium for Political and Social Research (distributor), 2000.

GLOBAL

The data in GLOBAL are from a variety of sources. The variable description for each variable uses the following abbreviations to indicate the source.

FITW: *Freedom in the World*, published annually by Freedom House.

HDR: *Human Development Report*, published annually by the United Nations Development Program.

HF: *The Index of Economic Freedom*, published annually by The Heritage Foundation and The Wall Street Journal.

IDEA: Institute for Democracy and Electoral Assistance. Turnout data are from the institute's *Global Report on Political Participation*. (Stockholm, 1997). Electoral system data and coding are from *The International Handbook of Electoral System Design* (Stockholm, 1997).

KIDRON & SEGAL: *State of the World Atlas*, 5th Edition, London: Penguin, 1995.

LE ROY: Coded and calculated by Michael K. Le Roy.

McCORMICK: Coded by John McCormick, *Comparative Politics in Transition*, New York: Wadsworth, 1995, p. 9.

NBWR: *The New Book of World Rankings*, 3rd edition, Facts on File, 1991.

PON: *The Progress of Nations*, UNICEF, 1996.

SAUS: *Statistical Abstract of the United States*, published annually by the U.S. Department of Commerce.

SWPA: Dan Smith, *The State of War and Peace Atlas*, 1st Edition, London: Penguin, 1997.

STARK: Coded and calculated by Rodney Stark.

TI: *Global Corruption Report*, published annually by Transparency International.

TWF: *The World Factbook*, published annually by the Central Intelligence Agency.

TWW: *The World's Women*, published by the United Nations, 1995.

WABF: *The World Almanac and Book of Facts*, published annually by World Almanac Books.

WCE: *World Christian Encyclopedia*, David B. Barrett, editor, Oxford University Press, 2001.

WDI: *World Development Indicators*, published annually by the World Bank.

WDR: *World Development Report*, published annually by the World Bank.

WR: *World Resources, 1994–1995*, World Resources Institute.

WVS: World Values Study Group. WORLD VALUES SURVEY, 1981–1984, 1990–1993, AND 1995–1997 [Computer files]. ICPSR version. Ann Arbor, MI: Institute for Social Research (producer), 2000. Ann Arbor, MI: Inter-university Consortium for Political and Social Research (distributor), 2000.

HISTORY

The data in HISTORY are from a variety of sources. The variable description for each variable uses the following abbreviations to indicate the source.

IHS: Brian R. Mitchell, *International Historical Statistics*, 1988–1995. A reference guide of historical statistics published on the Americas, Africa, Asia, Europe, and Oceania.

ISHIDA & KRAUSS: *Democracy in Japan*, Pittsburgh: University of Pittsburgh Press, 1995. 1998 Election data from "Elections around the World," http://www.agora.stm.it/elections/election/country/jp.htm

TAYLOR: *World Handbook of Political and Social Indicators*, Yale University Press: 1983.

TWF: *The World Factbook*, published annually by the Central Intelligence Agency.

WDI: *World Development Indicators*, published annually by the World Bank.

LATIN

The data in LATIN are from a variety of sources. The variable description for each variable uses the following abbreviations to indicate the source.

ALLEN: Paul Allen, *Student Atlas of World Politics*, 3rd Edition, Connecticut: Dushkin/McGraw-Hill, 1998.

FITW: *Freedom in the World*, published annually by Freedom House.

HDR: *Human Development Report*, published annually by the United Nations Development Program.

KIDRON & SEGAL: *State of the World Atlas*, 5th Edition, London: Penguin, 1995.

LE ROY: Coded and calculated by Michael K. Le Roy.

SAUS: *Statistical Abstract of the United States*, published annually by the U.S. Department of Commerce.

SWPA: Dan Smith, *The State of War and Peace Atlas*, 1st Edition, London: Penguin, 1997.

STARK: Coded and calculated by Rodney Stark.

TWF: *The World Factbook*, published annually by the Central Intelligence Agency.

WDR: *World Development Report*, published annually by the World Bank.

WDI: *World Development Indicators*, published annually by the World Bank.

WVS

The data in all files with the prefix WVS come from data collected by the World Values Study Group. WORLD VALUES SURVEY, 1995–1997 [Computer file]. ICPSR version. Ann Arbor, MI: Institute for Social Research (producer), 2000. Ann Arbor, MI: Inter-university Consortium for Political and Social Research (distributor), 2000. Selected variables have been collapsed or recoded by the author.